LEADERSHIP IN INDEPENDENT AFRICA, SIX DECADES ON

Dr. Kofi Vincent Anani currently wears multiple hats to drive his efforts in life. First, he is a co-owner of V&V Health and Wellness, an SME in Ghana specialized in providing lifestyle care natural remedies. Second, he is the managing partner of A&A (Anani–Afele) Network, a think-and-do tank on utilizing blended knowledge (traditional and global) for transformative development in Africa. Kofi is a former staff of the World Bank Group in Washington, DC, and the United Nations Mission in Kosovo (UNMIK). Dr. Anani obtained his bachelor of arts degree with honors in political science (1987) at the University of Ghana, Legon, and his master of arts (1992) and doctor of philosophy (1999) degrees in international development from the University of Guelph, Ontario, Canada. Kofi is also the immediate past executive secretary of the Ghana Refugee Board (GRB), 2015–20. Dr. Anani is proudly married and father of a twin girl and boy.

LEADERSHIP IN INDEPENDENT AFRICA, SIX DECADES ON

The Blended Representation Principle as a Cause for Afro-Optimism

Kofi Vincent Anani

LONDON • NEW YORK • OXFORD • NEW DELHI • SYDNEY

Zed Books
Bloomsbury Publishing Plc
50 Bedford Square, London, WC1B 3DP, UK
1385 Broadway, New York, NY 10018, USA
29 Earlsfort Terrace, Dublin 2, Ireland

BLOOMSBURY and Zed Books are trademarks of Bloomsbury Publishing Plc

First published in Great Britain 2024

Series design by Adriana Brioso
Cover image © cherryblossom77/Adobe Stock

Bloomsbury Publishing Plc does not have any control over, or responsibility for, any third-party websites referred to or in this book. All internet addresses given in this book were correct at the time of going to press. The author and publisher regret any inconvenience caused if addresses have changed or sites have ceased to exist, but can accept no responsibility for any such changes.

A catalogue record for this book is available from the British Library.

A catalog record for this book is available from the Library of Congress

ISBN: HB: 978-1-3503-7967-1
ePDF: 978-1-3503-7969-5
eBook: 978-1-3503-7968-8

Typeset by Deanta Global Publishing Services, Chennai, India

To find out more about our authors and books visit www.bloomsbury.com and sign up for our newsletters.

An ebook edition of this book is available open access on
bloomsburycollections.com. Open access was funded by the
Bloomsbury Open Collections Library Collective.

Bloomsbury Open Collections is a collective-action approach to funding open
access books that allows select authors to publish their books open access at no
cost to them. Through this model, we make open access publication available to a
wider range of authors by spreading the cost across multiple organizations, while
providing additional benefits to participating libraries. The aim is to engage a
more diverse set of authors and bring their work to a wider global audience.

More details, including how to participate and a list of contributing libraries, are
available from http://www.bloomsbury.com/bloomsbury-open-collections.

To my lovely and resourceful wife, Iris Rin Dzramedoa Mensah, and children,
Venus Esenam Anani and Vince Mawunyo Anani.

CONTENTS

Table	xii
Preface	xiii
Foreword	xvi
Acknowledgments	xxi

Chapter 1

AN OVERVIEW	1
Key Message	1
Distinguishing Characteristics of Tran-Serve Leadership	1
The Salient Features of the Blended Representation Principle	2
Background Development Landscape	6
Journey on Solutions Pathway	7
Representation and Participation in Governance: The Case of Ghana	8
Institutional Dividends with Operationalization of BRP	11
Better Governance Outcomes	12
Appreciable Sector Living Standards	12
Game-Changing Services Provisions	14
Organization of the Book	15

Chapter 2

ANALYTICAL FRAMEWORK	23
Introduction	23
Planting the Seeds of a BRP Construct	23
Restrained Capacity for Collective Actions	24
Access to Resources for Inclusive Growth	25
Institutional Resilience and Empowerment	26
The Centrality of Participation in Governance	26
Shared Prosperity Service Provisions Modalities	27
Key Values of Caring Governance	28
Anomaly in Governance Arrangements	29
Flawed Design and Operations Bias of the Administrative State	32
Conclusion	33

Chapter 3
EXISTENTIAL REALITIES   35
    Introduction   35
    Straddling between Two Worlds   36
    Navigating Life in Both Worlds   37
    Schooling to Embrace One Worldview and Shun the Other   39
    Laboring for Transformation   40
    The Odds Are Stacked against Millions   41
    Predatory Aligned Interests   42
    Pretensions at the Intersections of the Two Worlds   43
    Conclusion   45

Chapter 4
FUNDAMENTALS OF THE CONUNDRUM   47
    Introduction   47
    Grounded Leadership System   47
    Synchronous Rulership   49
    Transparency in Public Financial Management (PFM)   50
    Accountability for Policy Outcomes   52
    Participation in the Practice of Electoral Politics   53
    Unequal Distribution of Rulership Dividends   54
    Conclusion   57

Chapter 5
TOO BLESSED TO BE CHASING THE WIND   59
    Introduction   59
    The Critical Drivers of Success   60
    Visions and Values of the Path to Greatness   61
    Practice of Faith   62
    Communal Bonding and Institutional Synchronization   63
    Imbalanced National and Local Leadership Interests   65
    Curtailed Grassroots Participation and Involvement   66
    Breeding and Instigating Representative Leadership Underperformance   67
    Minimal Professional Rectitude in the Public Work Space   68
    Nation Life Choices and Alternatives   70
        Food Policy Strategy from Seed to Plate   70
        Appropriation and Application of Medicinal Properties   71
        Adaptation and Utilization of Technology   72
        Spiritual Materialism and Instant Gratification   76
    Conclusion   78

Chapter 6
THE CONCEPT OF BRP   79
  Introduction   79
  Conceptual Roots of Anecdotal Experiences   79
  Review and Reflections on Local Governance in Ghana   82
    Consensus and Contestations on the Mandated Leadership
       Arrangement   83
    Undermining Features of the Prevailing Local Governance
       Arrangements   83
    Misdiagnosis of Local Governance (LG) Subpar Performance
       Problematic   83
    Utterances on the Frontline Involvement of the Institution of
       Chieftaincy in LG   84
    Need to Eliminate Parallel Leadership Syndrome   84
    Indigenous Leadership for either Transformative or
       Regressive Politics   85
    Conscientious Patriotism   85
    Transformative Development Requires Proactive Involvement
       of Indigenous Leadership   86
  Salient Elements of BRP in Practice in the Case of Ghana   86
  Implications of Adopting BRP   88
    Structure, Composition, and Functioning of District Assemblies   88
    Reforms, Adaptation, and Strengthening of the Institution of
       Chieftaincy   88
    Customized Institutional Reforms across the Continent   89
  Conclusion: A Long-Range Lens on Solutions Pathway   90

Chapter 7
THE IDEALS OF TRAN-SERVE LEADERSHIP   91
  Introduction   91
    Summary reactions of target Stakeholder Groups   91
    Continuation of Organized Chaos as the Alternate Pathway   94
    Some Immediate Possible Outcomes   97
  Transformational and Servant (Tran-Serve) Leadership for Steering Affairs   99
  Distinct Profile of Tran-Serve Leadership as the Driver of BRP   102
  Conclusion   104

Chapter 8
OPERATIONALIZING BRP   107
  Introduction   107

Mission, Vision of Service, and Traits of African Personhood   108
    Essence of Mission to Build Blended Institutions   108
    Vision of Blended Institutions Service Provisions   110
    Virtues Underlying the Notion of African Personhood   111
Groundbreaking Readiness Actions   112
    National Command Papers   112
    Tailored Constitutional Amendments and Enactments   113
    A Plan of Public Education, Outreach, and Sensitization   114
    Orienting and Adapting the Institution of Chieftaincy   114
Other Pathway Measures   115
    Partnerships and Resource Mobilization Targets   115
    Likely Risks and Mitigation Measures   116
Conclusion   123

Chapter 9
CONTINENTAL DIMENSIONS OF BRP: THE AFRICAN TRADITIONAL
LEADERSHIP UNION (ATLU)   125
Introduction   125
The Rationale of ATLU and Synergy with BRP   125
    Strategic Opportunity for Enhancing the Ideals of BRP Continentally   127
    Center of Excellence on Tran-Serve Leadership   127
    Key Benefits for the Rollout of BRP   128
Supranational Structure for Boosting BRP   130
    The Embodiment of Collective Caring   130
    Fostering Altruistic Behavior at the Continental Level   131
    Energizing Grassroots Enthusiasm   133
    ATLU as a Harbinger of Renewed Leap of Faith in Collective
        Possibilities   133
    The Glitters of Light in the Africa Continental Free Trade Area
        (AfCFTA)   134
Conclusion   135

Chapter 10
WISDOM ON THE PRACTICE OF DEMOCRACY IN AFRICA   137
Introduction   137
1. Hopefulness because of the Undaunting Challenges   137
2. No Saving Grace in the Status Quo   139
3. Effective Participation in Democracy Reflects the Image and
   Realities of Society   140
4. Real Transparency Inspires Trustworthiness   142

5. Accountability is a Mirror of Belongingness   145
6. The Youth bulge is an Opportune Moment for Creativity and
    Innovations   149
7. Food and Nutrition are Not Outsourced Products of Benevolence   152
    Key Elements of the Seed-to-Plate (StP) Agriculture   153
8. Attributes of High-Value Education are the Bedrock of
    Transformation   155
9. Progress is not Clinging to Dogmatic Ways of Doing Things   158
Conclusion   161

EPILOGUE: AN ALTERNATE SOLUTIONS PATHWAY   163
Introduction   163
Practical Lesson One: Anchoring the Gains of Democracy Practice in
    Africa   164
Practical Lesson Two: State Structures of Governance Restricts
    Participation in Development   164
Practical Lesson Three: Foundation of Responsive Designs of
    Statehood Is Traditional Leadership   165
Practical Lesson Four: Multiparty Politics Is Not the Glue That Binds
    Africa Together   167
Practical Lesson Five: Empty Political Promise Destructs the Spirit
    and Soul of Society   168
Practical Lesson Six: Volunteerism Is the Supreme Sustainer of
    Compliance   169
Practical Lesson Seven: Acts of Impunity would be Rare Under
    BRP-inspired Regime   170
Practical Lesson Eight: A Child's Soil on the Lap is never Cleaned
    with a Knife   171
A Revolution of the Mind   171

Notes   173
Bibliography   197
Index   216

TABLE

1   Sample Results Framework: The Case of Ghana   117

PREFACE

This book is a memoir on solutions pathway for recommendations on tackling the leadership problems and challenges stemming from the critical principles of representation, transparency, accountability, and participation as the pivot and lever of democracy practice anywhere in the world. The journey commenced from the formative years of the author in communities with "no streets" in Ghana, and entailed academic, professional, and anecdotal engagement experiences on four continents—Africa, Europe, Asia, and North America—to Pennsylvania Avenue in Washington, DC, in the United States.

The style of writing broadly adopted in preparing this book is poetic-prose, which tends to enable imaginative or sensitive emotional style of expressions with less notice and attention. While this approach has the tendency to obscure objectivity of the document with unintentional elevation of subjectivity which ought to be less prioritized in an empirically informed book, it is mainly to invigorate Afro-optimism with wider appeal and readership.

The sordid situations of many African countries presently have given rise to somewhat widespread pessimism in the literature and daily life outlooks among several people. However, a major theme of the book is that Africa is too blessed to despair despite the trajectory of chasing the wind. It is the persistence and the seemingly intractability of the problems and challenges that there is space for such a title countering the Afro-pessimist tendency prevailing for quite a while. Making sense of the current situation of Africa and to offer constructive solutions is crucial to keeping hopes and the flames of Afro-optimism alive.

In this regard, this book has paved ways for ideas that have been under review in circles interested in a better form of the organizing and administering principles of life in Africa. Although this book may not become a manual on policy making, it has the prospects of widening a more positive pathway for Africa's future. There are no African problems needing African solutions, but there are problems in Africa which need an adequate response. Certainly, it is a step in the right direction to spell out such a pathway in a book published in all forms—print, audio, ebook, and translated into all languages of the world.

In fact, the major difference between this book and others of the same genre is that of diagnostics, treatment, and cure, to use a health metaphor. The literature is very heavy on diagnostics but quite light on treatment and cure. This book has devoted the bulk of its pages to treatment and possible cure. Because in Africa, things have long fallen apart (Achebe, 1958), and the army of the wretched of the earth (Fanon, 1963) has been increasing disproportionately on the continent. It is for such reasons that the blended representation principle (BRP) is a cause for Afro-optimism.

The book will be a great background reader for progressive solutions with appeal to a wider readership, including high schools, universities, libraries, research scholars, and development practitioners. It is possible that the conflation of BRP in the document may have the tendency to blur other processes that impact on outcomes within the African context. However, its widespread utility in various situations would not be understated. Instances of viable utilization include development practitioners, who would find the book useful in designing and implementing technical assistance interventions, and students for acquiring and broadening knowledge in the field of development and scholarly research in general. All these make the book a recommended library purchase and an excellent addition to a wide array of both private and public literary collections.

It is instructive to note the contextual differences between BRP and equation with related practices outside Africa largely for two main reasons: (1) avoid the trap of "perceptive sameness" in the development literature and (2) misconstrue the application of BRP in practice. From the outset, it is significant to emphasize that BRP is not adopted but originated out of personal experiences and observations of the leadership arrangements in Africa and the global village. However, it is possible to equate the tenets of BRP with practices outside because of the usage and application of the word "indigenous," and native reservation administration in some Western countries.

From the experiences of Navajo Nation in the United States, which is the largest native reservation administration like what pertains in Canada, Australia, and New Zealand, it is a misnomer to equate BRP with native reserve administration in Western countries. The governance practices at native reserves do not conform to the tenets of what is envisaged under BRP. There are vast differences between what are expected with the operationalization of the BRP in Africa and systems of native reserve governance—cultural, legal, economic, political, environmental, social in terms of fusion/assimilation, operational milieu, roles/responsibilities, and majority population receptivity and reaction.

For example, many native reserves are in remote areas and eke out living on least productive lands. The population of African countries is predominantly indigenous from coast to coast, and productive lands with allodial titles and rights are governed largely by indigenous norms, conventions, and practices. "Perhaps the main challenges facing Native American reservations are the socioeconomic struggles that many who inhabit them experience. Isolation, dependency, lack of career and educational opportunities, substance addiction, and many other ills affect many Indian reservations. Some of the most impoverished places in the US are on Indian reservations" (www.studysmarter.us). This reference to conditions of native reservation administration suffices to justify that BRP as construed is transformational and cannot be equated or viewed with the lens of native reservation administration.

An envisaged impactful outcome of this volume is that along the way it will galvanize many in the global village to pause for course corrections regardless of the complexities of processes and dynamics peculiar to the African context. In a post-pandemic world, the search for durable and sustaining solutions to the leadership problems and challenges in Africa will rally the world around actions in the manner and context of the Paris climate change agreement and the corresponding concerted focus on greenhouse gas emissions reduction, just energy transitions (JET), renewables in the forms of solar and wind power, and prevention of global disasters. It is thus the projection that the general appeal and acceptability of this book will be strengthened in the process.

FOREWORD

John C. Afele, PhD

"There is not one form of democracy; Africa needs to find its own form of democracy." This is quite a popular African refrain of the elite, intellectuals, and quasi pundits on the media circuit as well as of ordinary folk during their traumatic and long commute on rickety buses. This kind of talk is louder especially when an African country has failed at some critical democratic event—fighting over outcomes of elections, attempts to change the two-term limit of presidents, interference of one branch of government in the affairs of another, like executive manipulation of the judiciary. But these are just that—talks! Africans are good at that—talk, talk, and talk and loudly too. And it ends there, at the talk shop.

That is the reason this book is different. It gives a name to a possible African democratic arrangement. It points Africa to look within itself or, as Socrates (469–399 BC) would see it, for Africa to know itself.

If Africa could fashion or brand its own democratic system from within, why has this not been done in the six decades since decolonization swept across the African continent? By pretending to value, adopt, and practice Western democratic principles of governance on the continent, Africa has infected itself with a variant of the "Stockholm syndrome." Africa is so beholden to everything from external sources: from toothpick to the use of titles like "honorable" even for a local councilor that it shuns anything of its own.

In this book, the author stands on Africa's failed implantation of Western democratic norms within the administrative space and boldly hypothesizes that the most effective governance arrangement at the level of local organization would be that which is grounded in what Africa has as its own, has retained in very active forms, and is nurtured and revered by the people—the indigenous African leadership arrangement.

The indigenous African leadership structure is not entirely dusty and rusted, but it is also not actively utilized to the extent it can be effective at an instance. That leadership arrangement is used by the ruling elites when it suits them or when it is evident that the modern governance arrangements have hit a solid rock and critical solutions are needed, otherwise traditional or indigenous leadership systems have remained of cultural sentimental values—government appointees and elected officials trooping to traditional events to deliver speeches, court the masses for electoral votes, and so on.

A couple of anecdotes may elucidate the importance that ruling governments and citizens place on the indigenous or traditional leadership and their communities: Ghana, for example, is currently facing an environmental, social, and economic menace in the form of heavily mechanized small-scale mining, polluting major river bodies and leaching of heavy metals into the agroecosystem to the extent that one of the country's bedrock cash crop, cocoa bean, is threatened with export sanctions. The president of the country recently summoned traditional leaders from the affected ecological zones to urgent consultations. If these leaders can be consulted at such crucial juncture, suffice to say the indigenous leadership structure could be of value in other aspects of nation-building. Another manifestation of the importance of traditional leadership was evident when the global pandemic of Covid-19 got to Ghana: the state-imposed lockdowns. In the ensuing panic and uncertainties, the urban poor embarked on reverse migration, back to their villages, even in trucks used to ferry cattle, against the government order that banned movement of people out of the cities—it was a crisis of survival and home was the safest; that home was their village, where traditional leadership offered the sense of security with kin and access to land so at least they could get their basic needs.

Indigenous African leadership is by the people, for the people, and of the people. It ensures peace and access to productive resources, at least at the level of families and clans, and builds up to the level of paramountcy.

In that context, the blended representation principle (BRP) is a cause for Afro-optimism. The BRP simply means that the structure of governance should be arranged in such a way that while national leadership adheres to the principle of modern or Western forms of democracy, Africa's own principle of leadership and organization should prevail within the space of local government administration.

The author's works have dwelled on the pinnacle of the indigenous system, that is, the leadership arrangement that binds indigenous principles. I have been closely associated with the author's works since our graduate school education at the University of Guelph in Ontario, Canada, professional development through the Global Knowledge Partnership (GKP), and the World Bank Group in Washington, DC, and so on, much of which he focused on the search for a viable governance system, at least at the grassroots or what could be described as where the rubber of governance meets the people. I have therefore had a front-row seat in the author's dialogues and synthesis of the BRP.

The BRP would also reverberate in the consciousness of majority of Africans today, who have had their heritage and experiences of formative years with minimal direct contact with national government per se, except the public school system. Public security for coexistence, land for settlement and economic activities, social interactions and communal living, and environmental management for sustenance of the community were ensured under traditional norms with leadership of the institution of chieftaincy. Africans who are living witnesses to the visions, dreams, and hopes of African independence, and subsequent downward spiral of the fortunes of our national economies attributed by many scholars to bad leadership, would also be awakened by the BRP.

The search for solutions to Africa's leadership challenges is now more real and urgent. Africa at present is an amalgamation of Western models of democratic societies, and remnants of traditional African societies, and its systems of rulership and governance must adequately reflect such characteristics. The value proposition of BRP, that participation at the local level would be communal while multiparty systems operate at the national level, is at least worth an experiment and proving that "there is not one form of democracy; Africa needs to find its own form of democracy." The experiment would help find the most appropriate organizational principles of life in terms of representation, transparency, accountability, and participation through designs of statehood structures and institutions to meet the needs and realities of Africans, minimize impunity, and ensure good stewardship in management of public resources.

BRP has been conceived and constructed with the grounding mindset that indigenous forms of representation and participation while suitable for rural communities could be problematic in urban settings because traditional authority wanes in environments, where majority of residents have no grounds in the selection of the indigenous leaderships. Large urban communities would therefore be better served by the philosophical underpinnings of the Western versions of governance. Conversely, the wholesale application of Western forms of governance is inept in the rural space and semi-urban settings. This situation is evident in several attempts by successive governments in Africa to create, without much success, credible and responsible leadership structures and institutions.

A remarkable component element of BRP is the gendered requirement that when a male is chosen as a substantive occupant of public political position, the deputy is automatically a female, and vice versa. This is a centuries-old practice of many traditional leadership arrangements adapted to modern development administration, which served its purpose very well and could produce similar outcomes in terms of judicious management of the public purse. Regardless of its accusations of distortion of history and related controversies in its trail, the recently released Hollywood movie *The Woman King* (September 2022)—a story on the all-female army of the ancient Kingdom (early nineteenth century) of Dahomey—is linked to this practice of gendered balance in ensuring good stewardship of public resources.

Africa requires the combined values of transformational and servant (Tran-Serve) leadership, which are focused on fulfilling the needs of people and striving to manifest the blessings of success and greatness for everyone in a society. A Tran-Serve leader is the driver of government and national affairs under BRP. The wholesale replication of the Western models of democracy has not produced the leadership and robust institutions that are required to translate the visions of the early independence years into reality.

The author has done an in-depth treatment of the issues and themes, including expositions of the existential of the African in the global village and the fundamentals of leadership challenges, and maintained that regardless of the bleak picture and anomalies, the continent remained too blessed to despair. The book meticulously draws from the richly apt repertoire of literary observations to trace the intellectual origin of a BRP construct and emphasizes component elements as fit-for-purpose reform remedies for the leadership problems in Africa which could be embraced, adopted, and operationalized across the continent. A philosophical trilogy of Africa's development ills sheds abundant light on the concerns about the continent's future, especially for the idle and vulnerable young people coming of age in a time of great uncertainty.

The salient elements of the BRP concept, receptiveness of the idea among major stakeholder groups, and step-by-step guidelines on possible operationalization across the continent are detailed. The book provides ample reasons why embracing BRP is a commonsensical undertaking for Africa and the broader global community. Details of the necessary steps to operationalize BRP across the continent are provided. The critical driving task is to ingrain in the collective psyche of Africans and the international community that a systematic building of blended rulership institutions involving so-called formal and informal structures is the solutions key to the leadership malaise affecting the continent.

For appropriate directional insights in operationalizing BRP, an onset reminder is made to visit the mission, vision of service, and virtues underscoring the overall endeavor. A critical mass of BRP champions will not emerge by happenstance. The seeds must be sown and nurtured to fruition deliberately and proactively. In this regard, essential interventions establishing two basic forefront avant-garde structures—National Task Force on Operationalization (NATFO) and Communities of Learning and Practice (CLP)—are required to propagate and ground the philosophy of service to the mission of building blended resilient and strong rulership institutions. The ideals and values of Tran-Serve leadership are required to be learned and practiced as the driver of service and interactions. This undertaking is not a quick-fix, short-term process but a long haul of inspirational motivations and persuasive advocacies penetrating the spirit and soul of the African. The pivotal facilitating thread is grounding the champions of Tran-Serve leadership by encouraging widespread voluntary actions establishing communities of learning and practice at all public facets of society, including state organs, workplaces, schools, churches, villages, and townships.

The book outlines possible concrete steps, actions, and activities to be undertaken, including versions of planned constitutional amendment bills, partnerships, and resource mobilization, assigned agency, group or individual responsibilities, duration and completion of assignments, overall timetable, cost implications, likely risks and mitigation options, and sample case-based results framework. All this makes the BRP construct not only an analytical exercise but a crusading endeavor for changing the deplorable African leadership situation.

No doubt, African intellectuals are divided about the place, value, relevance, and effectiveness of the institution of chieftaincy or traditional leadership in modern Africa. In my opinion, this book will not change the minds of those who hold such views. The value of this book as I see it is that it opens dialogue on the subject and sets out parameters for the experiment to establish that "there is not one form of democracy; Africa needs to find its own form of democracy." In that experiment, Africa would also need to learn from the rest of the world, where indigenous peoples have been granted some room to manage some of their own affairs, to learn what has worked well and where the failure points reside. Things are not going in the right direction in Africa, despite the growing evidence of multiparty elections and term limits on the executive; something ought to give, and it is time for Africa to know thyself once again.

I am directly involved as a member of a team that is exploring the continental dimensions of BRP in the context of an ongoing initiative of African Traditional Leadership Union (ATLU) and its compendium executive arm, African Traditional Leadership Institute (ATLI), which seek to tap the power of communal togetherness inherent in traditional leadership and manifested through peace, love, unity, and development in local communities.

This book is highly recommended for wider appeal and readership. I have been a technician in development practice, playing various roles in institutional development for some of the most reputable global development institutions for more than two decades now. I can thus identify with the usefulness and relevance of this book for development practitioners in the design of technical assistance programs and governance interventions in Africa. Furthermore, the book will be a superb background reader in high schools and universities for acquisition and broadening of knowledge in international development. The book will also be an excellent collection for both private and public libraries across the globe as well as an invaluable resource for teaching and scholarly research.

Dr. John C. Afele is a consultant of the African Development Bank (AfDB) at the Secretariat of the African Common Free Trade Agreement (AfCFTA) in Accra, Ghana.

ACKNOWLEDGMENTS

To God be the Glory for the strength, energy, endurance, and discipline (SEED) to fulfill this generational obligation. My sincere gratitude to Guy Darlan, Daouda Sembene, John C. Afele, Andoh Obed Mensah, Emmanuel Yiridoe, Kofi Marrah, Baba Seidu Aziz, and Norbert Poga Anku for their reviews and comments which shaped the entire effort. Special appreciation goes to Togbe Afede XIV, Eric Chinje, and Ed Brown for their inspirational support. May you all be richly rewarded by the Good Lord.

Chapter 1

AN OVERVIEW

Key Message

This book is a memoir on solutions to the leadership problems and challenges stemming from the principles of representation, transparency, accountability, and participation (RTAP), which are central to the practice of democracy anywhere in the world. Such leadership problems and challenges in Africa are seemingly complex and intractable. Nonetheless, the corresponding solutions are commonsensical and evidence-based.

The key message is that the constitutional mandate to lead, rule, and govern is shared in a manner that allows leaders chosen through multiparty-based elections to be responsible for government affairs at the national level; and traditional leaders chosen based on indigenous norms, conventions, and practices to be responsible for local government affairs. In a sense, this will be the manifestation of the blended representation principle (BRP) for organizing the designs and shape of statehood according to the needs and realities of target societies.

Africa urgently requires the combined values of transformational and servant (Tran-Serve) leadership, which are focused on fulfilling the needs of people and striving to manifest the blessings of success and greatness for everyone in a society.[1] Tran-Serve is coined from the words "transform" and "servant," and derived from the combined ideals of transformational and servant leadership. A Tran-Serve leader is the driver of government and national affairs under BRP. The overall concept of BRP is an embodiment of the combined values of transformational and servant leadership. It is mainly a blending arrangement in this manner that can instill, inspire, motivate, and entrench these invaluable ideals of leadership and governance in Africa.

Distinguishing Characteristics of Tran-Serve Leadership

The following are the distinguishing characteristics of Tran-Serve leadership: (a) focuses on solutions, builds communities, and creates empowering spaces to uplift voices and mindsets around a common goal; (b) energizes people with improved outcomes, satisfaction, and performance to enhance political participation; (c) sets aside self-interests for the transformation of the whole to enable transparent policy decision-making; (d) operates with an underlying motivational value to serve others as a cardinal driver of accountable stewardship; (e) its consideration of every individual's needs and inputs shrinks distance between the ruled and rulers; (f) construes public service as a vocation to engender economy, efficiency, and effectiveness in the use of societal resources; (g) performs to earn respect and trust voluntarily rather than through real or imagined threat of coercion and force; and (h) high-level buy-in and a sense of belongingness by its very nature, existential traits, and operational characteristics.

For this purpose, Tran-Serve leadership encompasses all public office occupants, whose power, authority, and positions are rooted in the public purse. Every public officeholder can become a Tran-Serve leader by striving and aspiring to uphold the underlying values. For those at the helm of steering national affairs, the values of Tran-Serve leadership are a medley of the admirable attributes of Kwame Nkrumah of Ghana, Lee Kuan Yew of Singapore, and Mahathir Mohamed of Malaysia in terms of respective journeys of leading to serve and transform their various societies at a given point in time.

Africa presently is an amalgamation of hybrid variants of "Western" models of democratic societies[2] and remnants of traditional African societies, and its systems of rulership and governance must adequately reflect such characteristics. In truth, the agenda of wholesale implanting, superimposing, and replicating variants of "Western" models of democracy practice in Africa has caused more harm than good, and must be seen after six decades and more as wishful and an exercise in futility. This means that anyone claiming to have solutions while the established structures of "authoritarianism camouflaged in democracy garbs"[3] remain intact is either out of touch with the realities on the ground or taking the broader populace for a ride on vain and empty promises.

The Salient Features of the Blended Representation Principle

Specifically, BRP is a fusion of traditional African and "Western" principles of representation, transparency, accountability, and participation for organizing the designs and shape of statehood according to the needs and realities of target societies. The critical features are:

1. BRP is a mix of leadership systems with the constitutional mandate to rule and having an underlying superior capability to communicate, mobilize, and organize voluntarily for collective transformative development in a polity.
2. BRP connotes vertical and horizontal blending, whereby national leadership is determined by prevailing multiparty-based universal adult suffrage elections (Western); and local governance leadership is determined by leadership arrangements nurtured and guarded by African people for centuries and to which they continue to ascribe (indigenous).
3. Traditional chiefs (both males and females) would represent communities in their respective local electoral areas at corresponding designated district

assemblies (DAs);[4] a variation arrangement is applicable to the metropolitan assemblies (MAs).

4. One hundred percent membership composition by traditional authorities in DAs and municipal assemblies.
5. District chief executives (DCEs) and deputies would be elected from members of the DAs and municipal assemblies by representatives.
6. Guaranteed centrality of gender balance in the composition of the DAs—that is, if a male is elected as DCE, then a female is elected automatically as deputy and vice versa. This is a centuries-old practice in many indigenous African countries adapted to the present context of development administration. An aspect of this principle has been highlighted in the recently released Hollywood film *The Woman King*, which focuses on the ferociousness of the all-female army of the ancient Kingdom of Dahomey (now Benin).[5]
7. The DCE chairs the executive council; deputy presides over DA.
8. Comparable arrangements for the metropolitan assemblies will have to be considered.

The logic of the BRP framework is that the majority of the people in local communities will be better represented by their own chosen leaders based on familiar understandable norms and conventions in local governing arrangements. Many people would have access and influence control over their leaders to ensure transparency in policy decisions regarding the management of common resources. Collectively, the people would utilize their strengthened local governance structures and institutions to influence and exert control, and enable transparency and accountability for stewardship of national affairs, which would minimize or eliminate impunity and misuse of the public purse to engender shared prosperity.

Under BRP-inspired arrangement of democracy practice, participation at the local level will be communal, and at the national level, it will be based on multiparty operations. This means that representatives at the local level will be leaders of the communities chosen solely by members based on traditional norms, conventions, and practices for a term limit. Registered competing political parties will present suitable candidates to the communities constituting a constituency, and members of the communities will elect one of them by universal adult suffrage to represent the constituency at the national level. Once a representative is elected, the person becomes a consensual representative for all members of the constituency and not a representative of party members only for those who voted for him or her. The guiding mindset will be allegiance to community supersedes that of the party, and members of the community will have full rights and control of the power of recall, and not parties deciding the fates of representatives. If community members think their representative has underperformed, they will exercise the power of recall within the duration of term limits or wait till the end of tenure and vote for another representative. The same multiparty arrangement will be in place for the elections of the president to lead and govern at the national level.

Leaders of the local assemblies chosen by the community members will select among themselves occupants of the various district and municipal office positions with an important gendered caveat. When a male leader is selected for a substantive position, the deputy will automatically be a female leader and vice versa. The leaders will be supported by cadres of technical officials and experts assigned to the districts in the management of local governance affairs. Details of these arrangements will be included in the Constitutional Amendments and Enactments Reports, and Annexes of the National Command Papers will provide information on the adoption and rollout of BRP to be released by the respective countries.

Participation in communal and multiparty-based representatives' selection principles will ensure autonomy of local government institutions and serve as a bastion against leviathan executive overreach and abuse. Decentralization will have real meaning and ceases to be an extension of central government interests at the local level. Corresponding officials at lower levels will no longer exist and operate as poodles of national authorities by the fiats of appointments and dismissals. This manner of participation is geared at providing grounded checks and balancing of individualized and collective interests at both local and national levels.

As community members select their own leaders to constitute local government assembly members and occupants of corresponding offices, they are placed in unhindered positions to exert influence as checks on local performance of duties and responsibilities. This in turn would likely translate into collective strengthening and empowering of local government institutions and catapult them into spheres of influence to minimize or eliminate impunity at the national level. In this respect, local government will no longer be the weakest link in the ruling national-local partnership value chain in government transactions and operations across the continent.

For the regional ruling councils (RRC) of target societies, 50 percent of delegates will be chosen by the members of the DAs within the region, and 50 percent of delegates are chosen based on multiparty arrangements of electing interested individuals to represent the region at the RRCs with a term limit. Members of the RRC select the heads and deputies among themselves based on the aforementioned gendered balance principle.

BRP has been constructed with the grounding mindset that the indigenous forms of representation and participation would be problematic in urban settings because of the different philosophical underpinnings therefore various forms of the Western versions and formats would seem to provide the solution. Conversely, the wholesale application of the Western version seems inept in the rural and several parts of the few semi-urban settings. This state of affairs is evident in several attempts by successive governments in Africa to create, without much success, credible and responsible governance structures.

The inadequacy of the modern forms of leadership and governance in Africa has been neatly illuminated in the following comments:

> the first three decades of African independence have been an economic, political, and social disaster. . . . This sad state of affairs is not simply a consequence of an unfortunate coincidence of collapsing commodity prices

and mismanagement, but rather because of a fundamental flaw in the prevailing development paradigm. This was based on the erroneous proposition that state institutions derived from metropolitan models could be made the engine of development in the post-colonial era. In retrospect, it is all too obvious that the underlying cultural premises of these institutions were alien to the vast majority of Africans, and they started to crumble the moment the colonial administration left . . . [Even] most of the models introduced [afterwards] can be viewed more as attempts by African leaders to rationalize their authoritarian regimes than genuine efforts to construct nation-states on the basis of the communal and participatory principle found in traditional African societies. These leaders failed to articulate a process for nation-building understood by ordinary citizens, that could effectively mobilize them around a shared vision.[6]

This insufficiency of wholesale application of the borrowed forms of government across the length and breadth of the continent is further reflected in the conditions of the communities depicted in the following observation:

Independence brought with it an idealism that has been blasted apart by the brutality, looting and mismanagement of too many African governments. Whether they opted for multi-party democracies or one-party states has usually proved irrelevant for the majorities who have accustomed themselves to hunger, lack of education, unemployment, poor health, and brutal repression. Local democracies and freedom of expression are rare. And the communities are powerless to do anything but watch as the fruits of their labor are squandered on development follies, personal luxuries and weapons of war and repression.[7]

To buttress the observations, it is remarked that "both local politics and global economic factors conspired to produce a . . . political economy [in Africa] that not only conflicted with the existing philosophical and social systems of the [communities], but one in which they perceived little economic or social equity."[8] Accordingly, "while the twentieth-century events have changed some of the dynamics of the rural world view, the basic principles still exist and have retained their legitimacy. The development of local government structures since the 1950s has separated chiefs from control over local revenues, but the chiefs retain the moral authority to impose assessments and mobilize efforts for communal needs."[9]

Further, one perceptive author concluded that the crises in the global political economy and the rural-urban migrations of the last two decades have only disrupted but not destroyed the rural communal processes of coexistence.[10] In the opinion of another observer of the same genre,

for over three decades, both the African political class and development practitioners have failed to realize that the long-term efficacy of new socio-political institutions depends on an imaginative integration of modern structures with pre-existing institutions and practices at the grassroots level.[11]

The following pointed comments attributed to the former president of France, Jacques Rene Chirac, paint a vivid picture of the African situation with an indelible mark and implications for the post-independence leadership and governance arrangements: "We bled Africa for four centuries. We looted their raw materials, then we told lies that the Africans are good for nothing. In the name of religion, we destroyed their culture. And after being made rich at their expense, we now steal their brains through miseducation and propaganda to prevent them from enacting Black retribution against us."[12]

In another vein, the Minister for Parliamentary Affairs of Ghana noted that "our governance system needs retuning and fine tuning." From his perspective,

> The masses are not having the benefits of the wealth of the nations . . . Ghana, we are endowed with resources. In terms of resources, we are much more endowed than the UK, and yet our circumstances are not the best. . . . We must admit though that in the days of colonialism, they exploited our wealth to also develop their countries but how long has that been? The fault certainly is in ourselves. [This is not to say] I am not oblivious of the negative impact of colonialism but let us not keep blaming colonialism for our future development. We need to do better for ourselves. . . . Let us improve the governance architecture of our nation to really have greater transparency and accountability on the part of the governors, the rulers, and I think by that we will be able to spread the resources to better develop this country . . . improving governance, improving the ethos of transparency and accountability, parliament has a very great role to play. Our parliaments are not living up to expectations regarding providing proper oversight over the executive.[13]

All these comments are indications for a serious consideration of the indigenous leadership arrangements in any meaningful attempts to address the problem of leadership and governance in Africa. The critical issue is whether the African political class can provide a "viable system where local communities can harness the productive resources of these indigenous institutions within the context of a decentralized political structure. Such fluid political environment is likely in the long term to challenge authoritarian state control, extractive and corrupt bureaucracies."[14] The BRP construct could provide a classical answer to the search for alternate conceptualizations with flexible capabilities of enshrining the types of sociopolitical institutions urgently required for some semblance of long-range effectiveness.

Background Development Landscape

The book has been conceptualized through biographical reflections and observations of the African development landscape crisscrossing eras of policies, strategies, events, and episodes of domestic and external origins. This long-range gauging spans several decades of memorable periods, including the nationalist struggles, the joys of independence, and the abrupt end of the self-rule experimentation; the Non-Aligned Movement (NAM), regional organizations, and economic communities; the overthrow of the early visionary leaders, years of military dictatorships, and "strong man" rule; the unhinged activities of multinational companies (MNCs), the rise of 'Tied-Aid' industries, and the nongovernmental organizations (NGOs) phenomena; the Bretton Woods Twins' Structural Adjustment Programs (SAP) and Poverty Reduction Strategy Papers (PRSPs) globalization era; the "Perestroika" and the "Glasnost" years, and the simmering of the Sino-Soviet conflict on the continent; the fall of Apartheid, the emergence of Chinese benevolent autocracy, the Asian Tigers' narratives; the popular uprising, yearning, and demand for good governance leading to a series of peaceful transitions of power and multiparty intensified activities and vibrant civil society organizations; ascendancy of ruckus political participation, community empowerment, and social inclusion interventions; the Highly Indebted Poor Countries (HIPC) and Public Expenditure and Financial Accountability (PEFA) initiatives; the Extractive Industries Transparency Initiative (EITI); the Ebola outbreak, avian flu, SARS and the Covid-19 pandemic, African Continental Free Trade Agreement (AfCFTA), fintech, and the proliferation of social media platforms, to list some of the noteworthy interventions and challenges of the times.[15]

Central to these events and episodes are leadership and governance actions and inactions which induced the interventions. More often, it was the inactions and missteps which compelled the mounting of the policy and strategy responses. As such, there is a consensus "among the UN and development agencies, international financial institutions, and many Africans" that leadership and good governance are the banes of the developmental woes of Africa.[16] The legendary sage of African literature Chinua Achebe aptly summed it up for the continent in his words on Nigeria: "The trouble with Nigeria is simply and squarely a failure of leadership. There is nothing basically wrong with the Nigerian character. There is nothing wrong with the Nigerian land or climate or water or air or anything else."[17] Similarly, the economist Dr. Ishmael Yamson expressed "frustration over the country's [Ghana] slow pace of development and blamed the situation on bad leadership, corruption and greed."

Journey on Solutions Pathway

Navigating the nuances of these episodes and making intelligent sense of them entailed a painstaking journey of reflective observations by the author. This journey commenced from the formative years in neighborhoods of no-street communal communities in Kpandu;[18] undergraduate studies in political science at the University of Ghana, Legon in Accra—a variant urban city; graduate education in international development at the University of Guelph, Ontario, Canada, with academic work focusing on the winners and losers of the SAP; and the critical assessments of indigenous knowledge systems and leadership structures in modern-day governance in Africa. The journey also involved professional careers in international civil service at the United Nations Mission in Kosovo (UNMIK) and the World Bank Group in Washington, DC; a period of reaffirmation of thoughts at an executive position in Ghana entailing bird's-eye view interactions with high-level government officials in the political space on the continent.

The purpose of this book is to induce public policy reforms of building commonsense, resilient, and robust rulership institutions in the image, realities, aspirations and needs of Africa. The motivational intent is to enhance representation, political participation, transparency in policy decision-making, and accountability for resource use, misuse, and abuse of power and authority in democracy practice on the continent. Effective and efficient institutions are one of the four pillars of good governance as they are critical in fulfilling needs and propelling a nation to greatness. For example, in 2009, the former US president Barack Obama proclaimed in a speech to the parliament of Ghana that "Africa doesn't need strongmen, it needs strong institutions."[19] While this assertion is apt, and patience and time are prerequisites for building such institutions, Africa mainly needs rulership institutions based on its dualistic world life realities to be effective and efficient.

Representation and Participation in Governance: The Case of Ghana

It is appropriate to use a country case to illustrate the flaws in arrangements for representation and participation in governance across the continent. There seems to be no ambiguity that universal adult suffrage via competitive partisan elections regardless of inherent flaws is the acceptable means of representation and participation of Africans in governance at the national level. Ghana and many countries have chalked up relative successes by electing presidents and Members of Parliament through peaceful elections leading to successive alternate changes in party-based ruling governments. What seems contentious is the governance and leadership designs at the local level. With the 1992 Constitution, the local governance and leadership design have been based on the appointment of the district chief executives (DCEs), and the nonpartisan elections of corresponding district assemblies and unit committee members as the major actors.

Over the years, associated with this mode of representation and participation in governance at the local level are the undermining characteristics:

1. national executive overreach, influence, and control through appointments, inequitable allocation, and distribution of development resources
2. abysmal level of interests and participation by ordinary people in the governance arrangement
3. lack of transparency in decision-making and resource allocation, and inability of the ordinary majority to hold the local officials accountable for stewardship
4. arrested development aspirations of the communities.

As the development dividends of the prevailing local governance and leadership designs become increasingly elusive, there have been numerous calls for some reformative actions to redress the situation. What seems to gain groundswell consensus is a desist from the appointment of the district chief executives by the national executive and their direct elections by the people on competitive partisan basis alongside corresponding assemblies and unit committees.

To be precise, the call for institutional reforms at the local level is well-placed. However, whether to continue with the nonpartisan method or introduce competitive partisan elections seems to be missing the point that the inability of prevailing local governance arrangement to meet the aspirations of the ordinary populace is a *systemic leadership design anomaly* than either nonpartisan or partisan elections of the major actors.

Arguably, the backseat role assigned to the institution of chieftaincy in the local government design and operations is the root of abysmal interest and participation by people in the local governance, and the inability of these local structures to evolve into a bulwark for ensuring transparency and accountability in national governance operations.

As Ghana is branded a "beacon of democracy" in Africa, it could further strengthen its democratic credentials by contributing uniquely to designs of local governance systems for the region founded on the core principles and values of its civilizations. The persistence of poverty and the vicissitude of the poor majority continue to be an indelible mark on the capability of national leadership to stem the tide and lead the country out of the abyss of deprivations amid relatively endowed human, natural, and material resources.

A critical factor underpinning this scenario is the inability of the emergent national leadership (since independence and regardless of professed party-political leanings) to craft and institutionalize local governance and leadership arrangements capable of energizing the vast majority to participate vigorously in development efforts beyond recent periodic involvement in competitive partisan electioneering campaigns and voting. This situation at the local level affects the overall quality of governance in the country in terms of participation in decision-making, transparency, openness, and accountability for stewardship in the use (or abuse) of development resources.

On the way forward, guidance is needed on the country's experiential practice of competitive partisan politics, particularly at the national level, vis-à-vis the institution of chieftaincy and the corresponding indigenous knowledge systems which people continue to utilize for sustaining coexistence, as well as the psychosocial compositions of the communities with primordial ties to leadership and participation structures.

Certain critical hard facts are noteworthy in this context:

1. Competitive partisan politics per se is not the cure-all for lack of interest and participation of people in local governance, and the weak and ineffective capacity associated with these structures. More importantly, it has also not led significantly to transparency in decision-making and accountability of stewardship at the national level.

2. Incessant individualism engendered by the winner takes all character of partisan politics is tearing apart the social fabric of communalism which undergirds how people make living in their homes and communities.
3. Divisive and acrimonious tendencies associated with the forms of partisan politics practiced in the country have strangulated families and communities to become wary and suspicious of each other on the basis of party affiliations.
4. Competitive partisan politics is mainly one form of organizing principles of life in a polity and should not be construed as the only tool for governance arrangement designs, which merit the label of democratic accolade and behavior.
5. The institution of chieftaincy, regardless of its inherent flaws, remains the more cohesive governance and leadership structure at the local level with symbiotic capability to communicate, mobilize, and organize community members for collective development actions.
6. There is demonstrable high-level interest and participation of people in the functional operations of the institution of chieftaincy, and thus can be empowered and utilized innovatively to ensure transparency in local governance and decision-making, and hold officials accountable for stewardship of development resources at the national level.
7. The institution of chieftaincy (when reformed, adapted, and weaned of its anachronistic tendencies) can hold fort at the local level and progressively complement competitive partisan politics at the national level to build a nation-state capable of meeting the development aspirations of all Ghanaians regardless of party affiliations.
8. Development as a transformational process is predominantly political requiring energetic participation, transparency, and accountability to meet targeted goals. Majority of the people have to grapple with vacillations between two dominant and competing leadership structures at the local level at times to the point of paralysis.

Through constitutional and legal provisions, the structure which is more popular among ordinary people has been anomalously designated unofficial for the purposes of public policy decision-making, resource allocations and management, and stewardship at the local levels. There would not have been any concern if this arrangement has worked to fulfill the aspirations of the people. No questions would be asked if the people are able to participate effectively within such operational apparatus, and utilize the prescribed rules and principles of engagement to ensure transparency and accountability for the use and misuse of public resources on which subsistence depends. If politics as practiced in Ghana is the means by which development resources are translated into beneficial dividends to meet aspirations of ordinary people, then the constitutional provision barring chiefs from participating in politics has outlived its usefulness.

Paradoxically, the vast majority continue to rely more on the so-called unofficial and informal leadership arrangements and principles to make living within their family structures. And national leaders perceive such close ties and continuous relevance and influence as mainly veritable sources of access to votes and exploit them for self-serving purposes during competitive party election campaigns to boost vote-grabbing efforts and voter turnouts.

Even the relative peace Ghana enjoys amid a sub-region riddled with turmoil is arguably attributable to the ways and means the vast majority keep intact their unofficial leadership structures. Several people are therefore left in a quagmire as the imposed leadership structures could not unleash collective energies and know-how to seek and find solutions to mind-boggling problems of poverty confronting them in their daily lives of existence.

Now, the tangible dividends of the forms of democracy practiced in Africa have mainly dimmed hopes on the continent. The situation is such that several of the youth in particular want to leave the continent and not come back.[20] Hopes have been dashed, and dreams become wishful. The grind of eking out a living has taken a tremendous toll on the physique of many.[21] This institutionalized practice of democracy is captured in the following words: "Authoritarian and semi-authoritarian rulers, mindful of foreign opinion, have dressed their regimes with the forms of democracy, such as regular (if rigged) elections and de jure (not de facto) separation of powers. Presidential term limits, where in place, have been frequently circumvented through so-called constitutional coups."[22] Given widespread entrenched circumvention of rules, norms, and practices by vested interests under this institutionalized scenario, it is mainly BRP-inspired policy reforms which can bring about effective, resilient, and robust leadership and governance institutions in Africa.

In this respect, this book seeks to promote envisioned policies and frameworks which Africa could adopt and utilize for more resilient institutions and administration. The BRP approach could possibly cure the winner-takes-all, divisive, and alienating political economic ills currently in vogue across the continent. In a nutshell, BRP is a framework around which local and national government administrations can be reformed with more prominent roles of indigenous leadership.

The TAP (transparency, accountability, and participation) principles which are the principal motivating factors of good leadership and governance are yet to have strong footholds in the post-independence political, economic, social, and cultural organization of lives across the continent. Proactive efforts such as those undertaken by Singapore and Malaysia (under Lee Kuan Yew and Mahathir Mohamed respectively) to induce economic growth and poverty elimination are required to turn things around without acquiescing to the dictates of the few at the expense of the existential needs of many. It is mainly by redirecting efforts to address the deep-seated dysfunctionalities in the prevailing type of institutionalized democracy practice that the dividends of a caring and transformational society would be evenly spread among the population.

Institutional Dividends with Operationalization of BRP

Adopting and operationalizing the BRP will trigger some immediate possibilities resulting in likely specific outcomes. The first major possibility under BRP will be a tremendous rise in active genuinely enthused political participation by ordinary people because participation at the local level will be communal while at the national level, it will be based on multiparty operations. A second bold actionable possibility will be increased demand for accountability of stewardship at the local and national levels—approach will strengthen the practice of democracy through the effective use of guardrail channels and avenues. Third, there will likely be increased transparency in resource allocation, usage, and translations into dividends to fulfill needs and propel manifestations of blessings of success for all. This will mainly be due to the fact that actions will be technically knowledge-driven and wheeled by expertise based on genuine commitments to mutual benefits of society.

As community members select their own leaders to constitute local government assembly members, and occupants and managers of corresponding offices in collaboration with technical experts and advisors, they are placed in unhindered positions to exert influence as checks on local performance of duties and responsibilities. This in turn would likely translate into collective strengthening and empowering of local government institutions and catapult them into spheres of influence to minimize or eliminate impunity and misuse of the public purse at the national level. In this respect, local government will no longer be the weakest link in the ruling national-local partnership value chain in government transactions and operations across the continent.

Better Governance Outcomes

Possibly, these strategic measures and activities will lead to four key outcomes pertaining to better governance practices: (1) there will be deepened closeness of local and national ruling regimes to the majority from a distance gap, and these regimes will be imbued with a greater capacity to communicate, mobilize, and organize for collective purposes; (2) there will be increased administrative efficiency as related to resource use, service delivery, and overall leadership and governance performance record at the local and national levels; (3) several people will trust and respect the local and national administration operational procedures; and (4) majority of the people will express an increased sense of belonging and buy-in toward the leadership and governance arrangements. In a word, these governance outcomes have the potential to widen the prospects of a more positive path for African future.

Appreciable Sector Living Standards

The varied measures and activities will engender empowering environments to ensure that many Africans have fair and equitable access to resources for enabling with ease quality standards of living in the areas essential for peaceful coexistence—health care, education, agriculture, labor mobility, technology for harnessing and processing, housing with amenities, and enabling infrastructure for facilitating peaceful coexistence. Examples of actionable activities in the various realms will include the following:

First, health policy would be formulated with an overriding objective of ensuring availability of adequate financing[23] while reducing pressure and lessening overreliance on orthodox medicinal facilities and resources. The medicinal value of herbs would feature prominently in the outlook and projections of crafting effective responses to meet health demands and needs of the society.

Second, a cardinal feature of a thriving self-sustaining nation lies in the capacity to feed itself and assuring adherence to nutritional guidance for better quality living. It is beyond comprehension that Africa cannot feed itself and food imports dominate the budgets of all countries.[24] Growing an economy to be capable of feeding itself as well as optimize resources to engender and sustain an appreciable standard of living is a nonnegotiable responsibility of leadership. A future practice of democracy under Tran-Serve leadership will engineer social enterprises for seed-to-plate agriculture (StP) largely through systematic transformation of small-scale agriculture into highly attractive and profitable businesses covering the entire value chain of maximizing production, use, and consumption of food crops, fruits, fisheries, and livestock to handle the food and nutrition requirements of the continent.

Third, Africa is now practicing a runaway democracy partly attributable to an established post-independence education system, which churns out more self-serving public officials with mindsets that glorify other peoples' creative possessions and superintend over the hyper-exploitation of what belongs to them. The inherent wisdom of showcasing pride in cultural and heritage-derived belongingness has long been thrown into the dustbin. A pivotal feature of democracy practice under a Tran-Serve leadership will be dedicated education policy efforts of inspiring and motivating widespread consciousness and stimulation of generational responsibility for public goods and welfare in several dimensions of learning, knowledge acquisition, coexistence, growth, and development.

Fourth, Africa is currently experiencing a situation where a large share of the population is comprised of children and young adults, and it seems the leadership has placed both arms on its head and is resigned to the fate of dejection and hopelessness. According to the World Bank, 200 million people in Africa fall into this category, making up 20 percent of the population, 40 percent of the workforce, and 60 percent of the unemployed on the continent.[25] Although the proportion of the youth outnumbering the rest of the population is a critical challenge of economic management, this phenomenon is construed under a Tran-Serve system of rulership as a moment of creativity and innovations which would increase and expand the productive capacity of the economies. In this context, windows of opportunities enabled through digitalization, market integration to strengthen production of regional public goods, retail and commerce landscape, an accessible and affordable child- and elder care sectors, for example, would contribute immensely to ushering in an Africa of shared responsibilities, wealth, and prosperity.

Fifth, policy openings likely to provide pathways to the labor market for the youth and other able bodies are in the realms of feeding, clothing, sheltering, health and wellness, protection and guidance, education, training, and digital skills acquisition.

Each opening is an industrial boom for productive capacity, purchasing power, accumulation, and consumerism raining potential benefits on the economies that may not have existed before in adequate magnitude. African software developers, for example, are in global demand, and companies such as Microsoft and Amazon are leading big tech's push to relocate them outside the continent.[26] Avenues for substantial entrepreneurship, wealth creation, financing engineering, and capital accumulation are credible sources of inspirations and motivations in any society.

It is noteworthy to buttress such notions of possibilities with lessons of advanced economies that have "affordable, accessible child- and elder care sectors, and those economies have higher participation rates of the very people we're talking about."[27] It takes leadership visions, peoples' mindsets, attitudes, and behaviors to marshal societal energy; mold and direct toward creative and innovative solutions for tackling a particular challenge of a moment. Tran-Serve leadership will formulate policies geared at communicating, mobilizing, and organizing society to feed, clothe, and shelter the youth across the continent.

Sixth, Africa has endured and continues to endure its share of tragic woes within the global community—from its battered image, global stigmatization, and anti-blackness to flawed development paradigm embedded with colossal and rapacious looting of resources. Also, the present-day minimal trust and faith by the vast majority in the capability of leadership to uplift them out of the carnage and mess they find themselves—all these occurrences have taken a tremendous toll, unleashed untold hardships, and fragility by depleting the reservoir of coping and adaptive resources.[28] The continent is in need of replenishing coping and adaptive resources for building and sustaining strong institutional resiliency in all facets of organizational coexistence—political, economic, social, cultural, and ecological. Tran-Serve leadership is conceptually configured, designed, and crafted to steer societies in the directions of formulating appropriate policies aimed at replenishing depleted coping and adaptive resources.

Game-Changing Services Provisions

The vision of providing and delivering services under the guiding principle of serving first the needs of others rather than self, family, and friends is certainly a game changer compared to what pertains in the various societies at the moment. It implies a radical change in the image and modalities of how priorities are set and how service providers are organized and oriented to serve. Performance of the respective providers is raised as service delivery outcomes are improved and satisfaction of beneficiaries is increased without any disruptions to the social order. This then will be a true test of the envisaged leadership as its follower base is increased voluntarily and exponentially.

Envisioning service provisions and delivery in a new light will be liberating as this will be undertaken within a framework of ensuring that the core beliefs of the driving vision are not compromised. Those in positions of responsibility will produce based on engendered adaptation capabilities to increase the satisfaction for many beneficiaries and not just selected few or privileged in society. An atmosphere of humility will characterize and becloud service delivery processes as a major distinguishing feature of Tran-Serve leadership. In this regard, operationalizing BRP will be enhanced with tremendous support emanating from many people knowledgeable of the consistent possibilities of service provisions under the envisioned leadership and governance arrangements.

Crafting solutions pathways for tackling the problems of governance in Africa through the effective blending of traditional and national leadership arrangements furthers the discourse on prevailing leadership and governance fundamental problematics in the right direction. As noted, "first, at an intellectual level, it becomes imperative to develop further a discourse about governance for an illuminating basis from which to assess, and possibly criticize policies and institutional changes. Second, it is important to develop suited alternatives and options in order to re-animate political debates and counter the too often heard argument there is no serious alternative."[29] A BRP construct is thus aimed at creating an institutional framework which allows the emergence of new social relationships compatible with institutional empowerment in Africa.

Organization of the Book

This book is organized as follows: Chapter 2 traces the intellectual origins of a BRP construct to highlight the scholarly fountain from which BRP evolves as logical solutions pathway to address the governance problematic fundamentals in Africa. About half a century ago, some seminal works pinpointed worrying cracks in the post-independence African leadership and governance arrangements, networks, alliances, and trends within the global community. This observation deserves a befitting homage through recall reviews of such works.

A throwback recalling of the international development literature of the period reiterates the longitudinal background, character, and mark of origin of the BRP construct. As in this case, the bulk of the scholarly observations advancing the thoughts on BRP is culled from the formulations in pursuit of politics of sustainable livelihoods.[30] Relevant schools of thought paved way for a granular evolvement with expositions from the following literary nuances:

1. understanding the problem of leadership and governance from how people eke out living in homes and communities;
2. determining the formidability of available capacity for collective actions;
3. fairness of access to resources possibilities for inclusive growth, quality standards of living, and peaceful coexistence;
4. identifying and empowering tried and tested rulership institutions;
5. adapting participation arrangements to reflect real-world life experiences;
6. engendering shared prosperity service provisions modalities;
7. caring as the missing value of governance;
8. noticeable anomaly in leadership and governance arrangements;

9. retrofitting foundation design and balancing operational orientations of the
   African state.

The chapter meticulously draws from the richly apt repertoire of literary observations
to trace the intellectual origin of the BRP construct and re-emphasizes component
elements as fit-for-purpose reform remedies for the leadership and governance
problems in Africa which could be embraced, adopted, and operationalized across
the continent.

Chapters 3, 4, and 5 provide a philosophical trilogy of Africa's development
ills, which shed abundant light on the concerns about the continent's future,
especially for the idle and vulnerable young people coming of age in a time of
great uncertainty.

Specifically, Chapter 3 provides a conceptual narrative depicting the realities
of an African within the global community as an irrefutable entry point for
solution remedies capable of curing the leadership and governance maladies of the
continent. Acceptance of reality is a valuable skills trait of a good leader. Nothing
can change until it is accepted. Reality must be faced as it is and not as it was or
wished. "It takes courage to accept reality as it is, and only then can you . . . begin
to make changes."[31] Charting the realities of any situation creates consciousness
and awareness, develops the mindset for well-equipped coping and adaptive
capabilities, and sets the pace of response with swiftness and agility.

The chapter begins with the post-independence two-world syndrome reality
of the African life, which requires mental extrication to handle the exigencies
within the global community meticulously and successfully. It then highlights
the vicissitudes of navigating life in caricature societies supposedly functioning
and catering to the needs of both worlds categorized as superior and inferior.
Thereafter, the key aspect of schooling to embrace one worldview and shun the
other is discussed. In this context, the African is faced with the hard choice of
socialization, where the land of heritage and culture is continually depicted as
inferior and associated with all manner of ills, evils, wrongdoings, blackness, and
stigma. Meanwhile, the faraway land never to be seen by many in a lifetime is
labeled as crystalline superior and expected to be accepted by all as such without
any culpable links to contributions from episodes of plunder and sweats of forced
labor.

Laboring for transformation in a world pitted on grounds of pity and
hopelessness renders success and high achievement motivations the bellwether of
elusiveness, wishful dreams, and expectations. The aspirational goals of millions
from this world have been stunted and arrested. The chapter ends with a reflection
on interests of the political and economic magnates which have been aligned at the
global marketplace. Further attention is given to the realization that many of these
actors have acquired predatory accumulation characteristics with perfunctory
pretensions at the intersections of the two worlds.

Chapter 4 highlights the fundamentals of the confusing and difficult leadership
and governance challenges, and their corresponding effects on social living,
and postulates on the types of arrangements capable of addressing these issues
effectively for better outcomes. A conspicuous prevalence of leadership and

governing systems grounded in external aspirational beliefs has been exerting very high tolls on the majority's capacity to coexist harmoniously which recently prompted, for example, a usual toothless continental espousal without hitting the problem on its head.[32] The posture of dysfunctionality between the ruled and the rulers mainly enables increasing reliance on ever-lurking threats of coercion rather than the spirit of voluntarism as the basis of enforcing social contract terms defined in the image of the haves at the expense of the have-nots.

Transparency in public finance management remains another crucial point of concern. A tailored focus on high-profile institutionally commandeered initiatives in the extractive sector reveals up and downside results while the phenomenon continues to loom large in varied forms at the landscape. Aspects of accountability for related policy decision-making, actions, and choices do not fare better; and neither does participation in electoral politics which tends to fan more flames of divisiveness rather than integration and unifying around common reasonable causes. Furthermore, spreading evenly dividends of post-independence governing arrangements has remained elusive and hard to accomplish.

The chapter ends on the note that without a firmly rooted leadership system based on the beliefs and values of what constitutes goodness in the minds of the majority, all major high-profile response attempts at rectifying the situation to date have remained paper tigers and wishful. It is about a critical time the ruled and the rulers sing from the same hymn book because without synchronized measures driving reform, such related efforts regardless of intent and purpose would continue to be top-down and elitist in context and approach.

Chapter 5 explains the driving values of blessings for success against the background of the fundamentals of the governance conundrum to complete a philosophical trilogy of the trailing perils and woes of Africa's development trajectory. The objective is twofold: (1) elaborate on what the values entail, necessary actions and measures which would enable the surest guarantee of manifesting the blessings for success in a nation's existence; and (b) provide reminder insights into why Africa has been chasing the wind amid the ever-present principles of the blessings for success.

By completing the philosophical narratives of perils and woes of African development, the chapter serves as a bridge to appreciating the salient elements of the BRP concept and the dynamic ideals of servant and transformational leadership. The servant leader focuses solely on fulfilling the needs of society while the transformational leader views fulfilling needs as a vital preconditional means to manifesting the blessings for success and greatness in a society. The ideals of a servant and transformational leader are analogous. Africa requires the combined underlying values of these ideals for a potent cure of its dreaded leadership and governance illness seeping through the pores of the continent.

The chapter provides a dialectic of the ideals construed as the wheels of success and greatness in life. This is juxtaposed with certain policy practices, choices, and actions undertaken, which are inimical to fulfilling the needs of the masses and uplifting African societies to glory and greatness. The chapter ends on the note that regardless of the litany of illness, Africa is too blessed to despair and its potential is glaring—"a global economic driver, digital innovation hub, and model for green, resilient infrastructure." In this regard, there is an urgent need to come together within the global community "as public and private sectors, to ensure an inclusive, resilient recovery . . . unite around one shared and audacious goal: . . . create a more equitable and resilient world coming out of the pandemic."[33] The road to building the foundation for Africa's future could start with embracing, adopting, and operationalizing the BRP concept across the continent.

Chapters 6, 7, and 8 detail the salient elements of the BRP concept, receptiveness of the idea among major stakeholder groups, and step-by-step guidelines on operationalization across the continent.

Precisely, Chapter 6 outlines the constituents of the BRP as a groundbreaking conceptual framework imbued with a potent cure for the leadership and governance ailments ravaging Africa. To provide a contextual background, the chapter commences with conceptual roots entailing a three-phased series of professional anecdotal activities and experiences spanning over two decades. These varied activities include academic engagements in North America for graduate certifications, professional endeavors at the United Nations and the World Bank Group, executive assignments of high-level interactions with a bird's-eye view of government operations in Ghana, and an analytical reflective exercise of local governance subpar performance in Africa.

Furthermore, the salient elements of BRP are detailed, and the corresponding implications for necessary constitutional amendments, policy reforms, and country-level pathway adjustments noted. If African countries are expected within the global community to have strong, resilient institutions capable of fulfilling not only the needs of the elites but also those of the vast majority, the BRP concept could be embraced, adopted, and operationalized across the continent.

A major thrust of this manuscript is to translate the findings and lessons of background activities, interactions, analyses, and reform-implied interventions into tangible forms of blended representational principles on the ground. In this regard, BRP as an intellectual solutions pathway emanated from over two decades of empirical content, professional engagements, and experiences within the international community across countries on four continents including Africa, Europe, Asia, and North America.

Chapter 7 provides ample reasons why embracing BRP is a commonsensical undertaking for Africa and the broader global community. First, the level of receptivity to the concept of BRP by groups of stakeholders is purposely gauged during the period of executive high-profile interactions in Africa. And the expressed sentiments of these targeted stakeholder groups are categorized and summarized for literary convenience and insights. Second, instances are highlighted to demonstrate that without adopting and operationalizing BRP, the alternate pathway for the continent is the continuation of ongoing situation of organized chaos. However, it is always wise to stop digging a hole if sinking. Third, pertinent possibilities and outcomes bordering on the ideals of better governance on the continent which would be engendered by BRP are emphasized. Fourth, the sterling characteristics of the type of leadership arrangements—"Tran-Serve" (transformational servant)—which will steer the boat through the rough tides are noted. Tran-Serve leaders are those who lead to serve and transform by propelling nations to fulfill needs and manifest the blessings of success. A distinct profile of this notable leadership arrangement is constructed to reinforce the conviction that a BRP-inspired rulership is the potent cure for the leadership and governance malady in Africa.

Chapter 8 details the necessary steps to operationalize BRP across the continent. The critical driver is to ingrain in the collective psyche of Africans and the international community that a systematic building of blended rulership institutions involving so-called formal and informal structures is the key to the leadership and governance malaise afflicting the continent. An onset reminder is made to revisit for appropriate directional insights, the mission, vision of service, and virtues underscoring the overall endeavor. A critical mass of BRP champions will not emerge by happenstance. The seeds must be sown and nurtured to fruition deliberately and proactively. In this regard, essential interventions establishing two basic forefront avant-garde structures—*National Task Force on Operationalization (NATFO)* and *communities of learning and practice (CLP)*—are required to propagate and ground the philosophy of service to the mission of building blended resilient and strong rulership institutions.

The ideals and values of Tran-Serve leadership are required to be learned, imbibed, internalized, and practiced as the driver of service and interactions. This undertaking is not a quick-fix, short-term process but a long haul of inspirational motivations and persuasive advocacies penetrating the spirit and soul of the African. The pivotal facilitating thread is grounding the champions of Tran-Serve leadership by encouraging widespread voluntary actions establishing communities of learning and practice at all public facets of society, including state organs, workplaces, schools, churches, villages, and townships. This chapter outlines all the concrete steps, actions, and activities to be undertaken including versions of planned constitutional amendment bills, partnerships, and resource mobilization; assigned agency, group or individual responsibilities, duration and completion of assignments, overall timetable, cost implications, likely risks and mitigation options, and sample case-based results framework.

As is the case, conceptualizing and articulating a mission is not as rough as the occurrence and realization in practice which remain the most difficult part of the process. The substantive measures outlined in this chapter are guides and not meant to be prescriptive and must be followed by the letter and sequentially. "Flexibility" is the watchword, and countries will decide on the mode of adaptation without compromising or truncating the ideals and values which underpin the concept of BRP. It is crucial to uphold concept integrity in the operationalization process for envisioned results and impactful outcomes.

The leadership and governance mess in Africa requires well-coordinated rescue interventions. BRP provides the certainty of stopping the bleeding and paving way for a momentous redemption. Several cracks noticeable in the African statehood enterprises during the 1960s and 1970s have widened and rendered the whole structure complex, wobbling, and crumbling gradually under the pressure of present-day perennial challenges. Lo and behold, it is largely a BRP-inspired intervention which could provide the resilient and robust foundation for withstanding the onslaught and coming out with a win-win situation for all.

Chapter 9 explores the continental dimensions for boosting the operations of BRP through the prism of an ongoing initiative of the African Traditional Leadership Union (ATLU)[34] with an overarching goal of complementing efforts of the African Union (AU) in building the "Africa We Want"—a continental blueprint and strategic framework for ensuring inclusive growth and sustainable development by 2063 through the pathways of peace, unity, and integration.[35] The thrust of ATLU is more restricted in intent and scope than that of BRP. However, both seek to proactively tap the power of communal togetherness inherent in traditional leadership and manifested through peace, love, unity, and development in local communities. BRP is a continental intervention and will utilize the ATLU platform to articulate and disseminate the concept during planning and preparing to adopting and rolling out of the ideals across the various nations to facilitate the pursuit and attainment of the collective objective.

Strategic opportunities afforded by the ATLU platform and the key benefits to the rolling out of BRP ideals and values including a center of excellence on Tran-Serve leadership at the continental level (the African Traditional Leadership Institute—ATLI) are highlighted. Also, the propellers of such a supranational structure for traditional leadership with the potential to boost the BRP operations are identified and discussed with an end note on the glimmers of lights in the recently launched African Continental Free Trade Agreement (AfCFTA).[36]

Peace, unity, and integration are necessary ingredients for unleashing the continental potentials and capabilities of transforming and uplifting many Africans out of endemic poverty. Most Africans continue to rely more on the so-called unofficial and informal leadership arrangements—a pervasive scenario given the prevalence of entrenched primordial ties, the psychosocial composition of the populace, and the apparent ineffectiveness of the formal structures of development administration to reach the masses. It is therefore essential that the African ruling political class embrace, adopt, and roll out BRP which provides better mechanisms for maximizing the complementary development contributions and potential capabilities of traditional leadership in a Tran-Serve framework at national and continental levels.

In Chapter 10, carefully selected themes of wisdom which run through the book have been calibrated into enlightening insights on the practice of democracy with the rollout of BRP across the continent. These themes of wisdom collectively reinforce the key message that Africa needs to redesign the foundations of its democracy practice. The lines of thought which constitute the building blocks of this chapter are as follows: (a) Africa is hopeful because of its several problems and challenges; (b) promises of salvation are bogus and shambolic with retention and tweaking of the status quo organizational principles of life; (c) effective political participation is a reflection of the image and realities of society; (d) real transparency is knowledge-driven and wheeled by expertise; (e) accountability for good stewardship will be strengthened by maximal utilization of guardrail channels and avenues; (f) the youth bulge is an opportune moment of necessity for creativity and innovations; (g) food and nutrition are not outsourced products of benevolence; (h) valued education inculcates, instills, and inspires intergenerational care, duty, responsibility, and accountability; (i) progress is embedded in coping adaptive and resilient resources and not clinging to dogmatic ways of doing things.

The amalgam of these wise thoughts underscores the craft of BRP geared at invigorating for good the practice of democracy across the continent. With this approach of illuminating a topical subject matter for its policy relevance, implications, and consideration, the chapter reiterates the driving narrative of the book that adoption and rollout of BRP will inspire, induce, and instill hope in the dividends of democracy practice on the continent.

The epilogue serves as a final note on the BRP concept as an invaluable solutions pathway to conclude the in-depth discussions on a potent cure for the leadership and governance malaise in Africa. A reiteration of some key inconvenient truths about the design and shape of statehood in Africa ends the journey with corresponding parting thoughts on the moral lessons in the practical utility of a BRP construct. Some key inconvenient truths are:

1. Democracy practices can mainly flourish when derived from the needs, aspirations, and realities of the target societies.
2. African structures of statehood are not designed and shaped to exert influence and pressure on each other to ensure accountability in the use of the public purse.
3. The institution of chieftaincy in Africa is pivotal to the spirit of togetherness of constituent communities and cannot be marginalized in ensuring robust democracy practices on the continent.

Some corresponding moral lessons of such inconvenient truths are:

1. The gains of democracy practice can be firmly anchored with BRP.
2. Empty political promise destructs the spirit and soul of society.
3. Multiparty politics is not the glue that binds Africa together; rather, it is the institution of chieftaincy.
4. Voluntarism is the supreme sustainer of compliance.
5. Acts of impunity regarding the management of the public purse will be rare under a BRP-inspired regime.
6. A child does not soil the laps of a parent and is cleaned with a knife.

All these moral lessons double down on the inherent healing process of BRP as a suitable cure for the leadership and governance ailments on the continent.

Embracing, adopting, and operationalizing a BRP construct as a panacea for the leadership and governance problematics on the continent require a revolution of the mind both within and outside Africa. BRP is evidence-based, commonsense solutions pathway for transformational development in Africa. Tran-Serve leadership is an attitude of a mindset committed to long-term creativity and innovation for integrated plans capable of solving practical problems of life.

Deep-seated deprivations, plundering of the public purse, the privatization of public wealth; friends, family, sycophants, and bootlickers' regimes of control; internecine conflicts, senseless killings, forced displacement, deliberate creation of refugees, and the malaise of poverty which have become the development trajectory of Africa revolve around the post-independence operations of the modern state leadership and governance mismanagement.

The African majority needs real independence. Independence from colonial rule has been half-baked and silver-coated for the minority educated elites—civilian and military. A real independence is needed to free many Africans from their own internal ruling elites and external collaborators and financiers—that is, independence from the neocolonial arrangements presided over by African elites as part of the strategy to safeguard the interests of the major beneficiaries of the prevailing world order.

A revolution of the mind is about ideas, knowledge generation, integration, and innovation for collective wisdom to solve problems. African intellectuals need to awaken, become conscious of their fundamental obligations to their people, and strive to bring about far-reaching and drastic changes necessary to cure the ills of leadership and governance on the continent.

Chapter 2

ANALYTICAL FRAMEWORK

Introduction

About half a century ago, some seminal works pinpointed worrying cracks in the post-independence African leadership and governance arrangements, networks, alliances, and trends within the global community. This observation deserves a befitting homage through recall reviews of such works to highlight the scholarly fountain from which BRP evolves as logical solutions pathway to address the governance problematic fundamentals in Africa.

A throwback recalling of the international development literature of the period reiterates the longitudinal background, character, and mark of origin of the BRP construct. As in this case, the bulk of the scholarly observations advancing the thoughts on BRP is culled from the formulations in pursuit of politics of sustainable livelihoods.[1] Relevant schools of thought paved way for a granular evolvement with expositions from the following literary nuances: (a) understanding the problem of leadership and governance from how people eke out living in homes and communities; (b) determining the formidability of available capacity for collective actions; (c) fairness of access to resources possibilities for inclusive growth, quality standards of living, and peaceful coexistence; (d) identifying and empowering tried and tested rulership institutions; (e) adapting participation arrangements to reflect real-world life experiences; (f) engendering shared prosperity service provisions modalities; (g) caring as the missing value of governance; (h) noticeable anomaly in leadership and governance arrangements; (i) retrofitting foundation design and balancing operational orientations of the African state.

The chapter meticulously draws from the richly apt repertoire of literary observations to trace the intellectual origin of the BRP construct and re-emphasizes component elements as fit-for-purpose reform remedies for the leadership and governance problems in Africa which could be embraced, adopted, and operationalized across the continent.

Planting the Seeds of a BRP Construct

Understanding the problem of leadership and governance from how people eke out living in homes and communities is the first mark of origin of a BRP construct.

From the outset, the problem of leadership and governance in post-independence Africa as related to the basic requirements of organizing a society peacefully, and providing an acceptable quality of life for its members, induced calls for critical considerations of governing systems based on an effective blend of traditional and national leadership arrangements as a logical democratic mechanism. These exhortations and revelations laid grounds for a frame of thought in search of enabling and fit-for-purpose seedling conceptualizations. Essentially, the revelations commenced with the notion that

> peoples' ways of living in their homes, communities and environments present an important source for understanding governance issues in a more grounded way that challenges top-down institutional arrangements.[2]

Examining governance issues through the lens and prism of daily living conditions in homes, communities, and environments implies that any impactful approach to catalyzing change in response to a deep-seated social problem would essentially have to be political if it would "not benefit the rich at the expense of the poor, or the powerful at the expense of the powerless."[3] Such granular views opened politically oriented spaces for constructive engagements geared at addressing apparent failures in the prevailing dominant modernization "stages of growth" development paradigm, and inadequacies of countervailing "dependency" thought processes as part of the search for alternate and more appropriate conceptual options.[4]

Basically, the propensity to understand the problem of governance from how people eke out living in homes and communities is largely an outcome of analyzing the political economy of "the creation of world poverty."[5] These analyses exposed the deplorable conditions of "the wretched of the earth"[6] and emphasized the creativity and entrepreneurship inherent in communities as a veritable source for social improvement and transformation.[7] Simply stated, poverty as a contemporary African phenomenon directed focus to the questions of political, economic, and cultural oppression, and renders emancipation from these the primary political concern.[8] In the opinion of one critic, within the conventional modernization paradigm of development, "the poor and forsaken are . . . condemned to live in a world of terrible injustices, crushed by [unreasonable] and apparently unchangeable economic magnates on which political authorities, even when formally democratic nearly always depend."[9]

Restrained Capacity for Collective Actions

Determining the formidability of available capacity for collective actions is the second mark of origin of a BRP construct. As observed, the capacity for collective actions in Africa had been severely constrained because the world economic order and alliances defined the function of the mass of people to be pack hordes, while the function of their elites is to keep them under control."[10] In other words, "the participation of ordinary people in development was conceived as unidirectional top-down process: the leaders led and the people were supposed to follow."[11]

Clearly, the construct of BRP is rooted in advocating emphasis on the primacy of quality well-being for everyone, and the rejection of all predatory and exploitative colonial practices and behavior within the global system. In this respect, the formulation of BRP seeks a fundamental restructuring of the modern African state, the international markets, and civil organizations through which transnational elite interests are asserted and manifested within the global political economy.[12] The truth then and now is that the disposition of a Tran-Serve leadership arrangement would "fundamentally question the . . . inequitable access to resources, to power and knowledge, and the current institutions of governance embedded in globalism."[13]

The emergence of the aforementioned schools of thought provided the wherewithal to speak about politics, governance, and policies at local, national, and international levels through the lens of a BRP construct ensconcing the principle of blended representation. A BRP-inspired leadership and governance framework has been crafted to bring about the political organization of societies that would enable adequate fulfillment of needs and transformation to manifest the blessings of success for everyone. It is anticipated that this real-world life framework will possibly open political spaces for ensured access to productive resources on which livelihoods depend. Similarly, it will rekindle confidence in the relevance and effective utilization of local (indigenous) knowledge and vibrantly embrace convergent technologies in terms of appropriate science, know-how, and financing systems based on a blend of modern and indigenous knowledge for transformative development.

Access to Resources for Inclusive Growth

The third mark of origin is the fairness of access to resources possibilities for inclusive growth, quality standards of living, and peaceful coexistence. For the purpose of crafting a BRP construct, poverty is inextricably linked to the capacity for collective actions and production. Majority of Africans require fair and equitable access to resources for enabling with ease quality standards of living in the areas essential for peaceful coexistence—health care, education, agriculture, labor mobility, technology for harnessing and processing, housing and related household amenities. Emphasis on access to quality resources invites an examination of underlying organizational, management, and leadership principles utilized for forging caring societies and uplifting living standards. In this sense, a reappraisal of the unique knowledge embedded in traditional community governance approaches is necessary to unravel inbuilt collective wisdom and knowledge systems for decision-making and problem-solving. This appraisal is particularly important because within the post-independence development processes and the ongoing practice of democracy in Africa, "little serious attention is given to the possible enhanced role of indigenous knowledge and institutions in the improvement and transformation of livelihoods."[14]

Institutional Resilience and Empowerment

The fourth mark of origin as identifying and empowering tried and tested rulership institutions is the hallmark of BRP. The goal of a BRP construct is institutional empowerment—capable resiliency of ruling institutional arrangements to withstand the test of time, facilitate cooperation to identify problems, and organize toward a common objective of solving both immediate and future problems. Along this line, two interrelated mechanisms are essential in the quest for institutional empowerment: (i) the presence of community institutions/ associations for voluntary interactions and engagements, and (ii) availability of community leaders, actors, and entrepreneurs. In constructing the BRP, a lens is primarily zoomed on identifying and strengthening existing innovative and entrepreneurial local leadership and governance arrangements in the various communities and nations for embracing more inclusive, holistic, and empowered democracy practice.

Presumably, with proper organizational networks firmly grounded, collective actions are taken to meet immediate needs as well as the needs of the future. Actions to meet present and future needs are both pragmatic and transformative providing ultimately the basis for cooperation and the impetus for institutional empowerment. By cooperating in a constructive manner, trust, loyalty, dedication, a sense of belonging, and buy-in are inculcated and nurtured. These principles are utilized within the institutional arrangements for collective undertakings to continue identifying problems and organizing to solve them. The solving of immediate problems ultimately provides the encouragement and confidence to identify further problems to be solved—a spiraling syndrome of problem identification and finding appropriate solutions which, in essence, is the quintessential epitome of Tran-Serve leadership.

Empowerment is awakening of institutional power, and the capacity to engender this collective action is the social energy or "know-how" of the community. For institutional empowerment to unfold, there is the need for innovative ideas, knowledge, leaders, and political spaces or "sites of construction," that is, elimination of authoritarian rule which would normally prevent such situational social changes from unfolding.[15] BRP-induced participation, transparency, and accountability processes require organizational changes to enable persistent exercising of countervailing power. By and large, this exercise of power would permit commensurable assertiveness of rights to entitled resources, which in turn would pave way for the realization of institutional empowerment.

The Centrality of Participation in Governance

Adapting participation arrangements to reflect real-world life needs, realities, and experiences is the fifth mark of origin. The need to reorganize political spaces is very significant and urgent because in Africa, things have long fallen apart,[16] and most of the people continue to wallow in abject poverty. First, at an intellectual level, it has become necessary to develop further a discourse about governance for an illuminating basis from which to assess, and possibly criticize, policies and institutional changes. Second, it is important to develop suited alternatives and options in order to reanimate political debates and counter the too often heard argument there is no serious alternative.[17] Crafting solutions pathways for tackling the problems of governance in Africa through the effective blending of traditional and national leadership arrangements is bold and constructive. Also, it furthers the discourse on prevailing leadership and governance fundamental problems in the right direction. In this regard, a BRP construct is aimed at creating an institutional framework which allows the emergence of new social and political relationships compatible with institutional empowerment in Africa.

Clearly, vigorous and dynamic participation of most of the people in the planning and making of decisions which govern their lives is an essential molding ingredient in the construct of BRP. This scenario is practically possible with certain themes of thought geared at shaping the dialectical discourse. Such illuminating thoughts include: (a) harmonizing existing differential characteristics and philosophical orientations of the target population, (b) elevating principles of organizing human interactions of coexistence; (c) realigning the nature of majority participation in decision-making and resource management within a milieu; and (d) reconfiguring available leadership arrangements in the exercise of local political authority and day-to-day administration: As noted:

> Of central concern in any discussion of sustainable development [to engender shared prosperity service provisions in a society] in wider human terms is the issue of participation. It is a pretense to think that the crisis [Africa] is facing can be overcome, and that the reshaping of its societies, the development of its rural areas and eradication of the worst forms of poverty can be undertaken without the participation of the people, particularly the large numbers who are poor.[18]

Shared Prosperity Service Provisions Modalities

Participation engendering shared prosperity service provisions modalities is the sixth mark of origin of a BRP construct. As pointed out, participation requires leadership arrangements capable of mobilizing and organizing human interactions for enabling shared prosperity modalities to be rooted in societies. Participation and the strengthening of associational life are crucial to building viable leadership and governing systems capable of fulfilling needs and transformation to manifest the blessings of success for everyone. Both empower ordinary people, giving them the voice to demand more accountable government.[19]

Ethically, participation in this context would mean that all available leadership and governance arrangements in a particular polity are unified and geared to manage the resources upon which the people depend for their existence in a way that benefits everyone. The emphasis here is the role of the state to bring about political and economic organization of society in a peaceful manner as the foundation for sustaining and transforming lives. In this respect,

> governance is the use of political authority and exercise of control over a society and management of its resources for social and economic development . . . [Governance] encompasses the nature of functioning of a state's institutional and structural arrangements, decision-making processes, policy formulation, implementation capacity, information flow, effectiveness of leadership, and the nature of relationships between rulers and ruled.[20]

The resources for sustaining and transforming lives in ways that ground firmly shared prosperity modalities are both human and material. Therefore, any good leadership and governance strategy would be shaped and guided by culturally acceptable property ownership modalities, wealth generation and prosperity sharing avenues, caring mechanisms to promote unity and peace among residents, humane use conditions of natural resources, and human capacity building measures.

Key Values of Caring Governance

Honing the factor of caring for public goods, services, and interests as a cardinal value of governance is the seventh mark of origin of a BRP construct. From the foregoing, governance evolves out of the key organizing principles of a community's life and is basically a group and collective behavior. This assertion renders the shared cultural values embodied in the principles of organizing and managing resources upon which the existence of the majority depends crucial to inducing effective mechanisms for majority participation in decision-making and problem-solving.[21] These values are essential because they espouse local perceptions of "good" in terms of organization, mobilization, communications, roles, rules, regulations, responsibilities, transparency, and accountability regarding who gets what, when, and how in the various communities. Not only do the values "show the mode of thought and general principles used to direct personal and social behavior, but they also reveal the way Africans look upon the tangled web of human relationship and life, and chart in details the dangers of life and the perils of the human environment."[22]

The prevailing trend of coexisting traditional and multiparty forms of organizing society in Africa reveals principles of knowledge systems relating to the right and forms of representations, sense of responsibility, autonomy, accountability, transparency, and dissent. Both knowledge principles include types of empowerment modality that would ensure the making of decisions and choices with the probability of effecting positive political changes. As opined by Ayittey, the institutions of chieftaincy are generally democratic, with strong and viable inbuilt systems of accountability and participation.[23] And "checks and balances . . . exist in the form of chieftaincy institutions which largely prevent traditional rulers from being despotic."[24]

To buttress this viewpoint, it is important echoing a perceptive comment on the independence struggle era which was true then and remains so now:

> the so-called educated Africans are not divorced from the institutions and customs of their people regardless of the acquired mannerisms in dressings and language of communications regarding conduct of official business. What seems to be changing presently with worrying concern is the persistence assault and erosion of the communal system of living by the ruling elites through multiparty democracy activities which threaten to obfuscate the meaning and guidance inherent in the maxim of sink or swim with the family and community. It has been demonstrated that by and large individuals, whether civilians or military, have come to the top and grabbed political power into their hands with the object of exploiting the masses. Several instances of developments showed that nearly everywhere in Africa, exploitation of the masses by the better organized and more powerful middle-class men, civilian and military, has been the common experience.[25]

Furthermore, as pointed out, "what is wrong with the parties in the new states is not that they exist, but that their inheritance from European political philosophy is the language and tactics of the class war, rather than language and tactics of groups whose problem is to live in a coalition with each other."[26] Apart from the few urban enclaves, African societies were and remain largely communal societies, and it would be perilous to undermine and prevent this communalism from defining the people's perception of self-interest, their freedom, and their location in the social whole of organizing politically. In this sense, the wholesale replication of the Euro-American version of participation in governance arrangements would make little sense in Africa because "political parties do not make sense in societies where associational life is rudimentary and interest groups remain essentially primary groups."[27]

While in some cases both indigenous and modern principles are employed to regulate the use and management of resources upon which existential needs of the people depend, the use of indigenous African principles is still prevalent which brings to the forefront the place of indigenous knowledge (values) in a scheme of fostering good leadership and governance strategies in contemporary Africa. As a matter of fact, this situation presupposes that in the various communities something from the past has worked and continues to work.[28]

Anomaly in Governance Arrangements

Tackling the noticeable anomaly in leadership and governance arrangements is the eighth mark of origin of a BRP construct. The coexistence of modern and indigenous principles in organizational lives which shapes access to resources and relationships implies the existence of parallel leadership arrangements. This is a crucial phenomenon underlying the exercise of local and national political authority in day-to-day administration of target communities.

Under this arrangement, national leadership has been constitutionally mandated as the central government to exercise ultimate political authority and given responsibility for major development initiatives in the communities across the continent. In the same vein, the indigenous leadership arrangements, which constitute the political embodiment of values of governance cherished, protected, and preserved by the mass of the people, are relegated to the margins of modern day-to-day administration and restricted to peripheral roles in development initiatives undertaken in the communities. Clearly, this is an anomaly in modern political organization, planning, and administration, which does not augur well for inducing the form of leadership and governance arrangements capable of ensuring peace and transforming lives and existence which will enable shared prosperity in the communities.

The subordinate position of indigenous leadership in prevailing governance arrangements suggests the majority of the people are not included in making decisions and managing the affairs and resources of the communities. This sentiment is succinctly captured in the following:

> to the mass of the people, all the heated debates about (Western) ideology and political systems—one party or multiparty—are irrelevant. In most African nations, (the ordinary urban and rural dwellers) constitute the majority. Yet they have no voice in (modern) government, no protection before the law and no guarantees of human rights and freedom. Since independence they have been systematically exploited for the benefit of the tiny which dominate all (modern) political systems.[29]

Such a state of affairs is unfortunate because the values embedded in the indigenous leadership and organizational arrangements are mainly values of human security, community sustenance, property ownership, entrepreneurship, unity and peace, freedom, and well-being which are pivotal to institutional resilience, sustenance, and strength. It is appropriate that attempts to re-create participation to ensure good governance in the context of the sociocultural realities of Africans should engender an inclusion of relevant values which demonstrate the functionality of cherished ideas and practices instrumental in forging group and collective ties in the communities:

> The solution to the problem of democracy lies in the discovery and the forging of a new viable political synthesis which derive firmly from the African past, yet fully accepts the challenges of the African present. . . . Popular participatory democracy based on African concepts of community appears to be an essential element in any meaningful answer to endemic political and economic troubles in Africa.[30]

This perspective and need make the construct of BRP a logical mitigating antidote to the leadership and governance problematics in Africa worth attention and exploration.

Specifically, a BRP construct focuses on the pressing need to foster a critical review and reconciliation of the complementary ideas of rulership espoused in the indigenous African and Euro-American sociopolitical thought in vogue in Africa. The compelling motive will be to devise and elevate means of institutionalizing practices of participation based on the communal orientations of the people. It is thus important in the contemporary search for good governance in Africa to demonstrate how those areas of weaknesses in the forms of representation and participation derived from the Western model which have been institutionalized correspond to the strengths of indigenous forms of governance in the African world.

BRP has been constructed with the grounding mindset that the indigenous forms of representation and participation would be problematic in urban settings because of the different philosophical underpinnings so forms of the Western version seem to provide the solution. Conversely, the wholesale application of the Euro-American version seems inept in the rural and several parts of the few semi-urban settings. This state of affairs is evident in several attempts by successive governments in Africa to create, without much success, credible and responsible governance structures.

The insufficiency of the modern forms of leadership and governance in Africa has been neatly illuminated in the following comments:

> the first three decades of African independence have been an economic, political and social disaster. . . . This sad state of affairs is not simply a consequence of an unfortunate coincidence of collapsing commodity prices and mismanagement, but rather because of a fundamental flaw in the prevailing development paradigm. This was based on the erroneous proposition that state institutions derived from metropolitan models could be made the engine of development in the post-colonial era. In retrospect, it is all too obvious that the underlying cultural premises of these institutions were alien to the vast majority of Africans, and they started to crumble the moment the colonial administration left . . . [Even] most of the models introduced [afterwards] can be viewed more as attempts by African leaders to rationalize their authoritarian regimes than genuine efforts to construct nation-states on the basis of the communal and participatory principle found in traditional African societies. These leaders failed to articulate a process for nation-building understood by ordinary citizens, that could effectively mobilize them around a shared vision.[31]

This inadequacy of wholesale application of the borrowed forms of government across the length and breadth of the continent is further reflected in the conditions of the communities depicted in the following observation:

> Independence brought with it an idealism that has been blasted apart by the brutality, looting and mismanagement of too many African governments. Whether they opted for multi-party democracies or one-party states has usually proved irrelevant for the majorities who have accustomed themselves to hunger, lack of education, unemployment, poor health and brutal repression. Local democracies and freedom of expression are rare. And the communities are

powerless to do anything but watch as the fruits of their labor are squandered on development follies, personal luxuries and weapons of war and repression.[32]

To buttress this observation, it is remarked that "both local politics and global economic factors conspired to produce a . . . political economy [in Africa] that not only conflicted with the existing philosophical and social systems of the [communities], but one in which they perceived little economic or social equity."[33] Accordingly, "while the twentieth-century events have changed some of the dynamics of the rural world view, the basic principles still exist and have retained their legitimacy. The development of local government structures since the 1950s has separated chiefs from control over local revenues, but the chiefs retain the moral authority to impose assessments and mobilize efforts for communal needs."[34]

Further, one perceptive author concluded that the crises in the global political economy and the rural-urban migrations of the last two decades have only disrupted but not destroyed the rural communal processes of coexistence.[35] In the opinion of another observer of the same genre,

> for over three decades, both the African political class and development practitioners have failed to realize that the long-term efficacy of new socio-political institutions depends on an imaginative integration of modern structures with pre-existing institutions and practices at the grassroots level.[36]

Needless to say, all these comments are indications for a serious consideration of the indigenous leadership arrangements in any meaningful attempts to address the problem of leadership and governance in Africa. The critical issue is whether the (African) political class can provide a viable system, where local communities can harness the productive resources of these institutions within the context of a decentralized political structure. Such fluid political environment is likely in the long term to challenge authoritarian state control, extractive and corrupt bureaucracies.[37]

A BRP construct could provide a classical answer to the search for alternate conceptualizations with flexible capabilities of enshrining the types of sociopolitical institutions urgently required for some semblance of long-range effectiveness.

Flawed Design and Operations Bias of the Administrative State

Retrofitting the foundation designs and balancing operational orientations of the African state is the ninth mark of origin of a BRP construct. In a general sense, the major consequence of this anomaly in governance is the creation of a conceptually flawed modern African state in practice which, as pointed out by then and late Secretary-General of the United Nations Kofi Annan in a report to the UN Security Council, led to "colossal human tragedies."[38] The Secretary-General at the time blamed much of Africa's instability on its leaders and called on them to turn to political rather than military means to solve their problems—an unequivocal reference to the practice of politics of words and not swords which the construct of BRP portends to induce in varied manners.

This anomaly in governance has also created a situation whereby "the conduct of public administration and affairs is characterized by a displaced sense of purpose, an urban bias, an elite mentality, nepotism, distrust, paternalism, centralization, disregard for time and an absence of organizational loyalty."[39] As further elaborated "in almost all conceivable services, policies have been pursued that favor the politically influential urban populations. The result is that every service is urban based; urban areas are disproportionately more developed than rural areas."[40]

A Report of the Commission on the Structure and Remuneration of the Public Services in Ghana was cited to highlight the existing anomaly in public administration:

> it is strikingly obvious that development in Accra is quite disproportionate to what has taken place in other parts of the country. The rural areas in particular, appear not to have had their fair share of amenities and employment opportunities. . . . It is clear that much of the extensive construction in Accra could only have been financed at the cost of abandoning or deferring programs for the improvement of amenities or the development of the economy in the rural areas. This was possible because of the concentration of both power and facilities in Accra. In a properly ordered government structure, it should not be possible for one area of the country to be developed at the expense of the rest.[41]

Unambiguously, this referenced report was true then in its entirety and remains so presently. It is such narratives about the substantive directions of development interventions and the related performance of the public bureaucracies that the BRP is constructed to change with a compendium Tran-Serve leadership arrangement across the continent.

Conclusion

In the past, more than thirty wars occurred in Africa (mostly within states), and records of several attempted coups and successful military takeovers dotted the landscapes which are rearing their ugly heads quite recently mostly in the West-African sub-region. A rethinking of the so-called modern leadership arrangements is required if Africa wants to end a sixty-year legacy as the world's most strife-torn continent.

It is essential that the search for good leadership and governance strategies in Africa should involve an explanation of indigenous values and principles of participation in a manner that expresses their complementarity to the Western model in practice. Such a task could lead to considerations of infusing relevant indigenous knowledge, values, principles, and philosophy of participation in decision-making into community governance and leadership rearrangement initiatives in Africa. This is what the construct of BRP is about in mission, spirit, intent, focus, and goal.

In essence, African scholars have a fundamental obligation to deepen the understanding of the knowledge systems of their people, act as intermediaries in identifying problems and organizing to solve them. Opening political spaces for constructive collaborative endeavors and robust institutional strengthening in the genre of a BRP construct requires the conscious and honest engagement of African scholars to generate intellectual debates on the practice of democracy, and develop alternative plans on how to induce the collective empowerment of the majority of their people.

The construct of BRP is thus an intellectual obligation to the people of Africa—a choice which conforms with the common maxim that charity begins at home. Or, as Achebe puts it, "if the lizard of the homestead should neglect to do the things for which its kind is known, it will be mistaken for the lizard of the farmland."[42]

Chapter 3

EXISTENTIAL REALITIES

Introduction

This chapter provides a conceptual narrative depicting the realities of an African within the global community as an irrefutable entry point for solution remedies capable of tackling the leadership and governance challenges of the continent. Acceptance of reality is a valuable skills trait of a good leader. Nothing can change until it is accepted. Reality must be faced as it is and not as it was or wished. "It takes courage to accept reality as it is, and only then can you . . . begin to make changes."[1] Charting the realities of any situation creates consciousness and awareness, develops the mindset for well-equipped coping and adaptive capabilities, and sets the pace of response with swiftness and agility. The chapter begins with the post-independence two-world syndrome reality of the African life, which requires mental extrication to handle the exigencies within the global community meticulously and successfully. It then highlights the vicissitudes of navigating life in caricature societies supposedly functioning and catering to the needs of both worlds categorized as superior and inferior.

Thereafter, the key aspect of schooling to embrace one worldview and shun the other is discussed. In this context, the African is faced with the hard choice of socialization, where the land of heritage and culture is continually depicted as inferior and associated with all manner of ills, evils, wrongdoings, blackness, and stigma. Meanwhile, the faraway land never to be seen by many in a lifetime is labeled as crystalline superior and expected to be accepted by all as such without any culpable links to contributions from episodes of plunder and sweats of forced labor. Laboring for transformation in a world pitted on grounds of pity and hopelessness renders success and high achievement motivations the bellwether of elusiveness, wishful dreams, and expectations. The aspirational goals of millions from this world have been stunted and arrested. The chapter ends with a reflection on interests of the political and economic magnates which have been aligned at the global marketplace. Further attention is given to the realization that many of these actors have acquired predatory accumulation characteristics with perfunctory pretensions at the intersections of the two worlds.

Straddling between Two Worlds

Straddling between two worlds is basically freeing oneself from mental enslavement,[2] stemming from a systematic assault on culture and heritage.[3] From cradle, the post-independence African has to grapple with a bequeathed claims of two worlds which are pivotal to developing backbone self-confidence and esteem. Whatever is associated with the cultural practices of the Western world is superior and those associated with the culture of the African world is inferior. Thus, from the onset, this branding of the two worlds becomes the existential burden of the post-independence African.

Underlying this notion of the inferior African practices is a deep pattern of self-serving deceit, calculated lies, and contradictions. Anything from Africa which has to do with riches and wealth creation and can be used to adorn the streets, museums,[4] offices, and homes of the "superior" world is not bad. It is alright to inherit the riches and benefits of theft and plunder. No one should expect any remorse from the present generation of beneficiaries even if mechanisms rooted in the ravages of the past are still in place continuing the siphoning of resources from the so-labeled "dark" continent.[5] Prestigious scholarships and foundations have been created in the home capitals to honor those who took from "heathen" Africa with open hands in the name of the homeland what did not belong to them.[6] Evidence abound that many people have been knighted and celebrated for plundering the resources of the inferior world. Yet the expectation is to mute any criticisms that question the moral righteousness and integrity of such actions, and propagate them as glorified missions of pacifications of the downtrodden and the hapless.

The sad irony of all these distorted characterizations is that several Africans in the past and present bought into these chaotic mental schemes and have become what the "conqueror" wanted them to be—stooges, puppets, and praise singers. However, some stood firm at the peril of their lives and remained what they are, and their stalwartness interred with their bones. The later generations owe these stalwarts a ton of gratitude for paving the way with their heroics and lessons of pride in upholding the integrity of their rich cultural heritage.[7]

The systematic assault on cultural heritage has certainly created some upheaval in the mindset and economic operations of the post-independence Africa with the obvious being the divide-and-rule tactics of "official" language barriers. Another good example is the practice of the whole bunch of foreign earnings and reserves is deposited in the vaults of the central bank of the colonizer.[8] And the country has to go and borrow one's own funds whenever needed on the ground. Regardless of how such an arrangement flies in the face of common sense and logic, and reveals the insidious intentions of the mastermind, the peers, enablers, and compatriots see nothing wrong and have kept mute ever since. Numerous tales abound regarding how treacherous questioning such an anomaly could be in the realm of coexistence of individuals and nations.[9]

Institutional implications of this perennial assault on cultural heritage abound in varied areas of human progress and transformation, including health, education, agriculture, labor mobility, technology utilization and deployment, governance, and many more. Despite this systemic onslaught, many great things and practices of immense value survived which could be relevant for crafting viable solutions to the present-day predicament of many African societies. Emancipation from mental enslavement requires openness to both worlds, embracing, extricating, and blending what is potentially good and relevant from both realms and adapting such institutional knowledge, practices, norms, and values for crafting sustained solutions to overcome current challenges.

Navigating Life in Both Worlds

The two polarized worldview syndrome is further deepened by the structural delineations: formal-informal; rural-urban divide; national, regional, and local levels of governance and administration.[10] Access to public resources— appropriation, accumulation, distribution channels, quality services, business opportunities, and so on—is largely conditioned by where one resides, coexists, operates, or one's position and status in the societal structure categories. Overall, the degree of difficulty and steepness associated with the entire process of navigating life in society is shaped and influenced by such categorizations.[11] Given the historical experiences and circumstances, the societies created as nation-states post-independence were prototype enclaves of the "benevolent" societies with limited reach and restrictive penetration of space within a geographical boundary. There was little or no room for crafting entities which would build on or utilize time-tested elaborate structures, institutions, and norms in existence, which held the communities together for coexistence with each other. The "see nothing good" mentality in the African cultural heritage informed and shaped the narrative on nation-state building.[12]

Established societal structures for interactions with the state, for representations and participation in political and socioeconomic policy decision-making, ensuring voice and accountability in such processes, are largely functional in the formal sectors and urban spaces. The present-day state has become a behemoth, a leviathan whose presence is hardly felt in the informal and rural spaces. This means the mass of people residing and operating in such realms have minimal interactions with the formal state structures but coexist in harmony with each other utilizing organizational mechanisms which hitherto have been condemned to nothingness.[13]

State performance of "law and order" responsibilities in the informal and rural spaces is made possible through the lurking threat of force, coercive compliance apparatus, and enforcement mechanisms not necessarily reliant on sense of voluntariness and belongingness.[14] The likelihood of a post-independence African interacting with state structures is higher when resident in the formal and urban spaces. Navigating life under such scenarios is usually accompanied with ease and less frustrations, and higher prospects of accomplishments, success, and results.

Likewise, representation and participation structures are divergent in effectiveness and efficiency depending on space of residence, coexistence, and operations. It is relatively more difficult for residents in the informal and rural spaces to fuel and galvanize voice and accountability mechanisms in state policy decision-making processes at the national and regional levels using established formalized structures of communication and participation.[15] Particularly in the political arena, parties as units of mobilizing and organizing society for good have metamorphosed into entrenched cabalistic creatures where the ever-present predatory behavior of privatization of public wealth and postures as well as having exclusive monopoly of knowledge and wisdom become the norm.[16]

Nowhere is the African conflictual mental predicament stemming from the constant and calculated assault on cultural heritage is more prevalent than in the realm of religious worship and practice of faith and belief systems. Having been bombarded with lies at a point in time that even the Supreme Being was introduced to the African space from outside, there is the noticeable tendency of the post-independence African to oscillate between practices grounded in the much-maligned cultural heritage and external religious pastoral beliefs and inclinations.[17]

Similarly, navigating access to services in the sector of health, for example, speaks volumes of heavy reliance on a combination of orthodox and traditional medications and treatment procedures and processes.[18] In terms of agriculture, the age-long maniacal focus on so-labeled "cash crops" has blunted any reasonable spirited attempts at formulating and implementing coherent food policies. As a result, Africa cannot feed itself and its leaders have to rely on the embarrassing acts of resorting to charity and benevolence to meet such basic rights needs and obligations.[19]

Presently, navigating life under the various societal circumstances created several decades after independence poses serious risks and challenges for the youth in particular and the broader population at large. African societies are facing the "youth bulge" given its average age and several of them eking out a living in penury, idleness, and vulnerability.[20] The notion of servant leadership[21] is an anathema in the prevailing political climate rendering navigation of life a brutish venture particularly in the informal and rural domain for the post-independence African. Quick fixes and band-aid solutions for deep-seated structural problems are bandied around by politicians, who have become drains on national and continental coffers, and indelible scars on the consciences of the good people in the global community.

Several of the African societies have become ticking time bombs due to despondency and failures by an overwhelming geriatric leadership who erroneously believe longevity in office is the panacea of viable solutions for malfunctioning societies.[22] A troubling trend is re-emerging with the reappearance of the guns in the capitals of some societies, thereby complicating further the process of navigating sustainable life for many in post-independence Africa.[23]

Schooling to Embrace One Worldview and Shun the Other

The schooling system churns out graduates with elite mentality who believe and act broadly as "tin gods"—very greedy occupants of public offices who do not want to have anything substantial to do *with* the very communities they hail from except to visit and cajole for electoral votes, if running for public office.[24] They prefer the communities to remain informal and rural given the urban-bias and thrust of the so-called formal development strategies championed in respective countries.[25] The visionary traits of compassion and the urge to lead for good—characteristics of some of the leaders of the anticolonialism struggle—have evaporated and been replaced with the self-serving leaders desirous of turning public resources into private wealth. Occupying public office has become devoid of any notion of servant leadership and perceived as a license to "create, loot and share."[26] Graduates of the school system mainly construe public positions as honorable to the extent they serve as viable conduits for self-accumulation and aggrandizement. Public offices remain privileges so long as they provide the grounds for "shambolic respect" out of the ability to dole out favors to kinsfolks, colleagues, and friends.[27]

This attitudinal dysfunctionality is partly the result of the post-independence pyramidal school system which focused primarily not at problem-solving but on rote learning of content[28] and imitation of behavior rooted in the way of life of the "yardstick civilized culture." The exclusive selection process left behind a chunk of the populace and their corresponding communities along the way in a vicarious manner. As a result, the majority shuffled out tend to perceive the few who eventually have been crowned with glittering titles and certificates as "superheroes" with the wisdom and capability to lead and improve the lot of the population. It has also reached the point where the few graduates of the school system perceive themselves in the manner and prestige accorded to them by the majority of the populace to rationalize their miscreant attitudes and behavior whenever they occupy any esteemed public office.

The private apprenticeship system[29] which emerged to produce artisans and absorb the vast majority is geared to cater to the consumption needs and interests of the few so-labeled elites without the expansive capital foothold programs and assistance to serve the broader needs of society. A well-oiled patronage relationship of a "big man" syndrome[30] has been established, which makes the majority artisan groups dependent on the few elites for the practice and sustenance of their trade with serious consequences for quality service provisions, delivery, and revenue generation particularly in the public sectors. By so doing, exertion of pressure on public officials for accountability and good stewardship is either absent or minimal. In this respect, the majority often eschew the attitude to look the other way whenever there are violations of public ethics, especially if the public official is considered as one of their own.[31]

At the moment, there is a proliferation of learning centers across the continent with questionable status which continues the trend of schooling out of the cultural heritage.[32] The products are highly indoctrinated and brainwashed to conceive success as possible mainly through an external intervention and not anything which could be derived from their homes and communities. The resultant attitude is to deepen the stance of shunning efforts toward home-grown solutions for designs coated with the worldview of external conceptions. No wonder the school system, unlike in jurisdictions Africa seeks to emulate, has failed persistently to provide adequate solutions for the myriad challenges facing the generations of today.[33] What would serve better as a measure of success could largely be derivative of qualities and values of both worldviews.

Laboring for Transformation

Success at laboring for transformation by an African domiciled particularly in the informal and rural space is an uphill task and a mind-boggling life trajectory-altering phenomenon.[34] Communities and families in such settings usually live under the poverty line, and there is a pervasive lack of equity in terms of distribution of educational facilities compared to many urban spaces. It is an environment where the elementary school completion and graduation with flying colors' rate is palpable, and progression to higher phases of schooling may be limited to a handful of the very brilliantly endowed.[35] The whole effort toward transformation may be construed as acquisition of "borrowed" garments and transfer of privileges through formal education based on socioeconomically disadvantaged background of upbringing.

Access to higher social order is conditioned as the preserve of upscale upbringing and good life as the domain of elite education. Deeply engrained tensions, obstacles, and resentment would usually pave the way for efforts to climb the social ladder, as the guardians and enforcers of the "pecking order" intentionally or unintentionally engage in practices to dissuade people considered as not belonging or deserving of such supposedly bestowed social privileges. These sentiments would certainly induce internal struggles among people of lower-scale background in developing the requisite identity and mentality of toughness for seizing the opportunities to exceed social expectations. In so doing, the first casualty with the likelihood of deepening the conditions of informal and rural spaces is that the "beacon of hope" mainly leave behind the local schools and communities in the trail of developing and acquiring new attitudes, mannerisms, practices, and skills commensurate with the aspirations of attaining reserved privileged status.

The feelings of alienation in the process of attaining transformation pervade all aspects of lives. First and foremost, there would be little in common with peerage colleagues, acquaintances, and friends who hitherto did not have the opportunity of so-labeled elite education to climb the social ladder. Home communities usually seem distant and far away in imaginations while obligations from societal expectations may mount. Although such feelings of alienation may ease over time, the pride of attainment usually paves the way to a sense of overwhelming frustration and hopelessness given the entrenched deprivations and deterioration facing many of the communities.

Usually, the acquired privilege through education goes with the opportunity to observe from close quarters the extent of wanton dissipation of public resources into private pockets when not in cahoots with the progenitors. The political leadership seems to be on a planet of its own creation and somewhat oblivious to the plight of the masses, who provide the electoral votes in return for the misuse of public wealth. All over the continent, electioneering is mainly replacing one looter with another while expecting different results and outcomes. If this phenomenon is not insanity at its epic, then no one knows what it is, and something has to be done. Certainly, this may require changing the methods of leadership arrangements with the mandate to govern. This measure is possible through innovative ways of blending the knowledge base of the two worlds, which has ingrained in the post-independence African mindset the notion of twoness with the lingering impassioned internal conflict of self-worth and coexistence within the community of nations.

The Odds Are Stacked against Millions

Most of the three-quarters products of the pyramidal school system are half-baked literates with arrested aspirations and subpar work skills and ethics compared to globally accepted standards. These are people who largely roam the streets of the capitals and few urban centers with a "quick fix," "get-rich-instantly" mindsets and very economical with the cardinal principles of trust, loyalty, and sense of belonging in an organizational setup.

Having been uprooted from their cultural heritage with the taste and experience of some "formal" education, they constitute the loud and boisterous foot soldiers of the dominant political parties,[36] and serve as the conducive ignorant cover of support for the plunder of the very public resources which could have made their lots better. The urban bias of development focus and public resource allocation concentrations means the agriculture sector, for example, which could provide viable employment opportunities for many of these people, remains ironically undeveloped, and thus incapable and unattractive to their aspirational goals. Instructively, however, the counterparts who continue to reside in the informal and rural spaces are the bedrock of the local youth groups, who uphold in high esteem the indigenous leadership institutions and practices pivotal to the harmonious coexistence of the communities.

In a local parlance, "things have never been soft in the economy since time immemorial."[37] The vast majority of the multitudes of semiliterates and dunderheads eke out a living in nation-states with "jobless growth" situations the past several decades,[38] and perceive the political arena as the main source of opportunities for leapfrogging to their dream good lives. As practiced in its current state, the politics of avarice and prevarication does not hold any bright future prospects for the millions who are expecting the leadership of the continent to deliver on the promises of the independence cries, rallies, and clarion calls. The constant worsening of the political and economic plight of the people, the deeper the cultural heritage decadence and forward marching toward a societal Armageddon.

Changing the fortunes of million idlers and vulnerable is neither an option nor alternative for bureaucratic deliberations in a continent on the brink of implosion. Continental initiatives such as the African Continental Free Trade Area (AfCFTA) are long overdue.[39] However, patience is thinning when results are not easily forthcoming from such policy actions to ameliorate conditions. Measures toward realization of the ideals seem to be dangling in the same directions and manner of high-level forums, meetings, mission travels of principals of the predecessor generations.

The current generation of African leaders needs to wake up from the stupor, galvanize itself, listen, and act expeditiously when the alert bells are ringing on the rooftops with the message that time is running out for inactions and obliviousness. An account of the plight of a Nigerian before departure to the United States vividly paints the picture of the situation of millions eking out a living on the continent: "I had great hopes after graduating from the university, but four years afterwards, the only reality that stared me in the face each morning was the one of packing sachet water into bags and hanging on a moving truck to supply to customers, to make ends meet."[40]

Predatory Aligned Interests

One good thing about the world is it has become a global village and community with ubiquitous information and communications technologies (ICTs) particularly social media handles/channels. With this is the intensified alignment of interests of the global elites, which is non-concerning so long as it leads to good for the global community. The leaders of Africa and other developing countries have always been the "junior partners" of the global order. This has remained so until such aligned interests have been vicariously transformed into leakages of resources, which deprive the mass of the people critical resources for basic needs and improvement in living conditions across the continent.[41]

Globally aligned interests have become predatory in Africa leading to deprivation of valuable public resources in two major ways: mode of representation, and the practice and manifest of hegemonic activities. Western-oriented political parties and the accompanying acts of periodic elections of constitutionally mandated rulers, overseers, and managers of public resources have become the universally accepted mode of representation within the global community of nations. In Africa, it does not matter whether the manner of communicating, mobilizing, and organizing political parties is tearing apart communal bonds and unleashing divisiveness, acrimony, loss of lives, and avoidable depletion and wasteful resources.[42] It is even irrelevant if the process of party operations leads to the suppression, marginalization, and relegation of the remnants of indigenous leadership, which enabled harmonious coexistence of communities over the past several decades. Whether the whole gamut of political party operations and electoral processes have become a sham and charade of what pertains elsewhere, the mockery is fine and the outcome of irritable imitations acceptable for the conduct of governance.

The Bretton Woods twins[43] continue to manage the postwar global financial order with agility, which ensures that reckless, recalcitrant, or reneging actions and behavior are nipped in the global bud for conformity. This arrangement has suitably replaced the obtrusive "gun boat" policy with "pin-stripe suits" policy, while projecting a benevolent image of the "senior partners" of the global coalition. The mantra of sovereign debt and the associated management rituals of negotiations, rescheduling, capital flights, and siphoning remain a powerful instrument for compliance and recalibrating the global financial order. As recently noted by the World Bank president David Malpass, "we need a comprehensive approach to the debt problem, including debt reduction, swifter restructuring and improved transparency." Accordingly, "debt loads in low-income countries surged 12 percent to a record $860 billion in 2020 amid the pandemic . . . sustainable debt levels are vital for economic recovery and poverty reduction."[44]

Certain mind-boggling operations of some trust companies and locations in global metropolis metamorphosing into havens for illicit financial transactions have further muddied the waters of resource deprivation for millions in Africa and other developing nations. Revelations by the recently published "Panama Papers . . . expose a system that enables crime, corruption and wrongdoing, hidden by secretive offshore companies."[45] The scenario painted is truly a "destruction of the poor in their poverty."[46] What this means is that many children of the poor will continue to walk barefoot several kilometers to schools under trees; go to bed hungry; will not be attended to by a qualified health professional when sick; no dental visits, and vacations for roller skating, amusement and Disneyland theme parks. Yet these children are part of the same global community and expected to compete with counterparts and perform creditably with shinning outcomes.

Pretensions at the Intersections of the Two Worlds

The African development landscape is replete with pretensions and contradictions.[47] Recycled and severally debunked theories, policies, and strategies continue to be superintended without any substantial difference in results and outcomes. An avowedly but discredited strategy has been the structure of production and trade. African economies are conditioned to participating in global trade through concentration on the production of unprocessed raw material goods and products in which they have comparative and competitive advantage, and prices determined by the invisible marketplace forces.[48] It is a known fact that the "invisible hands" of the marketplace have always been tilted in favor of vested and powerful business elite actors.[49] And only economies with value-added processed goods and products have ever fared better at the global marketplace. However, trade based on comparative advantage has remained the pivot of the development projections of the African continent until the recent proclamations of AfCFTA, which have remained textual ideals and are yet to be grounded in practice.

Another eerie structural formulation of resource accumulation and wealth creation is noteworthy. The arrangement whereby several linguistic-bound African countries are compelled by an outdated colonial imposition to deposit foreign earnings and reserves at the central bank of the former colonizer in return for continuous so-called protections from volatility and instability at the global marketplace. And these countries would engage in borrowing their own money whenever funds are needed for expenses at home. It must be magical to the point of impracticality, despite intentions and goodwill, for any substantial transformations to materialize under the yolk of such an arrangement.[50] Notably, this is the rationale of the proposal in November 2019 by eight West African countries, including Benin, Togo, Burkina Faso, Mali, Senegal, Ivory Coast, Niger, and Guinea Bissau to withdraw their currency reserves from the French central bank to Senegal. As is the case, even though these eight countries had gained independence years ago, they continued to vest their foreign exchange reserves with the French central bank.

By design, the aforementioned conditions of production and capital accumulation are structurally fundamental and shape other vital indicators regarding the performance of an economy, including currency exchange rates, interest rates, inflationary rates, GDP growth, balance of payments, purchasing power, returns on investments, and related business transactions. The currencies of African economies are always referred to as "soft" and never "hard" ever since, and have fluctuated deeply compared to those of other jurisdictions at the global marketplace. For example, in the case of Ghana, the *Business Financial Times* (BFT) reported that recently "the Ghana cedi has experienced depreciation against the US dollar in the first week of October 2021, despite the inflows of foreign currency which have given the economy enough forex to cover imports for five months."[51] All the other indicators have mainly been on the astronomical high sides of the compendium in Africa. Countries with attractive trajectory of comparable lower rates in these varied categories of economic indicators are either "developed" or on the transformation track.

Of course, if a country devotes its most arable land and financial incentives to producing "cash crops," and concentrates on incurring very high food importation bills, stunted growth, underdevelopment, starvation, and deprivation would be the lot of the vast populace. Even the much-touted African Green Revolution has not changed the narrative in this regard.[52] A nation which cannot feed itself is a disgrace to humanity and remains a scar on the conscience and mentality of the global elites, who oversee and superintend pretentious development relations among nations. The aid industry would cease to be profitable if emaciated bodies of children are not paraded and beamed over on TV screens in many homes as rationale for donations and appeal to the benevolence of several "marauding" elites.[53]

Conclusion

This chapter provides the context of realities which will influence and shape the strength of leadership and governance arrangements capable as suitable solutions pathway for policy considerations across the continent. By so doing, the chapter sets the tone for the level of literary candidness and admissibility necessary for discussing the leadership and governance malaise which have afflicted Africa like a dreaded disease seeping through its pores with the intensity of ravaging it beyond repairs if timely action is not taken. The usefulness of any solutions intervention can be measured by the undergirding realism, courage, and hope it exudes. The envisioned blended solutions must have the requisite toughness to grapple with the vagaries of the double worldviews, the challenges of navigating life as an African within such setup, and socialization mechanisms which tend to alienate inhabitants from their cultural heritage and redirect energy and focus to appreciating anything coming from outside the continent. All this represents a tall order requiring swift, agile leadership and governance arrangement which inspires and motivates with the mindsets of fulfilling needs and manifesting the blessings of success for everyone.

Furthermore, the trials which accompany everyday hustles of eking a living in poverty to transition out of wretchedness whiles the odds are heavily unfavorable with predatory aligned interests and pretensions have to be taken into consideration. In this regard, familiarity and objective knowledge of the realities are essential for crafting suitable solutions which would withstand seemingly unsurmountable challenges for robust countervailing mitigating responses.

Chapter 4

FUNDAMENTALS OF THE CONUNDRUM

Introduction

This chapter highlights the fundamentals of the confusing and difficult leadership and governance challenges, and their corresponding effects on social living, and postulates on the types of arrangements capable of addressing these issues effectively for better outcomes. A conspicuous prevalence of leadership and governing systems grounded in external aspirational beliefs has been exerting very high tolls on the majority's capacity to coexist harmoniously which recently prompted, for example, a continental espousal without hitting the problem on its head. The posture of dysfunctionality between the ruled and the rulers mainly enables increasing reliance on ever-lurking threats of coercion rather than the spirit of voluntarism as the basis of enforcing social contract terms defined in the image of the haves at the expense of the have-nots.

Transparency in public finance management remains another crucial point of concern. A tailored focus on high-profile institutionally commandeered initiatives in the extractive sector reveals up and downside results while the phenomenon continues to loom large in varied forms at the landscape. Aspects of accountability for related policy decision-making, actions, and choices do not fare better, and neither does participation in electoral politics which tends to fan more flames of divisiveness rather than integration and unifying around common reasonable causes. Furthermore, spreading evenly dividends of overall gamut of post-independence governing arrangements has remained elusive and hard to accomplish.

Grounded Leadership System

The genesis of the governance conundrum in Africa is that leadership choices, avenues, and options are not grounded in the beliefs of the kind of society Africans want and dream about given the continent's cultural heritage and historical experiences.[1] For far too long, Africa has dangled between two dominant ideologies of organizing societies (capitalism and socialism) without much success of replicating either type for the good of its people.[2] The Africa of today is comprised of social entities far from their pristine communal roots under the leadership institution of chieftaincy which is inadequate to handle the exigencies of present-day needs and challenges facing the people.[3] However, Africa is paying the price of molding and fashioning leadership systems purely in the image of the outside world at the expense and neglect of utilizing as foundations leadership structures and institutions, which have held the communal societies together.

As a mark of its fiftieth anniversary, the African Union (AU) made some grandiose postulations of the "Africa We Want."[4] For our purpose, the "Agenda 2063," however, has left open the leadership types which would transition the continent into the promised land. In all honesty, many Africans wish the "goodies" capitalist societies provide in its wake without necessarily the "trickle down," "survival of the fittest," "weakling handouts" modes of resource accumulation, acquisition, distribution, access and control systems.[5] Undoubtedly, a society grounded in the tenets of communal mode of coexistence at the grassroots blended with a conscientious leadership to protect public wealth, values, and interests at the national and international levels would drive and serve better the ideals of the "Africa We Want." In this context, leadership systems appreciative of the complementarity of positions and roles in society would be more suited for promoting and attaining the ideals of the communities. Such systems likely operate with an adrenaline fortified by a deep sense of care, duty, and responsibilities to the mass of the people.

Leadership expressions of gratitude would go beyond engineering results for entrenched self-serving rule or routine "thank you" tours after solicitations and securing of electoral votes.[6] In truth, the gestures of gratitude will largely be significant and meaningful to the vast majority of people if they reflect real public recognition of efforts manifested in the provisions and delivery of due shares of public resources. And tours will specifically be exercises undertaken to boost morale and motivate while demonstrating full support of overall existential activities, and not eliciting hooting and rejections over electoral votes not delivering on promises.[7]

Rebuilding the "Africa We Want" would require leaders with demonstrable appreciation of the realities and not acting all-knowing as monopolists of wisdom. It would be leadership systems which would forge prosocial behavior by unleashing the innate social values, qualities, and capital of communities toward positivity, helpfulness, and intentions to proactively engage in activities geared at attaining the envisaged societal ideals. The purported structural leadership arrangements would be tolerant of diverse opinions regardless of the sources as a cardinal yardstick of unity and harmonious coexistence of the various communities under the umbrella of nation-states.

Furthermore, the society types which would deliver the ideals of the "promised land" would be fostered by ruling systems with the underlying driving philosophy of leadership for all and good based on the approach akin to servant leadership—a style of leadership which sees people's needs as the end. "Servant Leadership is defined as a philosophy and set of practices that enriches the lives of individuals, builds better . . . [societies] and ultimately creates a more just and caring world."[8] Notably, "servant leadership does not expect any outcome other than simply fulfilling the needs of people. It is implied that serving them will only do well for them."[9] The attributes of a servant leader were noted in the values of societal transformation espoused by Kwame Nkrumah of Ghana, Lee Kuan Yew of Singapore, and Mahathir Mohamed of Malaysia, to mention a few who demonstrated and implemented a compelling vision in this context.

Africa is in the throes of rulership confusion situations, which provide opportunities mainly to praise singers, sycophants, party apparatchiks, family and friends of the leaders in power.[10] There are usually no rooms to accommodate communities and individuals that happen to be on the opposite aisle regardless of the expertise, experience, and skills for contributions of substance.[11]

In the sense of rebranding and rebuilding the "Africa We Want," servant leadership would empower everyone in their homes and communities despite party colors and leanings. As it is, "the competitive future belongs to those leaders and [societies], which will have everyone on board empowered to identify and resolve [societal] problems . . . awards citizenship through servant leadership. [This] means that for [citizens] to show altruism and go beyond their call of duty, the servant leader must empower [everyone] to feel like a significant member."[12] Such a scenario is only attainable when the leadership of the society is concerned holistically with the care, well-being, and growth of everyone.

Synchronous Rulership

Another notable dimension of the leadership and governance conundrum in Africa is that the rulers and the ruled are not in sync. They are not on the same page, and neither do they sing from the same hymnal. The values of the rulers are different from those of the ruled.[13] To use an apt analogy, the head (elites) and the body (masses) are not working together.[14] The rulers are unable to inspire and motivate the ruled; they have a diminished capacity to communicate, mobilize, and organize society voluntarily for good (except sycophants,[15] praise singers, or party adherents) without the threat of force or the promise of doling out material favors. In the public arena, many officials have difficulty leading by example which is a critical embodiment of the foundational values of public servants. They cannot be servants to their values but rather engage in activities of privatizing public wealth.[16] Some officials literally interpret the concept of "public servants" as turning into "errand men or bowing to the superiors" and would rather encourage or engage in behaviors which create a culture that shuns and undermines such values in the execution of official duties.[17]

The first casualty of such rulership anomaly is closeness: that is, the organizational regime with the mandate to rule will not be close to the people; and the vessel of the state through which power and authority are manifested would become a distant hanging "Damocles"[18] with jittery footholds and no or fake imprints in the minds and hearts of the citizens.

Also, a collateral casualty is administrative efficiency and efficacy in terms of management of public resources for the provision and delivery of services to the people. Those in charge of the public offices are usually unable to encourage everyone to be on the same page, think outside the box, accommodate, and analyze diverse opinions before arriving at a decision for moving forward with a solution. In this case, these officials are unable to ensure that the final decision is a byproduct of a collective collaboration and exchange of ideas. In this sense, collective responsibility for a particular challenge of society, which requires attention, would be negated and sacrificed on the altar of self-serving individualistic power. Consequently, such acts of responsibility emanate from one person's mentality instead of everyone's contributions to the end results.[19]

Trust, respect, and loyalty (the cardinal ingredients of better governance) to the whole ruling structures become increasingly elusive, hard to forge, and instill. Under such circumstances, it becomes extremely difficult for the rulers to communicate the values people are expected to live by, and the overall vision of society which should be bought and ingrained in the minds of the ruled. The task of building a higher level of trust in society is shoddily executed and restricted to reaching mainly those who belong to the clique of ethnic backgrounds, family, and friends. Leaders are unable to lead the whole society and are rendered deaf and hardened to the plight of those who exist outside such tightly protected coterie. The purpose of ruling is then construed as limited to fulfilling the needs of those perceived to be deserving and are supposedly the loyal followers. As trust is earned and not given on a silver platter, the coercive instruments and tools are directed to clamp down on those considered hostile, disloyal, and untrustworthy.

A scenario of asynchronous rulership dents the mindset of the majority in nurturing and fostering a sense of belonging and buy-in of the much-touted agenda of one nation, one people, and one continent. Many of the present crops of African leaders tend to forget that ruling is not about them, and it was never and will not be but rather it is about the people who make it all thrive and worthwhile. As noted, great leaders "facilitate the success of others and make everyone feel valued and their contributions matter to the overall attainment of consensual societal goals. . . . Great leaders drive change in many ways, but unselfishness is what ultimately allows them to scale" their vision and create a long-lasting, memorable, and impactful legacy.[20] This implies that if a leader is perceived by the people as greedy, selfish, and uncaring with fuselage and adrenalin running on meaningless unfulfilled promises, there would be little or no excitement and minimal sense of belonging toward the endeavors undertaken during such rulership.

Transparency in Public Financial Management (PFM)

Africa's development landscape is riddled with numerous reports on financial improprieties with the debilitating consensus on lack of transparency in public finance management as a deep-seated governance problem.[21] The situation has been so worrisome that in the late 1990s onwards, a major pillar of the County

Assistance Strategy (CAS) and later named Country Partnership Strategy (CPS) of the World Bank and other related development agencies has been on strengthening public finance management.[22] On the requests of ministers of finance, the World Bank embarked on countless missions to help rectify the situation and organized seminars, workshops, and relevant series of learning events on this topical issue.

The focus and objectives of some of these learning events revolved around, for example, strengthening capacity for establishing open and orderly public financial management (PFM) systems, processes, and institutions in the country. Sample content details include guidance on international best practices related to the core dimensions of an open and orderly PFM system in terms of: (i) credibility of the budget, (ii) comprehensiveness and transparency of the budget; (iii) policy-based budgeting; (iv) predictability and control in budget execution; (v) financial accounting, recording, and reporting; and (vi) legislative and related external scrutiny and auditing of the budget.[23] In fact, the preoccupation of a whole department of the World Bank has been engagements and exercises to find suitable solutions to this canker of persistent leaks in public finance.[24] Reforms have been suggested, at times imposed, and the bank's assistance and assessment of country's creditworthiness have been shaped or conditioned by the extent, commitments, and results on public finance management.

The Extractive Industries sphere is a major culprit cited quite often. For the past two decades or more, the Extractive Industries Transparency Initiative (EITI) has been a bureaucratic flourishing business globally aimed at mitigating "the negative effective effects of resource abundance by promoting the transparency of resource revenues and accountability of the resource rich states."[25] The jury is out there on the effectiveness of the overall EITI.[26] What remains a fact is that the absence of transparency in this field is widespread and is a major contributive factor to the leadership and governance challenges facing African countries.[27]

Other features of PFM lacking transparency which are commonly cited include the award of contracts across all fields and sectors of endeavors but particularly in construction and the provision of infrastructure; sovereign borrowings (loans), assistance (credit), and donations (aid); procurement of public goods and services; project financing, foreign direct investments (FDI), and official responses to investigative revelations of financial improprieties.[28] The issue of concern here is that without transparency and failure to lead by example and a clear purpose, many would neither hold in high esteem nor emulate such leadership practices. Transparency forges trust as a cardinal principle of good governance and followership, which has a direct correlation to work performance.[29]

Without transparency in decision-making, the governing atmosphere is laced with doubts and constant second-guessing of motives and intentions, which hinder the ability of those in charge to foster leadership in others—a necessary ingredient of bridging and continuity in governance as related to the need to develop the next generation of leaders. The conscious and proactive act of passing the torch through molding the next generations to lead is an intergenerational responsibility of mentoring, coaching, and hand-holding. Lack of transparency in decision-making on resource use and allocation is an anathema to such thoughts and necessary action. It is important that the present generation gives back to the next, which is likely the only way to foster innovation and creativity for great leadership qualities in aspiring future generations of leaders.

Whether it is deliberate or not, Africa has experienced situations whereby after the demise of a long-serving octogenarian leader, the succession processes have been plagued with chaos, conflicts, anarchy, and destruction.[30] To ensure that such transitions are accompanied with peace and harmonious interactions among the successor generations, transparency in decision-making would constitute a hallmark and bedrock of governance norms and practices. A deliberate effort on the part of the older generation of leaders to instill and inspire the younger ones by giving more of themselves is not a choice but necessary acts of valuable statesmanship representing a potential legacy of history-making epoch.[31]

Accountability for Policy Outcomes

A veritable source of the leadership and governance conundrum is how public officials who exercise political power and authority are answerable for policy decisions, actions, and outcomes, which affect the vast majority of people. Other noteworthy dimensions are whether public officials are responsive to the needs of the people they are expected to care for in the process, and whether existing and available mechanisms and institutional arrangements are able to ensure enforcement of any disciplinary sanctions in cases of failure to satisfy expectations.[32]

Generally, the issue of accountability is a hydra-headed phenomenon, and the dynamics of the challenges are riddled with complexities.[33] The issue has been largely addressed with formal and informal mechanisms or with institutional arrangements in domestic and external contexts.[34] The approaches for suitable solutions have also taken the forms of vertical, horizontal, and social groups and individual interventions. At a point, external promptings from the donor community (World Bank and DfiD) took the forms of community empowerment and social inclusion initiatives. Many of these interventions were geared to catalyze civil society groups to be vigorous and vigilant, and other related programs, whose effectiveness in terms of moving the needle forward, were considered by some critical observers as doubtful.

Regardless of the entry point, certain facts are crystal clear and indisputable: holding African government officials accountable remains a huge challenge and finding effective solutions elusive. Attributed reasons are a combination of external factors such as colonial legacy, cold war, and neoliberal economic policies and internal factors entailing civil wars, military dictatorships, the lack of a vigorous civil society, and poverty.[35]

As noted,

> Africa is arguably a continent where the problem of accountable government remains most stark. The decolonization process of the 1960s promised an era of self-rule and independence in which the new governments would be both

responsive to the needs of the people and accountable to them. Yet the regimes that decolonization gave birth to did not meet that promise.[36]

The tactics of retreating from established commitments and undermining accountability structures including constitutional, legislative, and judiciary arrangements by the elites have been on display in the name of party politics dispensations and operations across the continent. The democratic wave of the 1990s and the proliferation of social media handles presently have seemed to resuscitate the public yearning for greater accountability. However, the widespread practice of politics of "create, loot, and share" as well as that of "friends and family" has eroded any gains which emanated from such laudable societal interventions in this cherished era.

Blurring lines between the public and the private spheres has remained a deeply ingrained practice, and the conduct of abhorrent behaviors with impunity by public officials is rampant. On several occasions, the offices of government are mute whenever the people are expecting explanations for certain actions and behaviors. What merits responses from government offices are usually determined arbitrarily or on ad-hoc basis and not by public consensus. Regardless of circumvention of societal needs and expectations for personal gains, and whether abuse of power or authority and misuse of public resources may have occurred in such instances, no official explanation or response would be provided. Too often the public may be expecting disciplinary sanctions regarding specific occurrences only to be met with complete stone-death silence, particularly if the person whose ox has been gored is highly placed in society.[37]

Without doubt, accountability is needed to ensure fairness, equality, and equity in public resource allocations and expenditure decision-making. Yet a multitude of culturally shaped and overlapping formal and informal relations determine citizens' ability to hold their public officials and representatives accountable. For example, in many cases, it has become an acceptable local norm and regular practices of parliamentarians to pay "school fees" of children of constituents, attend funerals, make contributions or donations to families, and preside over important events and celebration of festivals with monetary gifts in their respective constituencies.[38]

The nature of electoral votes solicitation and the practices of multiparty politics across the board in general have amplified existing multiple sources and overlapping forms of accountability. To a large extent, these actions undermine, diminish, and prevent public voices for accountability from becoming louder and more empowering. In this regard, it is logical and increasingly clearer that "some hybrid forms of local leadership have the potential to forge a degree of accountability," and society should be geared in this direction for a way forward.[39]

Participation in the Practice of Electoral Politics

Electoral politics, as practiced on the continent, has been debilitatingly divisive and drives the alienation of many people from those with the mandate to represent, rule, and govern.[40] Coexisting in societies which operate on the foundations of a weakened political culture[41] characterized by many unmet needs and expectations from political authorities have made participation of the majority limited and restricted to electoral cycles.[42] Interests in the periodic voting processes are shaped by partisan affiliations and the extent of involvement in the activities of a particular political party rather than awareness and understanding as acts of constitutional rights and obligations. Constitutional provisions in terms of regulation of relationships with the regime in power, and parties contesting outcomes of the elections as well as relations with fellow citizens, exert minimal influence or shape consciousness in this regard.[43] For example, it is noteworthy that the participation of the youth in general is similar across the board: "Africa's youth vote less and are more likely to demonstrate either no partisanship or attachment to opposition parties rather than to incumbent parties . . . and unlike older voters, the youth tend to vote less the longer an incumbent party has been in office."[44]

Further, in relation to women's participation, accordingly, "African countries are still far from achieving women's equality and effective participation in political decision-making. Women constitute only 24 percent of the 12,113 parliamentarians in Africa, 25 per cent in the lower houses and 20 per cent in the upper houses of parliaments."[45] Research has also debunked the claim that "political participation [in Africa] is costly and requires inputs in terms of individual resources . . . and citizens face comparatively high participation costs and have more limited resource endowments" than their counterparts elsewhere.[46]

The lack of enthusiasm toward voting has made the motivational force behind the decision to participate an essential component of the leadership and governance conundrum in Africa. There is a deep-seated knowledge deficit among many Africans to understand and internalize the complex and important relationships fostered through expectations of constitutional obligations, including the critical role played by elections in institutionalizing and entrenching such arrangements. Usually, nationwide civic education programs facilitate the governing processes which enable governments to provide and expose citizens to the necessary tools for appreciating the essence of such constitutional obligatory requirements. Examples of relevant tools in this case will include an independent judiciary; a free press; free, fair, transparent, inclusive, and credible election.[47]

Certainly, "addressing these issues will require grappling with longstanding grievances left untreated and often exacerbated by the poor, sometimes brutal governance that is all too common across the continent.[48]" As noted, "African governments can shore up their deficits and strengthen their responses to [such situations] by tapping into the political capital of informal leaders, such as religious and traditional leaders."[49] An effective response in this direction will require "true commitment to conserving and deepening domestic political capital, strengthening the social contract with their citizens and governing accountability."[50]

Unequal Distribution of Rulership Dividends

On the eve of its 2021 Annual Conference, the International Monetary Fund's (IMF) forecast on the operations of the global economy warned that "the outlook for the low-income developing country group has darkened considerably due to worsening pandemic conditions."[51] The bulk of the low-income developing country group comprises African countries, and so although this IMF forecast is quite worrisome, it is not surprising to many critical observers of the African development landscape.[52] At a point, many people in Africa subsisted on one dollar a day, and now this has increased to two dollars a day which means the progression needle has not moved that much.

The "quick fixes," commercially focused and commodity-based approaches, and short-term interventions to tackling Africa's economic development-fueled challenges continue to be in vogue on the continent. These approaches are the very stark contrast between how similar challenges are addressed in other related jurisdictions within the global system.[53] Such interventions remain what they are: cheaper in the short term, "provide a sense of direct and quick return on investment,"[54] operate with little or no efficacy span, and do not usually constitute the bedrock and mainstay solutions. No wonder nothing seems to work in several sectors of the economies in Africa after six decades and more.

On this day in 2022, things have not changed that much for the ordinary African, and conditions have been worsened further by the Covid-19 pandemic. As noted by the World Bank in its effort to ensure a strong recovery for developing countries, "the global economy is experiencing an uneven recovery, with the risk that it will worsen inequality and leave low-and-middle income countries behind. . . . Developing economies face challenges that could slow their recovery for years to come."[55]

Of course, if you are part of the ruling elites, well-connected in society and your party is in power, life cannot be better in Africa. Judging from outcome records of previous interventions, the ruling elites (politicians) will be the intended front and center of any assistance from the international community. As reported, the World Bank has "mounted the largest crisis response in its history . . . to help ensure that all countries can participate in a green, resilient, and inclusive return to stability and growth."[56] This response will certainly ensure that the ruling elites continue to have access to their chauffeured-driven four wheels convoys and other perk benefit guarantees under the conditions of public service rules inserted in the constitutions of the various countries.

However, from the grind- and brunt-bearing ends of the masses, for example, the health systems which severally crumbled with the onset of the Covid-19 pandemic have remained "death traps" ever since along the accompanying mantra that ordinary people go to hospitals not to seek cures but to die. More often, the coterie of elites, who are part of the transnational beneficiaries of such bandage interventions, are flown outside the continent for medical treatment. For the ordinary African, a resort to the combination of whatever is available within the orthodox and indigenous herbs spheres becomes the norm of medical recourse.

The public education system keeps churning out graduates with the few bright and talented well-versed mainly in theoretical concepts without corresponding applicable skills set and knowledge, and the large majority who can arguably be labeled as half-baked literates. Children of the elites are enamored with certificates from the best schools available locally or sent overseas by parents to attain the necessary education, which always put them at the top over their less-privileged counterparts in the job and career world. In fact, the cities of Africa have been turned into huge shopping malls dotted with Christian churches, prayer camps, mosques, and religious centers, many of which are deeply in the business of preaching and propagating "prosperity gospel.[57]" And these malls are often serving the material needs and acquired tastes of elites given prices of many items are out of reach of the poor masses.

The agriculture system has balked on its primary role of adequate food provisioning and rather engendered policies resulting in large-scale food shortages, periodic starvations and famines, food importations with astronomical foreign-denominated bills, chronic dependence on handouts, donations, and charitable organizations. Africa is even more at a very high risk with the present-day supply chain woes due to the Covid-19 pandemic and the never-ending Russian-Ukraine War rattling the global economy. As noted in an International Monetary Fund (IMF) report, food prices have increased the most in low-income countries where food insecurity is most acute, adding to the burdens of poorer households, and raising the risk of social unrest.[58]

Labor remains idle, vulnerable, and cheap as the continent recovers from the pandemic. This has deepened earlier ripple effects from decades of growth without jobs and continuing "tougher financing conditions as debt levels climb, inflation soars and currencies weaken against the US dollar—compelling . . . [raising of] interest rates in a bid to keep inflation expectations in check."[59] The practical situational outlook seems direr. As per a recent World Bank report released October 11, 2021, sub-Saharan Africa's "debt burden increased to record $702 billion in 2020—the highest in a decade," and the region has more debt than it can pay off.[60]

At its face value, and regardless of the uneven spread of infrastructure, the only bright spot with hidden social undercurrents is in the area of technology for communications.[61] Almost more than half of the population in Africa have cellphones and a vast number among them have social media handles. Many operate mobile money accounts and the unbanked seem to seize and enjoy the opportunities of digital money transfer transactions. The Telcos and Big Tech are making gigantic strides regarding handsets and internet penetration with the ubiquity of information and communications technology (ICT).[62] However, the promise of much-touted leap-frogging impact on the overall economic development efforts and the poverty-reduction agenda is yet to materialize.[63]

The rise in journalistic activities through media houses, television, FM radio stations, and online portals and podcasts regardless of partisan capture and leaning deserves a pat at the back in the right directions of press freedom. However, the quality of core journalism—news coverage and reporting—has not kept pace as it has remained in its mediocre realm. Similarly, the technology applications for construction, resource extraction, and related big-ticket interventions supposed to transform the "dark continent" have either lagged behind in terms of impact on the lots of the majority or underperformed with associated risks of conflicts, displacement, climate change-induced and related environmental consequences.

The housing sector has not fared better. Improved and affordable housing for all remains a dream-pipe fantasy and sloganeering of the ruling elites.[64] Household amenities meant to make life more bearable by reducing the raw energy spent on simple chores particularly for women who bear a disproportionate brunt in this sphere are either very expensive or above the pay grade of many. Soaring inflation rates have made access to utilities such as electricity, water, and hygienic sanitation services out of reach for many in the various countries.

Given the predicament of ordinary people, some critics painfully think after several decades of so-called independence and self-rule, "Africans have lost their minds" as the continent remains an "industry for weaponry for destruction, guns, and killing . . . industry of disease . . . the industry of displacement and dehumanization of human relationship" instead of a viable location for transformational development.[65]

Similar sentiments were revealed by the Nigerian diaspora sampled for thoughts and reactions on the occasion of sixty-one years of independence on October 1, 2021. Basically, the sum of the responses indicates there is "nothing to celebrate at 61; poverty, insecurity, poor leadership still thrive."[66] To reiterate the deplorable conditions in the country, "an Afrobarometer poll from 2018 found that one in three Nigerians wanted to move outside the country. This is especially so among younger, more educated males who typically leave in search of employment opportunities within and outside the continent, traveling to the Middle East, Europe, America and Asia."[67] The sentiments captured in relation to Nigeria speak volumes of the thought similarities and seemingly challenges of the post-independence continent. All of this is an attestation that a pattern of wobbling dividends and corresponding distribution channels constitute a critical component of the leadership and governance conundrum faced by Africa.

Conclusion

This chapter provides a somewhat somber analysis of what are arguably the fundamental elements of the leadership and governance challenges facing Africa. Without a firmly rooted leadership system based on the beliefs and values of what constitutes goodness in the minds of the majority, all major high-profile response attempts at rectifying the situation to date have remained paper tigers and wishful. It is about a critical time the ruled and the rulers sing from the same hymn book because without synchronized measures driving reform, such related efforts regardless of intent and purpose would continue to be top-down and elitist in context, approach, outcomes, and impact.

The RTAP (representation, transparency, accountability, and participation) principles which are the principal motivators and engines of good leadership and governance are yet to have strong footholds in the post-independence political, economic, social, and cultural organization of lives across the continent. Proactive efforts are required to turn things around without acquiescing to the dictates of the few at the expense of the existential needs of many. It is mainly by redirecting efforts to address the deep-seated highlighted dysfunctionalities would the dividends of a caring and transformational society be evenly spread among the population.

Chapter 5

TOO BLESSED TO BE CHASING THE WIND

Introduction

This chapter explains the driving values of blessings for success against the background of the realities to complete a philosophical trilogy of the trailing perils and woes of Africa's development trajectory. The objective is twofold: (1) elaborate on what the values entail, necessary actions, and measures which would enable the surest guarantee of manifesting the blessings for success in a nation's existence; and (2) provide insights into why Africa has been chasing the wind amid the ever-present principles of the blessings for success.

By completing the philosophical narratives of the perils and woes of African development, the chapter serves as a bridge to appreciating the salient elements of the BRP concept and the dynamic ideals of servant and transformational leadership. The servant leader focuses broadly on fulfilling the needs of society while the transformational leader views fulfilling needs as a vital preconditional means to manifesting the blessings for success and greatness in a society. The ideals of a servant and transformational leader are analogous. Africa requires the combined underlying values of these ideals for a potent cure of its dreaded leadership and governance illness seeping through the pores of the continent.

What follows is a dialectic of the ideals construed as the wheels of success and greatness in life. This, in turn, is juxtaposed with certain policy practices, choices, and actions undertaken, which are inimical to fulfilling the needs of the masses and uplifting African societies to glory and greatness. The chapter ends on the note that regardless of the litany of problems, Africa is too blessed to despair and its potential is glaring—"a global economic driver, digital innovation hub, and model for green, resilient infrastructure." In this regard, there is an urgent need to come together within the global community "as public and private sectors, to ensure an inclusive, resilient recovery . . . unite around one shared and audacious goal: . . . create a more equitable and resilient world coming out of the pandemic."[1] The road to building the foundation for Africa's future could start with embracing, adopting, and operationalizing the BRP concept across the continent.

The Critical Drivers of Success

As a grounded philosophy of human existence, everyone is blessed for success. This is applicable as individuals and collectively as nations, and is manifested in a lifetime or during a period on earth. How the blessings for success are manifested depend largely on certain fundamental principles, which can be appropriated, imbibed, and practiced to attain a reasonable measure of success as desired. Simply, success is a state, situation, or condition with the capability to pursue and attain wishes, desires, and aspirations.

Over the years in the history of humankind, the following principles have been the critical drivers of success at one point or the other in the existential trajectory of individuals and nations:

1. Belief and faith in God
2. Aspirations to do good
3. Heightened sense of excellence
4. Insatiable caring for people
5. Realization of human limitations
6. Availing to serve the nation (commitment, duty, loyalty, and service to the nation)
7. Glorification and replication of success.

While all these principles may not necessarily be at play the same time or practiced in a chronological order, their presence and practice in sync have proven to be the surest way to manifestations of the blessings for success in a lifetime or period of existence. Manifestation is not automatic or chance happenstance but driven by perspiration with clear mindsets of conscious deliberations, activism, and orchestrations.

As the undergirding principle, belief and faith in God is not an indication that atheist and nonbelievers are excluded from the blessings for success. Rather, it has been for many Homo sapiens the formative cornerstone of umbilical links of personifications molded through the nexus of family, community, church, school, and nation. Aspirations to do good is a cultivated and nurtured inner trait demonstrably revealed through intentions, words, deeds, and practice. Heightened sense of excellence is not settling for mediocrity and the inferior but knowledge of possibly available options or alternatives and the urge to surge for the ultimate superior in all endeavors. Insatiable caring for people is a mark of benevolence, philanthropy, shared, and concerned interests in the well-being of others. In a word, seeking the best for everyone and malice toward none. Realization of human limitations is the translations that human and societal needs are unlimited and some would certainly be overwhelming to remain unmet in a lifetime. Availing to serve a nation is about fulfilling obligations to society for its nurturing provisions of life and existence. And finally, glorification and replication of success is about giving thanks and praises, giving back to society, and creating enduring pathways for intergenerational extension of blessings for success.

Visions and Values of the Path to Greatness

Central to the notion of the ever-presence of God are the visions and values, which guide and propel a nation to pursue and achieve its goal of greatness compared to others.[2] The foremost values which shape the path to greatness always include purposefulness, belongingness, and the relentless surge to higher aspirational ideals.[3] Sense and consistency of purpose is a key driver in the life and existence of successful nations. Most undertakings and engagements are grounded and driven by a purpose and consistency in the focus of purpose. Consistency of purpose leads to excellence which is not just an act but habitual and requires hard work, dedication, and devotion in terms of time committed to fulfilling the purpose. In the context of consciousness of God which molds the pillars of greatness, the approach and attitude to any given work, assignment and responsibility would be consistent dedication, devotion, punctuality, and hard work to pursue and achieve excellence in purpose. Hence, purposefulness is an essential value and a defining strength of success. Kwame Nkrumah, Lee Kuan Yew, Mahathir Muhammed, and others, such as Nelson Mandela of South Africa and Julius Nyerere of Tanzania, at a point in their various journeys of leadership and governance have practiced to a certain degree of success consistency of purpose.

Sense of belonging is another essential value that drives a nation's vision of the journey to greatness.[4] In every dynamic workplace environment of a successful nation, corporate and community goals are pursued and met with much vigor, efficiency, and effectiveness if all the workers and members think and feel that they belong to the place.[5] Everyone would share and commit to the vision and mission of the corporation and community. The same goes for team and group pursuits. Sense of belonging engenders team and group cohesiveness and serves as the linchpin and glue for bonding for results. It is a conduit for ensuring the reliability, trustworthiness, and loyalty of team members, and enabling teams to avoid and resolve conflicts amicably and quickly. To inculcate a sense of belonging, many successful nations proactively make and enforce rules, norms, values, and mores, which guide, ensure, and encourage people to actively participate and avoid behaviors deemed hostile, rude, discriminatory, and disrespectful. Also, the value of sense of belonging enables people to be accommodating, friendly, polite, transparent, open, forthcoming, collegial, and accountable in dealings with each other.

Striving for higher aspirational ideals is a cornerstone value of professional endeavors and an intrinsic character trait in many successful nations.[6] The relentless urge to surge forward and reach higher ideals require thoughtful and purposeful intervening programs and activities with clearly defined targets, goals, results, risk calculations, and mitigating measures. This is an important value which regularly shapes and influences professional aspirations and undergirds roles and responsibilities of nurturing the pathway to pursuing and achieving a nation's goal of greatness.

In all African countries, the ever-presence consciousness and acknowledgment of God is abundant and needless to provide proof and evidence. At the dawn of independence, a vision of greatness was unleashed, hopes were astronomical, and the pathway well-lit and brushed by the nationalist leaders. However, along the way something seemed to be amiss with the undergirding values of purposefulness, belongingness, and aspirational higher ideals sidelined for a spiral descent to chasing the wind.

Practice of Faith

The practice of faith is an enshrined right of all people in nations either great and successful or desirous to be great and successful.[7] Widespread freedom of worship enables fellowships and communion among people of diverse backgrounds, and cultivates the seeds of loyalty, solidarity, alliances, links, and networks—invaluable ingredients required in a nation for effective communication, mobilization, and organization for success. Faith practice is made possible and guaranteed through institutional channels of the family, community, schools, and dedicated places of worship (churches, mosques, etc.). These channels provide opportunities for learning, knowledge acquisition, enlightenment, and awareness of aspirational potentials, possibilities, options, roles, and responsibilities in the immediate and external surroundings in the world.

Character formation to embrace the vision that engenders aspirational pursuits and contributions to achieving a great nation is at the core of interactions within the institutional channels that guarantee the practice of faith. In this context, faith practice for success promotes a character formation process that harnesses fully the inherent human potential capabilities to attain excellence.[8] This is a phenomenal feat, which requires nurturing and pursuing before attainment, and it is not merely given and attained because one is born of human seed. Thus, the eventual assumed character is basically woven by the vision of greatness into a texture or fabric of success. The collective harnessing of such formative character products, traits, and outcomes and transforming them into potent sources of creativity and innovations provide the impetus for shaping human inner strength capable of catapulting a nation to greatness.

The ethics of work, whether public or private, are molded and catalyzed by the practice of faith.[9] Fellowships and communion in faith do not hinder but rather embolden and enhance attitudinal inclinations toward work. Times for worship and work are not necessarily conflictual but balanced reinforcing nuances based on devotion, dedication, and punctuality. Professing to give all in faith for an anticipated goal requires extending the same in work including commitment levels. "Trust in faith" is not a synonym for "Wait in faith": the former urges to surge forward and attain the desired, while the latter beckons to stand still in expectation. Worship and work comingle in the spiritual but not physical realm where the self is extricated to the whims and demands of meeting a corporate or otherwise organizational goal within a given time period.

Some fuzzy trends are discernible in terms of practice of faith regarding Africa's march in pursuit of its vision of greatness and success. Constitutional guarantee of faith practice as an inalienable right is not necessarily implanting the seeds of loyalty, solidarity, and alliances in a manner that would produce the fruitful ingredients for communication, mobilization, and organization of society for proclaimed envisioned greatness and success. While the institutional channels which guarantee the practice of faith are intact, those of the corresponding learning and knowledge acquisitions at a point in time yielded the creativity and innovations to deliver some promising results but seemed certainly to have grinded to a halt presently. Collective visioning of greatness has become the enemy of individual character formation processes, and the pursuit of mass excellence has been sacrificed by gloating on the altar of mediocrity and sub-standardization. The absurdities seem more pronounced in the realm of work ethics and attitudes toward work. Worship has now been fused with work and assumes a prerogative over work.[10] Engaging time in work particularly at the public space is largely now a derivative of the time devoted to worship as people are affected if the balance between the two acts around them is upset and out of tune.

Communal Bonding and Institutional Synchronization

Communal bonding is a core element of social organization which belies the notion of sustainability. It is premised on the capacity of every individual to produce and regenerate one's existence under the principle of collective responsible reciprocity— an implied process of collective rights and actions, responsibilities, solidarity, accountability, collaboration, and concern for intra- and intergenerational equity.[11] The expectation is that each individual's responsibility and right to generate and regenerate one's existence would not conflict nor undermine those of others coexisting within the same milieu. In a word, each person and everyone is thy brother, sister, or neighbor's keeper. Thus, at the heart of communal bonding there is some sort of equilibrium, looking out for each other's interest, covering the back of thy fellow, transitional change, continuity, and a fundamental concern for the capacity levels which determine the quality of sustenance in the process. This value of communal bonding dovetails with some of the attributes which a Tran-Serve leader will exhibit under the operationalization of a BRP construct. A Tran-Serve leader operates to serve others first with the consideration of every individual's needs and inputs, sets aside self-interests for the transformation of the whole, focuses on building communities and creating empowering spaces for everyone within the polity.

At a point, particularly in the early period of a nation on the path to greatness, it becomes essential making the choices to strike a balance at all levels of humanity to attain the desired levels of bonding. This process requires undergirding institutions of the family, community, churches (or mosques), and schools to be in sync with each other for the pursuit and achievement of a collective purpose. Nations are then suitably and sustainably positioned in the transformational regenerative process to confront the realities and issues bordering on governance (political regeneration); production, distribution, consumption, investments, and surplus appropriation (economic regeneration); mobilizing and organizing relatively idle and vulnerable labor skills, expertise, and talents for a meaningful purpose (social regeneration); and the facilitative interpretation of natural and human environmental relations as related to the application, appropriation, and exploitation of natural resources for sustainable usage (balanced climate conditions or ecological regeneration). For example, in the context of reducing emissions and less reliance on fossils, Tran-Serve leadership would promote regional investments in polysilicon factories and domestic manufacturing of solar panels, inverters, batteries, and wind turbines in strategic locations across the continent.

The catalytic prowess of communal bonding and the synchronization of the corresponding institutional elements for the pursuit and achievement of collective endeavors in many African countries have been negated to the periphery and margins in the course of participation in the world economy. Although a cherished knowledge-based principle for shaping human interactions, relations, and adaptations with others in the world, Africa has neither fully integrated communal bonding as a capable principle for shaping interactions and participation in the global economy. Nor has measures been put in place for insulating citizens from the pressures due to neglect. With one foot in the global economy and the other in subsistence and informality, the principle of communal bonding has been debased in value with the complicity of actions and omissions by the administrative states, corporations, intellectuals, and experts seeking voices and places in the discourse and processes of engagements at the global market place.[12]

Africa's development trajectory has been shaped by a truncated form of communal bonding. The varied groups and classes within the various societies since independence seek to establish alliances and partners outside to craft economic strategies which have proven incapable of ushering benefits to majority of the populace. At some point, cracks emerged which deepened and weakened the sociocultural fabric that nurtured communal bonding as a principled bulwark against mass marginalization and alienation. The value of communal bonding is no longer a fortress for inclusion, transparency, accountability, and participation in the stewardship of societal resources. It has become an acceptable norm of nonconformity to the age-long mores of each person is thy neighbor's keeper. In other words, the value of communal bonding has metamorphosed into an unbridled penchant for trampling on thy neighbor to pursue self-serving and elevated individual goals vis-à-vis those which could propel the broader society to greatness.[13]

Largely as a result, the continent is now amid a ruthless struggle for socioeconomic fulfillment and improvisation with gradient-skewed minority winners and majority losers. The societies are unable to harness the elements of solidarity, responsibility, accountability, collaboration, and initiatives embedded in the norms and values highlighted earlier. The consequences of this anomaly are varied and profound. These include but not limited to (a) the design and operation of flawed nation-states which have lost in practice the sense of purpose and responsibility; and (b) an entrenched crisis of continuous undermined legitimacy and credibility of community leadership essential for mobilizing and organizing of labor for sustained livelihood activities to cure the malaise of poverty which has engulfed nations.

Overall, Africa is blessed for success with the open proclamation of the belief and faith in God. However, through largely leadership and governance omissions and inactions in the actualization of the fundamental principle of communal bonding, the corresponding blessings are manifested in drips and drops on the continent.

Imbalanced National and Local Leadership Interests

By dint of historical circumstances, leadership at the national level acquired the prerogative responsibility to determine the nature and forms of local-level leadership arrangements which would play lead roles in galvanizing the population to find solutions for the challenges of generating and regenerating existence with a sustained sense of collective purpose. The implementation of this prerogative turned out more as self-serving shortsightedness when it came to the tasks of institutionalizing local leadership arrangements capable of leading the vast majority to identify needs, set priorities, and mobilize resources geared at tackling and achieving desired goals.

National leadership interest has been more on creating a leviathan with concentrated power and authority at the national level. Local-level leadership arrangements have been construed in terms of control and perceived as an extended limb subservient to national leadership. To a large extent, this practice breeds sycophancy and incompetence in the management of societal resources. Across the continent, local level leadership structures have not been designed to function as checks on national state structures, or influence and shape behavior and actions of national state officeholders. This phenomenon deprives the national state of the foundational legs upon which cohesive institutions would thrive to inspire and rally citizens around a common sense of purpose, vision of development, and transformation of lives. Legitimacy of the nation-state and the justification of its existence as a representative structure are often derived from concepts, constructs, and practices which at times alienate majority of the citizens, or from the specter of real, imagined, and perceived threats of coercive apparatus rather than persuasion, trust, loyalty, and sense of belonging ingrained in the citizens.[14]

Furthermore, the scenario undermines the prospects of effective participation, transparency, and accountability of stewardship in the appropriation and use of public resources. The lower-level structures are the weakest links between the central-regional-local structure nexus. This phenomenon severely affects the participation of citizens in development governance decision-making with serious implications for deploying both vertical and horizontal accountability mechanisms to consolidate the dividends of democracy on the continent. Such a prevailing scenario translates into disconnect and distance (or at best tenuous/artificial relations) between the citizens and the state structures—a phenomenon which undermines the effectiveness of applying the principles of participation, transparency, and accountability to ensure that public resources are utilized efficiently by elected officials for the delivery of services and improvement of development outcomes (Chapter 4).

It is to rectify such practical anomalous scenarios that a BRP construct could be an essential antidote. The logic of a BRP framework is that majority of the people in target communities will be better represented by their own chosen leaders based on familiar understandable norms and conventions in local governing arrangements. These people would have access and influence over their leaders to ensure transparency in policy decisions regarding the management of common resources. Collectively, the people would utilize their strengthened local governance structures to influence and exert collective pressure, to enable transparency and accountability for stewardship of national affairs, which would possibly minimize or eliminate impunity and misuse of the public purse to engender shared prosperity.

Curtailed Grassroots Participation and Involvement

Participation and involvement in the stewardship of public resources are severely curtailed at the grassroots because the established participation apparatus and mechanisms are neither fully understood by many people nor are they familiar and comfortable with their effective usages. This situation gives rise to alienation, marginalization, and aloofness toward the behaviors and actions of leaders in terms of transparency and accountability for public stewardship.[15] Participation for desired results and outcomes requires trustworthy and respectable leadership structures capable of being utilized for communicating, mobilizing, and organizing—the rules of engaging people. For effective participation, the people must be pivotal in creating the leadership structures, be familiar and comfortable with the principles and rules of engagement, and understand the corresponding uses for intended purposes. And such structures must be rooted in their belief systems and ways of life derived from their communities of heritage.[16] Ownership, understanding, familiarity, and ease of usage of the participation structures are thus the linchpins of responsive governance, which strive to ensure that leaders are transparent and held accountable for the good stewardship of public resources in a society.[17] It is true Africa has completed some peaceful elections under the various constitutions and the investiture of new administrations (despite some disturbing trends recently).[18] By and large, elections are periodic events for holding elected leaders accountable for public resources held in trust and managed on behalf of the populace. However, accountability for stewardship of the public purse is not a periodic event or a one-time act but a continuous process of participatory relations with the electorate embedded in the operations of state governance structures responsible for the management of public resources.[19] The efficacy and effectiveness of these state structures at various levels in terms of involving the people in managing public resources would largely influence and determine the development prospects and transformation of lives in the nation.

The seemingly high voter turnout recorded in some of the completed elections does not mean or translate to high level of participation by the majority in the development governance of the nation.[20] In other words, high-level participation of the people is restricted to elections and not in the aftermath involvement in development governance. This is a serious anomaly which tends to retard efforts and progress toward transformational development. And there is a fundamental reason for this situation. Democracy does mean not only participating in elections but also partaking in the dividends of the aftermath development benefits which elections of leaders should engender in a nation.

Deliberate orchestration to curb grassroots participation for self-serving leadership ends has neither worked to fulfill aspirations of the rulers and the ruled nor has it ensured transparency and accountability for the use and misuse of public resources. It has also not led to national leadership structures, which command the trust, respect, loyalty, and confidence of the people without the lingering and overhanging threat of coercion or imagined authorized fear of the consequences of nonconforming.

Breeding and Instigating Representative Leadership Underperformance

The post-independence theme of "heritage nothingness" which emerged has been in display at its apogee with the formulations on representations and appointments under the various constitutions.[21] The framers and adherents have gone all length to justify copious adaptations of modalities for an externally oriented approach to selecting leaders. Only token consideration has been given to the thought of extracting anything good of value from the communities of heritage to strengthen the constitutional arrangements for organizing society.[22] In practice, one person is elevated to assume a "superhuman" character and wear several hats as a legislator, minister, board chairperson, and a host of others including roles as a parent, pastor, church elder, and so on. All these roles have demands, functions, expectations, and responsibilities, which require in many cases full-time undivided focus, devotion, and attention to pursue and achieve envisaged impactful results. The challenges and problems of these roles are so overwhelming that the scenario mainly breeds and promotes underperformance on the part of the incumbents and prevents broadening the horizon for more competent people to serve the nation in the various capacities.

Africa is afflicted with a deep-seated malaise of poverty and other societal ills requiring fundamental cures beyond tinkering or tweaking the institutional arrangements. In other jurisdictions the foundations of society are already fortified, and one legislator can double as a minister or perform other additional roles effectively and creditably. Extra efforts are needed in Africa for a fortified foundation, and dabbling in such inexplicabilities associated with the leadership selection and appointment processes tends to sway the mind to underlying vested interests and objectives beyond the sane purpose of institutionalizing leadership mechanisms capable of shepherding a nation to greatness (total absence of the ideals of transformational and servant leadership).

To engender the blessings of success in leaps and bounds, this way of selecting government business leaders which breeds and instigates underperformance needs to be substantively changed with pragmatism and inclusiveness in the governing styles of the nations. Regardless of party or regime in power, the prevailing tendency of most government leaders and members hailing from regional blocs or have familial relations with the chief executives underscores the ubiquitous ineptness in the conduct of government business falling short of smoothening the path to greatness. Under Tran-Serve leadership arrangements, participation in local governance by target communities would be communal. In this case, whoever is elected to represent target communities in the national legislative assembly would pay more attention to the needs of the constituents rather than the needs of the sponsoring party. In this respect, party ideology and dogma would not hamper the broadening of the leadership selection talent pool. Target communities would concentrate mainly on ideas and things which promote competency despite origin and affiliations, and support anything meritorious which advances the interests of the nation-states.[23]

For example, further innovations in ensuring the leadership selection process which would pave the way to greatness could evolve from institutionalizing gendered checks and balances and monitoring mechanisms in the governing arrangements for preventing abuse of office and inculcating a consciousness of accountability in the stewardship of public resources. A likely situation in this context would be if a male official is appointed to a leadership position, the deputy would be a female, and vice versa; if a female official is appointed, the corresponding deputy would be a male. This intuitively would be an affirmative case of looking back and drawing on an adapted version of an admirable practice valued in certain African communities of heritage geared toward strengthening the present pathway to greatness.

Minimal Professional Rectitude in the Public Work Space

There is a huge deficit of professional rectitude in determining and executing responsibility of a public office. Shirking of responsibilities for contributions to the nation's vision and match to greatness is pervasive in the public space. While public utterances with slogans and catchphrases indicate the desire to be great, many public officeholders and workers are reluctant to embrace the responsibilities for what it takes to build a great nation. Abysmal sense of purpose is displayed offhandedly, and many workers seek motivations from other obnoxious sources beyond stipulated remunerations before performing the tasks for which they are duly compensated. Associated attributes of high sense of purpose such as hard work, dedication, devotion, and commitment are minimally demonstrated in many public offices and the level of integrity not commensurate with what it takes to pursue and achieve greatness in a lifetime. There is no shortage of staging postures and payments to be serious about the pursuit of greatness.

Public officials regardless of level barely engage in self-introspection while assuming ownership of the dismal state in the conduct of public affairs amid the perennial elusiveness of the nation's quest to be great ever since setting up this goal at the dawn of independence. Several sources and causes of hindering problems are deemed exogenous without much thought to the complicity of endogenous actions and actors. Transnational interests have submerged and superseded any local interest. It is foolhardy not to subject such actions to objective test and verify the truth, trust, respect, and integrity in the transactions undertaken by public officials on behalf of the nation. Several transnational transactions at the global marketplace are shrouded in secrecy and circumvent the legal and regulatory approval processes. Transparency, competitiveness, and value for money have remained normative concepts in many dealings public officials execute on behalf of the nation. Terms like cooked, conspiracy, connivance, duped, conflict of interest, defensive fearmongering, preferential treatment, and so on, pervade the empirical storyline to the point of questioning whether the nation's journey to greatness is either facilitated or hindered by many of these transnational transactions.

The ideals and values of Tran-Serve leadership are required to be learned, imbibed, internalized, and practiced as the driver of service and interactions. This undertaking is not a quick-fix, short-term process but a long haul of inspirational motivations and persuasive advocacies penetrating the spirit and soul of the African. The pivotal facilitating thread is grounding the champions of Tran-Serve leadership by encouraging widespread voluntary actions establishing communities of learning and practice at all public facets of society, including state organs, workplaces, schools, churches, villages, and townships.

Using a simple model of educating the educators in the ideals and values of Tran-Serve leadership, proactive efforts would be geared to stimulate society intellectually on the sterling qualities, generate public discussions, steer opinions and debates, and provide impetus for individualized learning and practice considerations, shaping and influencing the trajectory of occurrence of the mission almost anywhere in society. For example, schools from the formative stages to tertiary levels would have weekly sessions devoted to civics educating pupils on the ideals and values of BRP. Likewise, church leaders will be encouraged to utilize the pulpits to preach and disseminate the rationale and particularly, the spiritual undergirding elements constituting Tran-Serve leadership.

The insatiable urge at the public space to outwit and outsmart the collective consciousness of what is right and good for the nation has made some groups of individuals, particularly those who are in the elite class, to think, believe, and act as belonging more than others to the nation-state and therefore more entitled to any accrued benefits.[24] Media houses and personnel are contracted to defend what is unfathomably indefensible and utterances which fly in the face of collective sense of reasoning. This truncated sense of belonging tends to alienate and deprive the nation of the unflinching drive and energy of everyone in a situation when all hands are needed to roll the boulders off the pathway to greatness. This phenomenon is demotivating and affects how credit is accorded and rewards shared to induce exemplary behavior. It encourages attitudes of holding back on potentials and prospects, dampens spirits, and prevents stimulations to aim and reach higher laurels. In sum, high professional rectitude in the public space is the cog in the machine which drives a nation on the path to greatness. If this performance character trait is exemplified minimally in practice, the blessings of success can mainly be manifested in drips and sips.

Nation Life Choices and Alternatives

Life choices are pivotal props to success depending on the options and alternatives available to choose from when a nation is faced with making greatness-driven decisions. Choice determines the pathways which lead either to desolation, deprivation, and depression, or propelling, progress, and prosperity. The types of choices made in certain existential areas of a nation would be indicative of which pathways are able to propel the blessings of success in leaps and bounds. *A perusal of the types of choices made by Africa in the critical areas of food strategy, appropriation, and application of medicinal ingredients, and technology adaptation and utilization seems to impede progress toward success.*

Food Policy Strategy from Seed to Plate

Over the past several decades, Africa made clear choices to be on the route of not able to feed itself, and greatness eludes any nation unable to feed itself.[25] As pointed out earlier, food strategy and interventions have been notable more in sloganeering, catchphrases, and absentee politico-elite meddling tactics than well-targeted strategies of hoisting on solid footing all stages and aspects of the value chains of food provisions from seed to plate. For a start, the continent is stubbornly stuck with the bequeathed misconstrued designation that food crops are not cash crops and should merit secondary attention in policy dispensations. Hence, structural and institutional setups and arrangements in support of a coherent food strategy and interventions have to date been wobbly and porous. This blatant choice means reliance on other sources to feed the nation with ridiculously astronomical food import bills and beckoning bowls of outstretched hands in the trails.

The chosen pathway has rendered the whole food value chain in derision. From the seed chain through the entire processes to the plate for consumption have overwhelmingly remained subsistent. Not a single component of the value chain has received widespread uplifting to engender engagement of a sizable number of the population in a sector which holds the promise of expansive capabilities and opportunities toward greatness. What is needed to rectify such a deep-seated self-inflicting anomaly in food strategy is an agriculture-based seed-to-plate initiative tailored to support communities and provide numerous jobs/employment opportunities as business engagement and conducive ways of life for the many idle and vulnerable youths and young adults across the continent.

A seed-to-plate food strategy (see Chapter 10 for details) is an undertaking of transforming small-scale agriculture into highly attractive and profitable businesses covering the entire value chain of maximizing production, use, and consumption of food crops, fruits, fisheries, and livestock. For example, under Tran-Serve leadership, the seed-to-plate lens would mean and require that business service support facilities would be established to aid throughout the value chain. In the case of food crops, tailored assistance will be provided for seed lots, land preparation, tilling and nurturing, makeshift irrigation, harvesting, storage, processing, packaging, marketing, and distribution for widespread internal uses and export. Same goes with the other product categories. The smallholder farmer in the various agriculture zones of the nation would be targeted and supported to maximize productivity in the products of choice within the space of cultivation. The compendium skills, tools and equipment upgrade, retooling, and automation regarding productivity, capacity enhancement, and extension support services in the value chain will create myriad jobs and employment opportunities for the many youths and young adults able and willing to be engaged as private business owners and partners, and/or formal employees of business services entities. Given the realistic potential of food agriculture capable of fundamentally altering positively the fortunes to propel the manifestations of the blessings of success in leaps and bounds, the seed-to-plate concept is a compelling strategy which could be considered in the continent's quest for greatness.

Appropriation and Application of Medicinal Properties

Africa to date has been unable to craft and implement health care systems capable of delivering solutions to the health needs of the population. And to reiterate, greatness eludes a nation incapable of meeting the health care needs of its people. A fundamental reason is the inability of health policy to provide a balance of attention on resources from both orthodox and plant or herbal medicine. "Africa is endowed with up to 45,000 plant species—about 25% of the world's plant genetic resources."[26] Yet, official health policy and practice overemphasize the pursuit of orthodox medicine to elusive sophistication and mastery while plant/herbal medicine is negated to secondary consideration in terms of education, training, research, and institutionalization of knowledge for widespread practical usage, appropriation, and application.

A typical African community comprises entities with dual health care and treatment procedures, where sickness and diseases are euphemistically categorized in terms of what could be treated with orthodox or plant/herbal medicines. Depending on the conceptual diagnosis and related factors of affordability and availability, either the orthodox or herbal medicine is used. Nevertheless, it is demonstrative of the attitudes of the people that they continue to use herbal medicine as they have done for several centuries. It will be expected that a continent striving for greatness will provide equal attention to the development and deployment of resources from both sources beyond the institutional lip service and cosmetic focus of appropriation and application, which pertain in the domain of herbal vis-à-vis orthodox medicine.

It is known that remedies for many out-patient department (OPD) visitations could be drawn from increased learning of nutrition, herbal medicine, and other forms of natural medicine and yet the domain remains peripheral in health policy thinking and formulation in search of effective solutions to meet the health needs of the population. Health policy needs to be formulated with an overriding objective of reducing pressure and lessening overreliance on orthodox medicinal facilities and resources. Under a Tran-Serve leadership, the medicinal value of herbs would feature prominently in the outlook and projections of crafting effective response to meet health demands and needs of the society. This means the subservient attention provided to the herbal medicine domain would pave way for standardization of the entire value chain of learning, education, training, research, extraction of active ingredients, processing, packaging, dispensing, and usage. The pathway to greatness would be smoothened and the journey facilitated if a proper balance in attention and importance is struck between orthodox and herbal medicine especially given the latter's prevalence, availability, affordability, and deep rootedness in the sociocultural psyche of the people.

Actions in the direction espoused here will also enhance the ecological footprints of African societies and engender invaluable country-level contributions to addressing some of the phenomenal effects of climate change. Uplifting herbal medicine to the standard of orthodox medicine in public policy formulations would increase the preservation of plant species and strengthen frameworks of ecological knowledge, rights, responsibilities for ensuring and preserving biological diversity.[27] Such endeavors of ecological resource regulation and management regimes induce better land use planning and management practices, and enable deepening and dependability of the core elements of social organization—solidarity, responsibility, accountability, collaboration, and initiative—all at the crux of many nations' journey to greatness. In essence, Africa's health care policy, planning, and management choices cannot remain at this state of institutional disparity and discordancy between orthodox and herbal medicine if the strive toward greatness is expected to yield the desired results and outcomes.

Adaptation and Utilization of Technology

The climb to "mount greatness" requires widespread and maximum adaptation and utilization of scientific knowledge to enhance purpose in what are arguably the "vital signs" of a nation—health, education, agriculture, labor, household amenities, and governance. From basic filing, record-keeping, registration at health facilities to the delivery mechanisms of preventive, curative, and nutritional health care, sanitation, and water, the level and quality of technology deployed in these spheres determine the efficiency, effectiveness, and reach of the services purposefully meeting intended needs. The abundant tales and sights of patients carrying files back and forth, abysmal lack of surgical gloves and auxiliary first aid kits, careless disposal of clinical wastes, overflowing garbage dumpsites, and potable water-deprived communities foretell the palpable levels of technology utilization to enhance the purposeful functioning of health care systems in the societies.

Puzzling features of the education system amid the ubiquity of technology are the chronic lack of learning, reading, instructional and teaching materials; computer-deprived libraries and depleted laboratories; delivery methods and formats devoid of industry-readied practical skills; innovation labs, simulations, and incubation spaces and parks. Thus, over the past several decades, the education system has increasingly churned out half-baked literates fed with leap-frogged technology spoils of social media platforms, where many have invented grammarless sentence constructions for communication and exchange of information, and are woefully ill-prepared for industry and corporate life.

Nowhere are the attendant effects of the minimal adaptation and utilization of technology more pronounced than in the field of agriculture. Allusions were made to this anomalous situation in the section on food strategy. But it is suffice to state that the pace toward greatness will quicken when bellies are full through the release of requisite energy, creativity, and innovations inherent in the utilization of technology to spur the tide ensuring sufficiency and security in the realm of agriculture.

Idleness and vulnerability are the banes of minimally utilizing technology to catapult labor toward industry readiness. The refrain that labor is abundant and cheap on the continent is more an indictment of the incapacity of the countries to create avenues for skills training and acquisitions commensurate to the needs and demands of industry. While such a situation stifles growth and expansion in industry, it also serves as a propitious ground for increased deviant behavior in the wider society. Avenues of wealth creation become limited for many with unhealthy aggressiveness and decadence pervading the social and moral fabrics of society. All over the continent, there are signs of incipient entrepreneurships which if harnessed with technology will unleash the impetus required to hasten the nations' pathway to greatness.

Critical aspects of power generation and transmission seem technology-driven and enabled notwithstanding the attendant contentious and vexatious lingering issues of inadequacy in the value chain. However, the aspect of distribution seems to be in dire need of technology infusion and enhancement to have a semblance of efficiency and effectiveness in responsible company delivery performance. Vast swaths of areas with connectivity and regular supplies are undoubtedly captured in periodic underwhelming revenue projections and declarations simply due to inadequate use of technology-aided approaches of determining usage and user compliance with bills and payment collection arrangements. Segments of the population and sectors of the economy are spuriously categorized as underperforming which overwhelm underwriters that assume the disproportionate burden of covering the energy consumption costs. Such an existing scenario is not a mark of match to greatness.

It is a truism that the proliferation of cellphone and social media technology has exponentially enhanced communication and widespread information-sharing capabilities of the populace across the spectrum. Long before the explosions in mobile and social technology, nations which attained the greatness feat had used and appropriated technology to induce engineering innovations, deepen communications and interactions, facilitate knowledge acquisition modalities; They also engaged in trend and pace-setting research for solutions to life-changing challenges, propelling smart skills and training undertakings. This has been done with such level of sophistication, widespread access, benefits, and impact that it becomes luxurious for such nations to just overly be concerned about the negativities which come with the ubiquity of mobile technology.

Smart mobile technologies are two-headed conundrum for nations in Africa. While they provide leapfrogging moments of by-passing aspects of infrastructure build-up, access, and reach, efforts are needed to (a) harness a mobile phone with an internet to induce innovations, facilitate knowledge acquisitions, learning, and research; and (b) address the negativities which accompany the proliferation of such technologies. The need for such efforts can be gleaned from one significant outlet—the public bureaucracy responsible for implementing and translating government visions into concrete actions and impacting results. Government business transaction communications is still heavily dependent on the conventional paper trail and less use of electronic channels. For example, although public servants do have official and private email avenues as well as widespread access to social media channels, the issue of concern is the preponderance reliance on paper trails to conduct and communicate government business transactions.

Leapfrogging has left the public bureaucracy behind in mastering computer technology for conducting and facilitating government business before massively embracing mobile and social technology. Such a phenomenon will be less bothering if social media channels are harnessed to fill the gaps exacted on the transaction communications performance of the public bureaucracy. The nations' path to greatness will be greatly enhanced by utilizing the opportunities provided by the proliferation and widespread embrace of social media to facilitate sharing of not just social trivia but also serious formal government work. Fulfilling this endeavor remains a trying challenge to overcome in nations' desirous quest to pursue and achieve greatness.

Minimal use of technology is also prevalent in the construction business with attendant effects on levels of productivity. Artisans engaged in the construction sector are barely equipped with the requisite simple tools to reduce the raw energy expended to produce an expected output within a given time period. This deficiency makes entry, recruitment, outputs, and rewards for engaging in the field and practicing the trade unattractive for many would-be interested hands. Artisans in the construction business are the main builders of nations' infrastructure; their levels of sophistication in the usage of technology to enhance productive engagement are major determinants of the status, conditions, and availability of the infrastructural foundations which underscore prosperity and greatness.

Deployment of technology for conservation, protection, and judicious harnessing of natural resources whether on land, air, and sea is an essential driver of survival and regeneration of a great nation or those yearning to be. Performance indices of conservation regarding utilization of the basics in the specific realm must be spectacular. For example, operating safe, efficient, and profitable airline industry over a prolonged period will be a notch toward excellence in the harnessing of airspace resources. Likewise, having the capability to preserve marine resources and prevent overfishing in territorial waters is a mark of ensuring ecological balance and sanity. Furthermore, persistent orderly application and enforcement of mining regulatory rights assist in avoiding uncontrollably hazardous exploitative tendencies and recklessness in harnessing mineral resources. Where a nation lies in relation to such basic measures usually shapes its pathways toward greatness.

Among strategies to consider under a Tran-Serve leadership is the utilization of regional public goods, which will be a key catalyst in the transformation of African economies in general, and boosting fragile, conflict, and violence (FCV) abatement investments in green and technology-enabled infrastructure to rectify some of the anomalies of the pathways to achieving greatness. Such regional public goods include building transport corridors, managing river basins, establishing cross-border digital connectivity, managing climate risks, and controlling outbreaks of pests and disease. Priority FCV zones in this context will involve: (a) Horn of Africa, (b) Lake Chad Basin, (c) the Sahel, and (d) the Great Lakes region. The driving issues of investment interventions in these zones will include drought, flooding, extreme heat, deforestation, degradation, displacement, and pest invasion.

This strategy would be implemented by establishing Project Development Fund Facility (PDFF) to undertake the following regional public goods in specific FCV zones:

1. **Horn of Africa:** The multiple groups of countries are Somalia, Ethiopia, Eritrea, Djibouti, Sudan, and South Sudan. The primary means of economic activity is agro-pastoralism. Investment opportunity is to establish a regional industry for widespread manufacturing of animal feed, animal husbandry products and services, meat processing and packaging activities.

2. **The Lake Chad Basin:** Involved countries are Cameroon, Niger, Nigeria, Chad. The main livelihoods of communities dependent on the lake are fishing and agriculture. Investments opportunity will be to establish a regional industry for an efficient fish supply value chain promotion. A key focus of the industry would be to enable improved access to regional markets for reviving cross-border economic activity.

3. **The Sahel region:** The G5 Sahel countries include Mauritania, Mali, Niger, Burkina Faso, and Chad with claims to three main rivers—Senegal, Niger, and Nile—and a great potential for renewable energy. Investment opportunity is to establish a regional industry for polysilicon and the manufacturing of solar panels, inverters, batteries, and wind turbines. This will enable creating National Green Banks in each of the countries that help leverage private-sector funding for clean energy projects in low-income communities. The location of the regional industry will be strategic to create jobs and boost shared prosperity.

4. **The Great Lakes region:** It comprises seven lakes covering areas in the countries of Burundi, Rwanda, northeastern DRC, Uganda, northwestern Kenya, and Tanzania. As the largest freshwater system in the world, the investment opportunities with a regional value chain dimension seem abundant. The more obvious investment opportunity with an economic sense will be to establish a regional industry for bottling freshwater and producing nutritious beverages for catering to the health and wellness needs of the region. Africa is a "treasure trove of medicinal plants," and this regional industry can be geared to be a leading provider of eco-friendly, healthy herbal drinks for consumers across the region. This will create jobs within the value chain and generate spillover economic benefits of employment for several people in the region.

Intensive utilization of technology to meet household amenities needs of the country is lacking. For example, Ghana has very rich deposits of clay and perennially rudimentary pottery industry. The widespread use of technology to refine the clay texture, upgrade products, and transform the entire industry with the capability to produce durable and competitive quality household products will be a step in the direction toward greatness. Every successful nation in this era and time has been able to reduce its import of porcelain products by building domestic capacity for meeting household needs. With several technical institutes dotting all over the landscape, and some rapidly transformed recently into universities even if in name only, it still remains a mystery why this basic feat of utilizing technology to refine and improve clay texture has not been attained in the musings to build great nations.

An important undertaking under a Tran-Serve leadership arrangement to address the minimal deployment of technology could be investments to increase access to digital skills training, through creating affordable, accessible solutions that provide learners with the relevant knowledge and skills they need to thrive at the job market. In 2021, Africa had 716,000 developers—Nigeria, South Africa, Egypt, and Kenya are the countries with the most developers.[28] Combined, they received 81 percent of venture capital in 2021.[29] This could be done by establishing venture capital fund to support implementation of investments in learning and training platforms to enable Nigerian companies at the frontline to mount training and skills acquisition activities in the ECOWAS sub-region; Kenyan, South African, and Egyptian companies do the same in EAC, SADC, and AMC respectively. The dearth of tech talent across the continent will be addressed with a regional lens, which will allow funding of equity into tech companies from North Africa and sub-Saharan Africa. An analytical tool could be used to easily identify such companies and understand the developer landscape on the continent to define a skills gap matrix. The skills gap matrix will feed into capacity enhancement training and learning programs to address types of skills required.

Spiritual Materialism and Instant Gratification

Belief and faith in God as a cardinal principle underscoring the blessings for success has metamorphosed largely into belief and embrace of spiritual materialism and instant gratification in the societies. Miracle churches proliferate in all corners and preach instant wealth accumulation and delivery from poverty over conventional notion and wisdom of hard work, dedication, devotion, and commitment to the pursuit and fulfillment of purpose on earth.[30] The very fabric of religiosity of the African has been turned headlong. And the preponderance overconcentration on mainly the spiritual realm to the neglect of the realities in the other equally essential spheres of life and human construct has rendered the average follower and worshipper at these miracle churches captives of misery and palpably pathetic. It is like déjà vu all over again: the gun-boat policy cunningness has not left the continent—the bible in one hand, the sword in the other, and proselytizers embarked on conversions. While the locals were busily acclimatizing to their new faith, their resources were speedily whisked away. However, this time around, it is not an outsider visiting this predicament on the unsuspecting and gullible locals but their own sons and daughters who parade themselves as the saviors, chosen and anointed ones ordained to deliver them out of the ravages of poverty and deprivation with superhuman powers and prophecies.

The gospel of sowing seeds and tithes for the self-proclaimed deliverers and leaders to build wealth and reside in luxury while the vast followers eke out a living in penury awaiting the miraculous day is propagated and justified as the new norm in the belief and faith in God. One United States-based comedian put it succinctly that unlike Jesus Christ who fed 5,000 poor and hungry,[31] this time it is the other way around when the 5,000 poor and hungry are feeding their pastors and prophets. Avarice, self-centeredness, personal gain, and doubtful integrity are the halos that encircle and follow several leaders of these miracle places of worship.

As religious leaders of avowedly captive followers, they have very critical roles and responsibilities to ensure that belief and faith in God is turned into remarkable blessings of success for the good of the nations the way it could be. First and foremost, these leaders could see themselves as the mouthpieces of progress and transformation by minimizing sermons on instant miracles and gratification and amplify emphasis on purposefulness, consistency of purpose, hard work, responsibility, dedication, devotion, staying the course, commitment, and perseverance in the pursuit and achievement of goals and targets. Sowing seeds and tithes will not change the deleterious effects of neglecting the preventive steps and nutrition necessary to avoid certain illness and sickness in life amid the absence of the fundamental tools and equipment to provide basic curative responses. All-day fasting and all-night prayer sessions will not bring good drinking potable water and useful sanitation and waste management practices into the community. Neither will a clean city and community emerge through constant prayers; it takes purposeful planning and good development governance to accomplish such feats.

The churches could cease espousing laziness through expectations in instant miracles and gratification and rather promote education with creative and innovative skills acquisitions imbued with entrepreneurism. They could encourage testimonials of job creation and employment delivering essential services and products to the community. Ensuring food on the table regularly will not come through the permission and generosity of the church leader but largely a function of "dirty hands" operating in a milieu of supportive policies throughout the entire agriculture value chain. The churches could acknowledge and propound that if able-bodied men and women are in church all day and all week, it is a worrying manifestation of idleness and vulnerability with all its attendant effects. It is equally important for the leaders to espouse and exhort members to explore and harness for upliftment the potential benefits of social media beyond just sharing and exchanging of trivial videos, gossips, and jokes. Furthermore, it could be extolled that for many of the followers, deliverance from the scourges of poverty lies in adding value to the very resources surrounding them in their homes and communities.

Preaching and practicing the gospel of spiritual materialism through miracles, prophecies, and instant gratification have placed the continent at the pedestal of a callous and careless leadership drive toward a horrifying outcome of institutionalizing blessings for the success of the few. The hapless populace of ardent worshippers has been negated to a constant struggle in worship and praise of their predicament—acceptance of fate or destiny while in wait of the miraculous deliverance. Belief and faith in God as a cardinal principle of the blessings for success can certainly lead to outcomes better than what is currently prevailing, and things need not be in such overdrive if the climb to mount greatness will be real and evident.

Conclusion

A philosophical trilogy of Africa's development ills sheds abundant light on the concerns about Africa's future, especially for the idle and vulnerable young people coming of age in a time of great uncertainty given "conflict is on the rise, and the number of countries falling into instability is increasing."[32] In the face of such stark realities, it is not out of place for a sigh of despair. But as succinctly noted, "if we do nothing, we risk losing them . . . we cannot allow this to happen."[33] And the call for a united front to confront this dilemma is in the right direction. However, the fact remains that capable solutions will not emerge from the same trodden pathways of the past. There seems to be a necessary need for more audacious and commonsense innovative ways to have a leap of faith in operationalizing concepts such as BRP for organizing the design and shape of statehood according to the needs and realities of target societies. Evidence for the belief in this vision is overwhelmingly abundant and irrefutable. The continent cannot continue leaving things to chance and commandeering public and private funds into the same leaking bowls and expect transformational results and outcomes.

Chapter 6

THE CONCEPT OF BRP

Introduction

This chapter outlines the constituents of BRP as a conceptual framework. To provide a context, the chapter commences with conceptual roots of anecdotal experiences entailing a three-phased series of activities spanning over two decades. These varied activities include academic engagements in Ghana and North America for tertiary certifications, professional endeavors at the United Nations and the World Bank Group, executive assignments of high-level interactions with bird's-eye views of government operations in Ghana, and an analytical exercise of reflections on local governance subpar performance in Africa.

Furthermore, the salient elements of BRP are detailed, and the corresponding implications for necessary constitutional amendments, policy reforms, and country-level pathway adjustments are noted. In sum, the chapter concludes on a note that if African countries are expected within the global community to have strong, resilient institutions capable of fulfilling not only the needs of the few elites but also those of the vast majority, BRP could be embraced, adopted, and operationalized across the continent.

Conceptual Roots of Anecdotal Experiences

The concept of BRP derives its roots from a long-range three-phased set of activities spanning two decades as follows: (1) early scholarly work and engagements, 1990–99; (2) professional mission visitations to over twenty African countries, 2000–2015; and (3) residential Executive interactions in Ghana, 2016–21. The early scholarly works involved an academic study titled *"Transnational Elites Interests as Manifested in the Socio-Economic Programs in Sub-Saharan Africa,"* as part of the requirements for an MA degree at the University of Guelph, Ontario, Canada, and a PhD dissertation, *"The Pursuit of Politics of Sustainable Livelihoods: Focus on Governance in Ghana,"* at the same university. Engagements in this context included interactions with the Africa Leadership Forum (ALF)[1] and the Global Knowledge Partnerships (GKP)[2] initiatives of the UNDP and other international development organizations. Professional mission visitations were part of the

World Bank Group programs in Africa. Among the African countries visited were Ethiopia, Kenya, Tanzania, Uganda, Sudan, and Somalia in East Africa; Senegal, Cote d'Ivoire, Togo, Benin, Nigeria, Gambia, Sierra Leone, Liberia, and Ghana in West Africa; South Africa, Lesotho, Seychelles, and Mauritius in the Southern Africa region. Residential executive interactions involved government appointment as the Executive Secretary (CEO) of the Ghana Refugee Board (GRB), which provided unfettered access and interactions with senior-level public sector officials, politicians, informal traditional and religious leaders, and ordinary citizens.

The MA studies afforded an opportunity to examine the roles, interests, and responsibilities of African leaders in relation to counterparts within the global community in the context of the design and implementation of Structural Adjustment Programs (SAPs) spearheaded by the IMF and the World Bank to ensure stability of the global economy.[3] Safeguarding investments and related economic operations within the global economy requires transnational partnerships, cooperations, alliances, and affiliations. Sometimes, inadvertently, or otherwise, cementing transnational interests becomes vested to the detriment of the masses in African countries.

Using Ghana as a case study, the PhD dissertation established two interrelated issues pivotal to innovations to forging better leadership and governance practices for the fulfillment of needs and propelling the nations to greatness: (a) traditional leaders have a greater capacity than any leadership institutions to communicate, mobilize, and organize ordinary Africans voluntarily for collective purposes; and (b) traditional leaders are marginalized and relegated to minimal roles in local governance arrangements in present-day practices of development democracy.

It became clear that Africa urgently needs robust institutions to enhance political participation, enable transparency in policy decision-making, and ensure accountability for public expenditure, resource use or misuse, abuse of power and authority. Institutions are efficient and effective if they are reflective of the needs and realities on the ground. Time and patience are required for building strong institutions, particularly to engender constituent elements of a freer press, independent judiciary, loyal and efficient public servants, and reliable taxation and revenue generation systems.[4] Former US president Obama referred to this essential task of building strong institutions in his visit to Ghana in 2009, and the aftermath White House undertakings in the context of the "Open Government Partnership" he launched in 2011 to secure commitments from African governments for transparency, accountability, and empowered participation.[5] Although laudable, such efforts mainly follow the scripts of the discredited superior-inferior worldview and not molded in the image or based on the realities of existence of ordinary Africans.

It has been sixty years and more that post-independence Africa has been crafting and experimenting with Western-type institutions for representation, leading, ruling, and governing that marginalize leadership institutions which ordinary people utilize for coexistence in their communities. The results have so far not been impressive and the jury is out there on the outcomes of tangible dividends. It is about time to revisit the institutions-building and designing the shape of statehood efforts and ensure that ordinary people are at the front, center, and back of the process especially at the grassroots level.

Engagements with the Africa Leadership Forum provided the opportunity to interact with former presidents, incumbent leaders, and senior public officials at that time, and groups of individuals currently in the driver seats on the continent. Many of the discussions and platforms focused on building the capacity of the successor generations of leaders with notable emphasis on emulating or replicating external innovations on leadership institutions-building. Such efforts by the ALF are similar in focus and intent like the Obama-era "Young African Leadership Initiative" (YALI),[6] which has been invigorated by the Biden administration. All these efforts are evident of the leadership and governance deficits at the African development space.

Interactions under the auspices of the Global Knowledge Partnerships for Development (GKD) induced moments to delve deeply into indigenous knowledge systems, which undergird African leadership and governance institutional arrangements. The GKD initiative created and opened the space for articulating "blended" knowledge solutions to improve the one-way approach of "doing development in Africa" without much success. Blended knowledge approaches are what could instill resilience in rulership institutions in Africa with the capability of not crumbling at the cracking footsteps of self-imposed gatekeepers clothed in uniforms of brutality, or under the folly and greediness of counterparts in suits or African traditionally designed clothing.

Professional mission visitations were undertaken to several African countries under the World Bank-supported "Mobilizing the African Diaspora for Development" program. Although not an explicit priority of the Diaspora program, determining the position and role of traditional leaders in local governance arrangements was an issue of investigative focus during visitations to any African country. And in line with earlier scholarly findings, the story has basically been the same all over the continent—constitutional guarantee of recognition and presence, and backbench roles in local government despite need and relevance.

In addition to Ghana as a case study for the PhD dissertation, a few more country cases[7] are worthy of note as follows:

1. **South Africa:** There is constitutional recognition of the role and status of traditional leaders according to customary law, but they occupy the bottom rung of the local government ladder. More importantly, service delivery is the responsibility of the formal local governance structure.
2. **Zimbabwe:** The constitution provides for National and Provincial Houses of Chiefs; nomination of 10 members as part of the 150-member National Assembly; and a provision for qualification to stand for elections on political party tickets.

3. **Namibia:** Traditional leaders were excluded from political office after independence and their traditional and colonial status reduced from that of political leaders to cultural agents.
4. **Botswana:** There exists constitutional recognition of the status, powers, and roles but subjugation under legislative bureaucratization to peripheral responsibility in local governance.
5. **Sierra Leone, Cote d'Ivoire, Liberia, and Benin among others**: All have constitutional provisions which recognize the existence, role, and status of traditional leaders but are assigned marginal responsibilities in local governance.

Without doubt, the backseat role assigned the institution of chieftaincy in local government designs and operations is the root of abysmal interests and low political participation by ordinary people in governance arrangements across the continent. Africa's post-independence participation in democracy practice has been largely based on wholesale adoption of models and mechanisms from outside. There may not have been any concern if this arrangement has worked to fulfill the needs and aspirations of the people. No questions would be asked if the people are fairly represented in national deliberations, able to participate effectively within such operational apparatus and utilize the prescribed principles and rules of engagement to ensure transparency and accountability for the use and misuse of public resources. Furthermore, all would have been deemed well if the successive leadership structures command the trust, respect, loyalty, buy-in, and confidence of the people voluntarily and without threats of coercion, and are utilized to manage the basic resources upon which existence and subsistence depend.

A blended approach could provide the watershed solutions pathway because it seemingly constitutes a potentially viable and robust antidote to the leadership and governance challenges of the continent. The BRP principle makes room for multiparty-based elections and leadership at the national level and traditional leadership and communal representation arrangements at the local level.

Serving as an executive secretary of a government agency in Ghana provided a bird's-eye view of the intricate operations of government and machinations of the public sector. The period afforded the opportunity to undertake a thorough review of the literature and objective reflections on the performance of local government structures, as well as the role of traditional leadership in facilitating harmonious coexistence of communities. The outcome of this review is a *critical analysis and reflections on the situation in Ghana* which provides compelling reasons to adopt a blended approach to addressing the leadership and governance challenges confronting Africa.

Review and Reflections on Local Governance in Ghana

This analytical review is organized around the following themes: (a) consensus and contestations on the mandated leadership arrangement; (b) undermining features of the prevailing local governance arrangements; (c) misdiagnosis of local governance subpar performance problematic; (d) utterances on the frontline involvement of the institution of chieftaincy; (e) need to eliminate parallel leadership syndrome; (f) indigenous leadership for either transformative or regressive politics; (g) conscientious patriotism; (h) transformative development requires proactive involvement of indigenous leadership.

Consensus and Contestations on the Mandated Leadership Arrangement

By now, there seems to be no ambiguity that universal adult suffrage via competitive partisan elections regardless of inherent flaws is the acceptable means of representation and participation of Ghanaians in governance at the national level. Ghana has chalked up relative successes by electing presidents and Members of Parliament through peaceful elections leading to successive alternate changes in party-based ruling governments.

What seems contentious is the governance and leadership designs at the local level. With the 1992 Ghana Constitution,[8] local governance and leadership designs have been based on the appointment of the district chief executives (DCEs) and the nonpartisan elections of corresponding district assemblies (DAs) and unit committee (UC) members as the major actors.

Undermining Features of the Prevailing Local Governance Arrangements

Over the years, associated with this mode of representation and participation in governance at the local level are the undermining characteristics: (i) national executive overreach, influence, and control through appointments, inequitable allocation, and distribution of development resources, (ii) abysmal level of interests and participation by the vast majority of people; (iii) lack of transparency in decision-making and resource allocation, and inability of the majority to hold officials accountable for stewardship; and (iv) arrested development aspirations of the communities as the overall gamut of governance arrangements through appointed district chief executives, district assemblies, and unit committees are unable to provide and deliver services to the satisfaction of the people; and (v) inertia largely due to the phenomenon of relegation of traditional leadership to peripheral roles and positions.

Misdiagnosis of Local Governance (LG) Subpar Performance Problematic

Contestations on the mandated leadership arrangements have been based on diametrical views leading to a misdiagnosis of the LG problematic in the country. Core viewpoints are to have either nonpartisan or partisan-based district assemblies and unit committees. The main focus has been on holding a referendum to amend Article 55 (3) of the Constitution (Organization of Political Parties) to permit the introduction of partisan politics into local government. The driving belief is the seemingly underlying consensus on the direct elections of the DCEs, and their nomination has largely been the cause of the LG problematic. Amid the contestations, however, there seems to be missing the point that the inability of prevailing LG arrangement to meet the aspirations of the populace is a *systemic leadership design anomaly* than either nonpartisan or partisan elections of the major actors including the DCEs.

Utterances on the Frontline Involvement of the Institution of Chieftaincy in LG

The LG challenges have prompted many calls from eminent personalities including the Asantehene,[9] Okyehene,[10] Asokorehene,[11] and the Agbogbomefia,[12] among others, for the frontline involvement of chiefs beyond prevailing constitutional provisions of guaranteeing recognition and presence, and consultations (jointly with other interest groups) by national executives on 30 percent nominations regarding the composition of the district assemblies (1992 Constitution—Chapters 20 and 22). These utterances have mainly remained pronouncements so far without corresponding blueprints on "HOW" this necessary and uncontestable feat can be pursued and achieved. Such a scenario spurred Togbe Afede XIV (the Agbogbomefia of Asogli State) to announce the establishment of an African Traditional Leadership Institute (ATLI) to be headquartered in Accra.[13]

Regardless, a committee of experts[14] charged with the formulation of proposals for the 1992 Constitution recommended that (a) chiefs should be made ceremonial heads of the DAs; (b) a percentage of the DAs set aside for chiefs; and (c) cooptation of some chiefs as members of the DAs. It is important to note that these recommendations would mainly be cosmetics in practice and not adequate to induce fundamental changes.

Similarly, the Legal Affairs Committee of the National House of Chiefs' suggestion to cede the constitutional stipulation on 30 percent nominations of the DAs by the national executives solely to Chiefs is also inadequate to alter the fundamental dynamics of parallel leadership which arguably is the root cause of the LG malaise.[15] Although, the Legal Affairs Committee rightly pointed out that "the introduction of an electoral system should not be used to deprive traditional authorities of their role as effective partners in development and governance."[16]

Need to Eliminate Parallel Leadership Syndrome

Parallel leadership syndrome stems from people having to grapple with vacillations between two dominant and competing leadership structures at the local levels at times to the point of paralysis and inertia. One structure is the chieftaincy institution, which the people have meticulously created, nurtured, guarded, and sustained. The other structure is the panoply of the DCEs, district assemblies, and unit committees, which have been constructed and superimposed as features of the post-independence LG arrangements

Through constitutional and legal provisions, the structure which is rooted in customs and thus more understandable and pliable among the majority of people has been anomalously designated unofficial for the purposes of public policy decision-making, resource allocations and management, and stewardship at the local levels. National leaders perceive continuous relevance and influence as mainly veritable sources of access to votes and exploit them for self-serving purposes during competitive multiparty election campaigns to boost vote-grabbing efforts and voter turnouts in national elections. There is the urgent need to eliminate the phenomenon of parallel leadership which has bedeviled local-level administration since independence.

Indigenous Leadership for either Transformative or Regressive Politics

Indigenous leadership manifested as the institution of chieftaincy (entailing both male and female chiefs) is a powerful mainstay of the Ghanaian/African society and should not be considered a relic of the past. Rather, the institution is an underutilized bastion for catalyzing mass participation, transparency in resource management, and accountability of stewardship for transformative development. The institution of chieftaincy, regardless of its inherent flaws, remains the more cohesive governance and leadership structure at the local level with symbiotic capability to communicate, mobilize, and organize community members for collective development actions.

The institution of chieftaincy as a home-grown, time-tested leadership institution can be reformed, adapted, and weaned of its anachronistic tendencies to hold fort at the local level. And this same leadership institution can progressively complement competitive partisan political representations at the national level to build nation-states capable of meeting the development aspirations of all Ghanaians/Africans regardless of party affiliations.

Conscientious Patriotism

Now, Ghana (and ultimately Africa) is in dire search of solutions for the LG problematic, which has partly contributed to the prevailing winner-takes-all, divisive, and alienating electoral politics regardless of the impressive successes in peaceful elections of presidents, MPs, handing over of power and change of ruling governments. Certainly, these are sterling actions which have provided the basis for the country to be branded within the global community with the accolade as the "beacon of democracy in Africa." Regardless, it cannot be refuted that unbridled partisanship is increasingly marching the country off the plank and into the abyss. Families and communities have been strangulated and become wary and suspicious of each other along party lines. This is not to say that ascension to the throne under the institution of chieftaincy has been devoid of bitter clashes between "royal gates" or families vying for recognition and legitimacy regarding the leadership in a community.

Conscientious patriotic interventions are needed to calm nerves and remind the public that partisan politics is mainly one form of organizing principles of life and crafting the design and shape of statehood according to needs and realities in a polity. Thus, it should not be construed as the only tool for governance arrangement designs, which merit the label of democratic accolade and behavior. Competitive partisan politics per se is not the cure-all for the LG malaise in the country as it has also not led significantly to transparency in decision-making and accountability of stewardship at the national level.

Transformative Development Requires Proactive Involvement of Indigenous Leadership

Development as a transformational process is predominantly political requiring fair representation, energetic participation, transparency, and accountability to meet targeted goals. The relegation of the institution of chieftaincy to purely ceremonial roles may explain the inability of associated local structures to evolve into a bulwark for ensuring transparency and accountability in national governance operations.

Ghana has about 40,000 settlements across the country and over 30,000 rarely experience a regular presence of formal government as they make living in their homes and communities. Given the prevalence of entrenched primordial ties and psychosocial compositions of the populace, the vast majority continue to rely more on the so-called unofficial and informal leadership arrangements.

The relative peace enjoyed by Ghana vis-à-vis neighboring countries in the subregion is largely due to the existence and functional operations of the institution of chieftaincy albeit its marginalized role in LG and development. Participation is key to development so the involvement of the leadership structure which arguably has superior capability to communicate, mobilize, and organize the majority of the people for collective actions is fundamental and critical.

In this context, the constitutional provision of Chapter 22, Article 276, of the 1992 Constitution of the country barring chiefs from taking part in active party politics has outlived its usefulness. Politics, as practiced in Ghana and elsewhere on the continent, is the avenue by which public resources are allocated, managed, and translated into beneficial dividends to meet the needs and aspirations of people in the polity.

Salient Elements of BRP in Practice in the Case of Ghana

As in the case of the background narrative, it is essential to unravel the tenets of BRP in the context of a specific country's practices for better understanding of the leadership and governance relevance and the corresponding reform implications. Ghana provides the most appropriate sociocultural milieu for close reflective observations of the anomaly in the constitutional mandate to lead, rule, and govern to fulfill people's needs and interests. The main reason underlying Ghana's appropriateness for a case study is the visible presence and roles chiefs (males and females) play in grassroots development through communication, mobilization, and organization of communities for collective endeavors, and peaceful and harmonious coexistence. Arguably, the relative peace enjoyed by the country in relation to neighbors in the subregion could be attributed to the resiliency and robustness of the institution of chieftaincy rather than arrangements of coexistence fostered through party politics operations. Ghana is also suitable for this analysis and reflections, given its geographical position as the major transport hub of the inglorious slave trade evidenced in the numerous forts and castles which dot its coastlines as well as the history of its frontline role in the struggles for independence.

During the earlier post-independence period, Ghana experienced many military takeovers and armed insurrections more than any African country. In the present era, Ghana is heralded within the international community as the "beacon" of democracy for its relatively peaceful transitions of power from a ruling to an opposition party based on a series of nationwide electoral balloting and universal adult suffrages.

Furthermore, and more importantly for our purpose, the resilience of the institutions of chieftaincy is highly visible and the continuous relevance for harmonious coexistence easily observable amid the glamour and glitters of partisan bickering and divisiveness. In fact, the saying that all politics is local has a more significant meaning in the context of Ghana, as every present-day politician standing for elections has to go all length to secure the implicit or explicit endorsement of traditional leaders within the respective communities.

Generally, BRP is a fusion of traditional African and "Western" principles of representation, transparency, accountability, and participation for organizing the designs and shape of statehood according to the needs, aspirations, and realities of target societies. The critical features are:

1. A mix of leadership systems with the constitutional mandate to rule and having an underlying superior capability to communicate, mobilize, and organize voluntarily for collective transformative development in a polity.
2. BRP connotes vertical and horizontal blending, whereby national leadership is determined by prevailing multiparty-based universal adult suffrage elections (Western), and local governance leadership is determined by leadership arrangements nurtured and guarded by African people for centuries and to which they continue to ascribe (indigenous).
3. Traditional chiefs (both males and females) would represent communities in their respective local electoral areas at corresponding designated district assemblies[17]; a variation arrangement is applicable to the metropolitan assemblies (MAs).
4. 100 percent membership composition by traditional authorities in DAs and municipal assemblies.
5. District chief executives (DCEs) and deputies would be elected from members of the DAs and municipal assemblies by representatives.
6. Guaranteed centrality of gender balance in the composition of the DAs— that is, if a male is elected as DCE, then a female is elected automatically as deputy and vice versa.[18]

7. The DCE chairs the executive council; deputy presides over DA.
8. Comparable arrangements for the metropolitan assemblies will have to be considered.

The logic of a BRP framework is that majority of the people in local communities will be better represented by their own chosen leaders based on familiar understandable norms and conventions in local governing arrangements. These people would have access, influence and control over their leaders to ensure transparency in policy decisions regarding the management of common resources. Collectively, the people would utilize their strengthened local governance structures to influence and exert control, and enable transparency and accountability for stewardship of national affairs, which would minimize or eliminate impunity and misuse of the public purse to engender shared prosperity.

Implications of Adopting BRP

The implications are manifested in two areas: (1) structure, composition, and functioning of the district assemblies; and (2) reforming, adaptation, and strengthening of the institution of chieftaincy (IoC).

Structure, Composition, and Functioning of District Assemblies

1. The need for the promulgation of constitutional amendments, reviews, enactments, and local governance reforms. Relevant chapters and articles of the Ghana 1992 Constitution and the LG Act are as follows:
   • Chapter 20—Decentralization and Local Government:
   • Article 242—Composition of District Assembly
   • Article 243—District Chief Executive
   • Article 244—Presiding Member
   • Chapter 22—Chieftaincy
   • Article 270 (1)—Enhance Effectiveness of IoC
   • Local Government Act, 1993
2. A suitable formula-based variation of BRP in the metropolitan assemblies is required given the cosmopolitan character, population, and spatial configuration of the cities.[19]
3. The composition of the executive committee of the DAs and extending membership to the heads of the requisite technical departments with the right to vote.
4. Replacing the duplicative administrative nomenclature—urban, town, area, and zonal councils with the more grounded and far-reaching traditional councils.

Reforms, Adaptation, and Strengthening of the Institution of Chieftaincy

1. Tenure limitations of representation and participation of traditional leaders at the DAs[20]

2. Delegation of representation (representation can be delegated in case a community considers a chief not capable of participation)
3. The structure, composition, and functioning of corresponding traditional councils would require retrofitting for centrality of gender balance, resource support, and capacity enhancement to assume the roles and responsibilities of urban, town, area, and zonal councils of the DAs.
4. The structure and composition of National and Regional Houses of Chiefs to accommodate suitably balanced integration of female traditional authority counterparts (National and Regional Associations of Queen Mothers, for example). This is notwithstanding some notable scholarly contestations on the positions of female chiefs in societies which are predominantly patriarchal.[21] Regardless, women chiefs are rooted and widespread in several societies.[22]
5. Documentation for codification of essential practices of the institution including enstoolment/enskinment and destoolment procedures, consensus-building, mass participation inducement, accountability for stewardship and transparency in resource allocation and management, and conflict resolution

Customized Institutional Reforms across the Continent

From the foregoing, to make BRP functional, African countries would, first and foremost, embark on constitutional reforms to amend articles and chapters of the various constitutions on the structures, composition, formation, and functions of the state at the national and local levels particularly relating to the roles and responsibilities of national and traditional leadership. Countries would be required to revise relevant chapters and articles on decentralization and membership of the constituent assemblies, and reconfigure overall local government arrangements. These revisions would reflect requirements and conditions for a functioning blended leadership and governing structures capability to communicate, mobilize, and organize society voluntarily for collective purposes.

In the same vein, countries would embark on deep reflections and introspections to reform the Institutions of Chieftaincy so that they are better equipped to handle the expected roles and responsibilities adoption of BRP confers and requires. Notable areas in this regard include (a) lifetime tenures, (b) restrictive leadership selection pools and choice options, (c) gendered roles, visibility, and responsibilities clarifications, (d) shrouded mythical operational procedures, and (e) limits of adjudicative capability.

In all reform areas, care would be taken to ensure that good practices do not become the enemy of the best in attempts to adapt and conform to the exigencies of governance challenges confronting the societies. For example, tenure limitations would apply to participating in local assemblies, membership, and steering of policy decision-making task groups and committees. Also, established traditional norms, conventions, and practices regarding selection choices, options, and alternates would be documented, acknowledged, and accorded the due recognition and respect. Furthermore, the vital roles and responsibilities of women would be amplified in a manner that reverberates in the entire reform process to rectify the misleading conceptions that the institution of chieftaincy in Africa only revolves around males in the communities.

Conclusion: A Long-Range Lens on Solutions Pathway

A major thrust of this manuscript is to translate the findings and lessons of background activities, interactions, analyses, and reform-implied interventions into tangible forms of blended representational principles on the ground. In this regard, BRP as an intellectual solutions pathway emanated from over two decades of empirical content, professional engagements, and experiences within the international community across countries on four continents including Africa, Europe, Asia, and North America.

Good governance is the lynchpin of development as a transformational process. This process entails (a) fair representational arrangements and robust institutions steering the wheels for fulfilling aspirations and needs of people; (b) transparency in decision-making, public expenditure, resource allocation, effectiveness, and efficiency of resource use, (c) access to information and knowledge, application of appropriate technologies, and adaptation to changing dynamics, (d) accountability for stewardship, and (e) participation in governance arrangements, to mention some of the mechanisms which make development transformational, resilient, and sustainable. It is possible that good governance and sustainable development in Ghana/Africa could be grounded more firmly in a blend of indigenous and modern knowledge principles and values.

In this respect, this book seeks to promote envisioned policies and frameworks according to needs and realities which Africa could adopt and utilize for more resilient institutions and administration. The BRP approach could possibly cure the "winner-takes-all," divisive, and alienating political economic ills currently in vogue across the continent. In a nutshell, BRP is a framework around which local and national government administrations could be reformed with more prominent roles of indigenous leadership.

Chapter 7

THE IDEALS OF TRAN-SERVE LEADERSHIP

Introduction

In real life, every new medication is tested, tried, and approved by a regulatory body before releasing for use by the public. This chapter provides ample reasons why embracing BRP is a commonsensical undertaking for Africa and the broader global community. First, the level of receptivity to the concept of BRP by groups of people is purposely gauged during the period of executive high-profile interactions in Africa. And the expressed sentiments of these targeted groups are categorized and summarized for literary convenience and insights. Second, instances are highlighted to demonstrate that without adopting and operationalizing BRP, the alternate pathway for the continent is a continuation of ongoing situation of organized chaos. However, wisdom provides to stop digging a hole if sinking. Third, pertinent possibilities and outcomes bordering on the ideals of better governance but elusive on the continent which could be engendered by BRP are emphasized. Fourth, the sterling characteristics of the type of leadership arrangements—"Tran-Serve" (transformational servant)—which will steer the boat through the rough tides are noted. Tran-Serve leaders are those who lead to serve and transform by propelling nations to fulfill needs and manifest the blessings of success. A distinct profile of this notable leadership arrangement is constructed to reinforce the conviction that a BRP-inspired rulership could be the potent cure for the leadership and governance malady in Africa.

Summary reactions of target Stakeholder Groups

Any proposed change to the status quo in society has a price and so it is strategically wise to gauge the responses of those who would be impacted in various ways by the envisaged dividends of such a measure. In this regard, and as part of the resident executive interactions, opinionated responses to the adoption of BRP by segments of the population in Ghana were gleaned through purposive conversations and insights from secondary sources (media utterances—print, online, and social) on the topic. Overall, no outright condemnation of the BRP idea was countered, but there were mixed reactions in opinions, ambivalence, skepticisms, and "who cares" or "nothing much" will change attitude among the population group.

The following summarizes the key points of sentiments expressed by target groups as follows:

1. **Ruling elites/political class:** This group is startled by the possibility of sharing power and privileges and would rather divert attention to the numerous chieftaincy disputes and land litigations engendered by some chiefs across communities in the country. Quick reference is made to the constitutional provision that chiefs are not allowed to partake in partisan politics. In their opinion, sharing the mandate to lead, rule, and govern would be a drain on the public purse monetarily as chiefs would have to be paid salaries which the national coffers cannot sustain.

2. **Traditional leaders:** For some of them, it seems quite difficult to fathom the kind of change implications envisaged under the BRP concept. As the institution most battered by the continental historical experiences, the continuous relevance is construed in terms of tweaking the status quo to allow more active official forefront participation in development. Even if this perspective is logical and commonsensical, it is never projected as a conferred right by the fact that it is the leadership institution closest to the people in the various communities. Although traditional power and authority importance is flexed particularly during the solicitation of electoral votes by the national elites, adoption of BRP would fundamentally alter entrenched leadership and governance relationships on the continent.[1]

3. **Women:** Many women who reside in communities in semi-urban and rural areas practice their livelihoods in the markets and so opinions on adoption of BRP are influenced and shaped by the perceptions of local governance performance and how their roles are perceived in keeping the communities together or harmonious communal coexistence. Women may not be the head chief in a community, but the position of the chief of women is revered and whoever chosen is usually leader of the search task force to identify, nominate, and choose the head chief whenever there is a vacancy. Women consider themselves as the glue which binds the communities together, and without their vital roles, the communities would not thrive and may have "withered" away long ago. For this essential purpose of existence, they exude much pride and signal unusually strong preference of BRP given the abysmal performance of prevailing local governance arrangements in the communities.

4. **Youth:** Mixed reactions in opinions are amplified among the youth, particularly those residing in urban areas, educated, internet-literate, and are social media-active. On the one hand, the yearning to be "westernized" is highly noticeable, and given their minimal and truncated knowledge of cultural heritage, they mainly consider the institution of chieftaincy as a relic of the past and thus not relevant in the current dispensation of searching for viable solutions to present leadership and governance challenges of the continent. On the other hand, in the semi-urban and rural areas, the youth constitute the "asafo" groups and actively participate in community undertakings spearheaded by the chiefs and elders. The urban residents often join their counterparts in the rural areas in adhering to the sanctity

and reverence of the traditional institutions. They do not openly disrespect the chiefs of the communities and rally to condemn anyone perceived to do otherwise. The youth of this latter category and attitude expressed muted enthusiasm and willingness to embrace the concept of BRP.

5. **Public sector officials**: As the cogs in the wheels of administrative efficiency, effectiveness, and economy, public sector officials generally bemoan the situation in the various economies without necessarily considering themselves as partly responsible for the prevailing situations. They are wary of the possible disruptions in their positions and roles which the BRP concept may induce, and so expressed skepticism and ambivalence about the efficiency and effectiveness of such a measure. Although the yearning for positive changes in their fortunes and personal lives is visibly high, BRP is welcome if it does not lead to losing their jobs. Given that some of these public sector officials are the same people who constitute the elderships of the traditional establishment, the tendency to give the concept a try has been clearly evident in many of the interactions.

6. **Ordinary Africans:** The mere fact of the "unimaginable" possibly occurring in terms of elevating their home-grown and time-tested leadership institutions was enough to induce some enthusiasm and hope that change could be on the horizon with the adoption of the BRP concept. However, given the weight of immediate conditions of deprivations and marginalization in the midst of so perceived abundant resources, and that the expected changes may take time to be felt in pockets, some expressed resignations and "who cares" attitudes. To many, it is possible change may occur but may not impact positively or improve their lots directly and individually. There seems to be the conviction on the part of this category of the population that any change would be better than the current situation in which they find themselves.

7. **The African diaspora:** They are the most vocal and critical of the African countries; are in dire search of a cure for the leadership leadership and governance situation on the continent, and yearn for replicating the conditions of current residencies back in their homes and countries of heritage. Their frustrations with the leadership of the continent are quite high but not sure whether they should embrace and believe BRP type of changes would bring about the expected remedies. Some in the diaspora, however, take comfort in the operations of their respective hometown associations (HTA). Those with philanthropic tendencies have acknowledged that channeling resources through HTAs under the respective chiefs for community improvement undertakings is the only surest guarantee of fulfilling wishes. In this context, it is posited that BRP as a solutions pathway could be thrown the welcome mat.

   The international community: This is the case of ambivalence predicated on adherence to strict dogmatic preference for familial solutions pathways even in the face of not-so-good abundant evidence of progress and positive gains. The linear pathway of replicating the successes of Western societies in Africa is always right and cannot be circumvented. No other way could produce the so-called dividends of democracy and any recommendations otherwise could be diversionary and disruptive. However, BRP is an ardent advocate of the principles and values of both worlds which have become the hallmarks of present realities of Africa. Dogmatic insistence on adherence to one particular mold has never been successful in the past six decades and more, and will not now miraculously generate the expected dividends for the people. Some in the international community, albeit perhaps in the minority, have expressed the desire of adopting the concept of BRP with the hope and belief that it could induce the required fundamental changes for leadership structures that would produce leaders who will lead to serve and propel the societies to fulfill needs and manifest the blessings of success.

There are some noteworthy underlying threads in all the reactions:

1. The current leadership and governance situation is sinking the fortunes of the continent and something concrete must be done to change the narrative.
2. In the midst of abundant natural and human resources, there is no excuse for the African continent to remain impoverished after several decades since independence.
3. Africa's current deplorable condition is a testament to the failure of leadership both domestically and within the international community.
4. Well-trusted, respected home-grown actions and measures, and not externally imposed cosmetic, short-term palliative interventions are required to turn things around for the better.
5. Enough is enough so far, time is running out, patience is on a short leash, and the yearnings are high for momentous leadership that will lead to serve and transform in terms of propelling the societies to fulfill needs and manifest the blessings of success for everyone.

Continuation of Organized Chaos as the Alternate Pathway

African countries are in dire search of a cure for the leadership and governance subpar performance on the continent. This search largely includes ideas of "sound strategies for sustaining and expanding the benefits of economic growth to all people of Africa in the years ahead."[2] BRP represents a conscientious patriotic intervention of sociopolitical engineering capable of inducing energetic political participation, transparency, and accountability for collective endeavors. In the absence of a BRP type of rescue, the alternative for the continent is to continue with the current predicament of organized chaos in all spheres of life—politically, economically, socially, and culturally.

Politically, sham and fraudulent elections are organized under the banner of democratic ideals across the continent. More often, the periodic electoral events have partly contributed to the prevailing "winner takes all," divisive, and alienating partisan politics. This is regardless of the impressive successes in peaceful elections providing the basis, for example, for Ghana to be branded within the global community as the "beacon of democracy in Africa."[3] As noted earlier, unbridled partisanship is increasingly marching countries on the continent off the plank and into the abyss. Families and communities have been strangulated and become wary and suspicious of each other along party lines.

BRP-inspired interventions are necessary to calm nerves and remind the public that partisan politics is mainly one form of organizing principles of life in a polity and should not be construed as the only tool for governance arrangement designs, which merit the label of democratic accolade and behavior.[4] To reiterate, competitive partisan politics per se is not the cure-all for the leadership and governance subpar performance at local levels in the various countries as it has also not led significantly to transparency in decision-making and accountability of stewardship at national levels.

Widespread imitations making fuss and charades of what prevails as democratic norms and practices elsewhere have become commonplace across the continent. African parliaments are miniature "House of Commons" in the UK, Canada, or whatever they are in France and the United States, sometimes making caricatures of the deliberative processes. Independence of the judiciary seems to be thrown to the wind as the invincible arms of the executive branch of government is perceived as influencing and exerting pressure through the constitutional prerogatives of appointments and doling out favors.[5] Freedom of the press is tolerated so long as the ox of the powerful in society is not gored. It is a common joke that the more vocal a journalist is, the deeper he or she is in the pockets of a benefactor, and the practice of stomach journalism is the order of survival and sustenance.

Maintaining law and order by the police forces and related security establishments is pursued in the context of protecting and preserving the status quo ruling regimes. Double standards are the mainstay of policing and enforcement of rules—one for the powerful and well-connected, and the other for ordinary Africans. Quite recently, military coups are rearing heads again as if the continent is back in the 1980s, where strongmen occupy the seats of governments; or in other related cases, some countries fending off the shenanigans of the elites in uniform.[6] Indeed, this situation is the epitome of organized chaos.

Economically, the ravages of the Covid-19, climate change, fiscal pressures, mounting debt levels, high interest rates, rising inflation, depreciating exchange rates, downward spiraling currencies, eroding purchasing power, joblessness, chronic poverty all combine to make mockery of economic management strategies and interventions on the continent. The economic narrative of Africa has always been mired in "economic recovery," and the projected forecasts have followed similar headlines or same patterns—jobless growth. "The IMF expects Sub-Saharan Africa to grow 3.7% in 2021 and 3.8% in 2022"—a growth and expansion projection amid liquidity strains, which depicts a picture that African economies are making some strides but obliviously not enough to make a dent in the fortunes of the ordinary African.

Quality education is compromised on the altar of mushrooming of educational institutions of questionable capacity and the visible specter of the policy-makers increasingly sending their wards and children outside to avoid the domestic schools.[8] The ruling elites prefer not to invest in health infrastructures at home but would rather be flown outside for treatment at facilities which sometimes are administered by medical practitioners and nurses of African heritage. It is a known fact that a large proportion of personnel at several of the hospitals and clinics in the metropolis of the advanced economies are Africans who left the continent because of lack of opportunities at home. And many of these people are yearning to go back home and contribute their quota to the development efforts if only decent health facilities are available. However, they are not prepared to practice their trade and profession in setups described euphemistically as "death traps."[9] This situation is organized chaos at its apogee.

Another seeming feature of organized chaos is the business of churches evangelizing "prosperity gospels" amid high levels of unemployment.[10] There are tales of abandoned factories and buildings remodeled into churches. Many congregants could choose to spend their days all week in these churches and praying for miracles to put food on the table or pay children's school fees or hospital bills. It is possible churches outnumber manufacturing facilities making the owners and operators very wealthy while pauperizing the worshippers. Commonsense is sometimes thrown to the wind when it comes to miracle churches purporting to fulfilling needs, which obviously could be made possible through sheer hard work and perspirations in a factory. And when the fasting and prayers do not provide the instant gratifications expected, then it must be the cause or curse from someone who is an enemy of progress. What can be deduced from such thought processes if not outright foolery exhibited in chaotic trances?

The embodiment of African culture is the institution of chieftaincy. As noted, development as a transformational process requires embeddedness in the cultural practices and the realities of life of the people for outcomes fulfilling needs and propelling to manifest the blessings of success. The relegation of the institution of chieftaincy to purely ceremonial roles on the continent may explain the inability of post-independence Africa to evolve and build strong and resilient rulership institutions into bulwarks for elevating political participation and ensuring transparency and accountability in national governance operations.

Given the prevalence of entrenched primordial ties, the psychosocial compositions of the populace, and the ineffectiveness of the formal post-independence structures, the vast majority continue to rely more on the so-called unofficial and informal leadership arrangements. There is abundant truth in the observation noted earlier that the relative peace enjoyed by Ghana vis-à-vis neighboring countries in the sub-region is largely due to the existence and functional operations of the institution of chieftaincy albeit its marginalized role in local governance and development. Participation is key to development so the involvement of the leadership structure which arguably has superior capability to communicate, mobilize, and organize the majority of the people for collective actions is fundamental and critical.

The foregoing scenario paints a picture of a heavyweight boxing champion with hands tied to the back and thrown into the ring to defend title from being taken by a rival counterpart. Such is the state of the leadership and governance situation of Africa. The concept of BRP could be embraced domestically and externally, and indigenous leadership is given a new leap of faith for more active position in present-day political activities. This is not a nostalgic recommendation but a factual statement of the missing link in African transformation efforts. Politics is the avenue by which public resources are allocated, managed, and translated into beneficial dividends to meet the aspirations of people in a polity. And engaging in this vital practice with one foot in and the other out while expecting transformational dividends is organized chaos at its best posture.

Some Immediate Possible Outcomes

Adopting the BRP will trigger some immediate possibilities resulting in likely specific outcomes. The first major possibility under BRP will be a tremendous rise in active genuinely enthused political participation by ordinary people. Activities to inspire a rapid march and arrival at this destination will include (besides the proactive enactments of constitutional reviews and amendments to effect the necessary structural changes in governance arrangements) public education and sensitization, release of high-profile country position papers on BRP, capacity enhancement and retrofitting of the traditional leadership structures, and reorientations of both leadership institutions—traditional and national.

The second bold actionable possibility will be increased demand for accountability of stewardship at the local and national levels. Indigenous channels and spaces of interactions will become integral to the structure and composition of local government arrangements. Intimidation of ordinary people will be eliminated or minimized as they will likely be empowered through the use of familiar and easily understandable means of communication and deliberations. Emergent special advocacy and pressure groups orchestrations at all levels will ensure persistency of demands and request for adoption of BRP. Ordinary people will utilize such opportune mechanisms for engendering appreciable transformational and servant (Tran-Serve, see later section) leadership behaviors and qualities. Furthermore, regular community mass actions on the need to promulgate BRP-based reforms, civic accountability forums becoming a permanent feature, and collectively emboldening local leadership through elimination of national executive outreach and patronage would serve as formidable checks on abuse and misuse of power and authority by national leadership.

Third, there will likely be increased transparency in resource allocation, usage, and translations into dividends to fulfill needs and propel manifestations of blessings of success for all. Activities to be embarked upon in this context will include revising the formula of respective resource categories, adapting protocols on the utilization of indigenous knowledge and leadership, and formulating applicable resource allocation arrangements based on a ratio of more equitable modalities between national and local government.

Possibly, these strategic measures and activities will lead to four key outcomes pertaining to better governance practices. There will be deepened closeness of local and national ruling regimes to the majority from a distance gap, and these regimes will be imbued with a greater capacity to communicate, mobilize, and organize for collective purposes. The vexatious issue of parallel leadership syndrome will be eliminated in local governance, and community-owned selected leadership will exercise local political authority based on voluntarism and consensus and not fear of coercion or reprisal. Direct leader-to-people communication, mobilization, and organization will become the norm rather than the exception, and the distance gap is drastically reduced through majority involvement and familiarity with the operations of governance arrangements.

There will be increased administrative efficiency as related to resource use, service delivery, and overall leadership and governance performance record at the local and national levels. This will commence with, for example in Ghana, technical heads of applicable public sector departments becoming members of the executive committee of the district assemblies with the right to vote.[11] It will mean curtailing the practice of concentrating development resources always at the few urban centers/cities and widespread extending to the hinterlands at the local levels.[12] It will also mean negating the practice of relegation of technical expertise in resource use decision-making, and majority opinions shaping and influencing prioritizations of deployment of available resources and interventions. In practice, service delivery response and quality, performance record of the administrative bureaucracy, and access by the majority to local officials will all be rated highly satisfactorily by beneficiaries; and there will be noticeable improvement in timeliness of interventions related to public requests and demands.

Several people will trust and respect the local and national administration's operational procedures. These attitudinal response outcomes will be revealed through periodic assessments of civic duties responses; local bye-laws compliance and violation occurrence rates and analysis of majority perceptions of experiences with operational procedures; and regular conduct of motivation response polls in selected communities. Also, any analytical data on leadership motivation capacity and response rate of community members gathered will attest to an improved condition. Besides, more than half of the population will indicate a high level of trust and respect for the local administration arrangements.

Majority of the people will express increased buy-in and a deep sense of belonging toward the leadership and governance arrangements. Evidence in this context will reveal exponential demonstration of pride in being citizens of the communities and increased concern for the collective welfare in terms of minimized aloofness toward place-based symbols and insignia. Overall, development impact assessments and level of enthusiasm polls will demonstrate impressive awareness of respective national political cultures, energetic leadership enthusiasm capacity, and community members' expressions of attachment to the governance arrangements.

In sum, the key takeaway messages on pertinent possibilities and outcomes of embracing and adopting the concept of BRP are:

1. Parallel leadership syndrome underlining subpar performance of leadership and governance arrangements at the national and local levels of statehood will be uprooted to pave way for leadership arrangements grounded in the socioeconomic realities, cultural existence, practices, and experience of the people.
2. Familial indigenous avenues, channels, and spaces will be elevated and opened for the majority of the people to have fair representation and

participate in local and national decision-making. This will have the effects of enhancing transparency in development resource allocation, use, and translation into dividends for the benefit of not only the privileged few but the majority.

3. Majority of the people will be empowered to engage in measures for ensuring accountability of stewardship at the local level, which in turn will translate into exertion of collective pressure for accountability at the national level.

4. Overall, the "TAP" principles of governance—transparency, accountability, and participation—will be strengthened to minimize "winner-takes-all," divisive partisan-based politics and steer the continent toward the path of transformative development that fulfills needs and manifests the blessings of success for not only the privileged few but the majority.

Transformational and Servant (Tran-Serve) Leadership for Steering Affairs

The concept of BRP is an embodiment of the values of transformational[13] and servant (Tran-Serve) leadership arrangements. A Tran-Serve leader will be at the driver's seat under the BRP. Tran-Serve is a play on the words—transform and servant, and derived from the combined ideals and values of transformational and servant leadership.

Research identifies four main distinctive components of a transformational leader: "intellectual stimulation, inspirational motivation, individualized consideration, and idealized influence."[14] As pointed out, "no one component is more important than the other, and all four makes for the idealized transformational leader."[15] The transformational leader has one main goal: "better the team's productivity and collective identity." However, while working toward this common goal, he or she cares for people as individuals by striving to manifest the blessings of success for everyone. Wearing the hat of a transformational leader as per the distinctive components, the Tran-Serve leader urges followers or underlings to think outside the box; gears or energizes passion and excitement toward the collective goal; considers everyone's contributions or inputs; focuses on the whole; refrains from narcissistic/self-serving behaviors to earn respect and trustworthiness and not through vain promises, doling out favors or lingering threats of retaliation and coercion.[16]

In a similar vein, "servant leadership," with its antecedent in biblical times exemplified by the life of Jesus Christ of Nazareth, sets aside self-interest for the betterment of followers—the collective or common goal. Servant leadership has been researched extensively in contemporary time by Robert Greenleaf and several others.[17] This is a style of leadership that places the needs of others first and fosters a conducive environment for follower's growth.[18] Here the leader is first a servant who wants to serve others first before leading, an approach which differs with leaders that lead first and who may be motivated by the need to secure power.[19]

Accordingly, the ten most respected characteristics[20] of servant leadership include "listening, empathy, healing, awareness, persuasion, conceptualization, foresight, stewardship, commitment to growth, and building communities." These characteristics are influenced and shaped by the three dimensions of operational performance capabilities of a servant leader: execution skills, people skills, and cognitive skills.[21] And depending on attitudes, skills, and domain knowledge, the level of strength and capacity of the servant leader can be predictably demonstrated, whether low, medium, or high. Execution skills refer to tolerance of ambiguity, resilience, and attention to details; people skills are about behavioral integrity, emotional intelligence, and proactive feedback; and cognitive skills relate to analytical reasoning, measured collaborative-consultative approach, and strategic thinking.[22]

Servant leadership is solutions-focused leadership which is key to success in life. Through "continuous learning and evolving, openness to change and opportunity, calculated risk-taking and receptiveness to other perspectives," strong servant leaders offer a "framework that facilitates crisis management."[23] Such characteristic traits or tendencies of servant leadership serve as veritable fountain of wisdom for the values which undergird the BRP concept in terms of Tran-Serve leadership arrangements. "This web of interconnected and mutually reinforced characteristics helps empower individuals to lead effectively through a diverse set of conditions and circumstances."[24] The traits of adaptability, flexibility, and versatility which underlie servant leadership position the Tran-Serve leader to operate with efficacy not just in crisis situations but in all contexts to tackle the challenges confronting the continent with dexterity and fulfill the needs of the people.

Furthermore, research has demonstrated synergistic relationship between servant leadership and various dimensions of spirituality.[25] This has tremendous relevance and significance in the African world as spirituality permeates many aspects of life. Proactive education of servant leadership style is essential for grounding the concept of BRP in rulership tradition as a vocation—serving the needs of others. As noted, a belief system that acknowledges the presence of God, Creator, or a high Power contributing to a more meaningful life and adds to an individual's well-being is the first principle of a transformational leadership manifesting the blessings of success in a society for everyone. Thus, charting a path of construing workplace spirituality as "the recognition that employees have an inner life that nourishes and is nourished by meaningful work that takes place in the context of community"[26] is illuminating, commendable, and a step in the right direction.

BRP is predicated on the actions of leaders who will lead to serve and transform societies. In this respect, Tran-Serve leadership refers to the actions of leaders who will lead to serve and transform by propelling societies to fulfill needs and manifest the blessings of success for everyone. For our purpose, Tran-Serve leadership encompasses all public office occupants whose power, authority, and positions are rooted in the public purse. Every public officeholder can become a Tran-Serve leader by striving and aspiring to uphold the underlying values. Figuratively for those at the helm of steering national affairs, the values of Tran-Serve leadership are a medley of the admirable attributes of Kwame Nkrumah of Ghana, Lee Kuan Yew of Singapore, and Mahathir Mohamed of Malaysia in terms of respective journeys of leading to serve and transform their various societies at a given point in time.[27]

Broadly stating, Africa requires the "head" and "body" (elites and masses) to be in sync to strive for a Tran-Serve leadership and come out of its current doldrums. The continent urgently needs all public officials who are in leadership positions to have a change of mindset—be they presidents, cabinet members, ministers, members of the legislature, judiciary, electoral bodies; media, police force, national security, military, teachers or professors, CEOs, and executive secretaries of the bureaucracies and local government assemblies—to forge and strive to become Tran-Serve leaders—that is, leaders who will lead to serve and transform with one common goal of fulfilling needs of society and propelling to manifest the blessings of success for everyone. This audacious calling includes as well indigenous leaders as custodians of the land and customary heads of the local communities. It is a vision and mission of building rulership institutions resilient and robust enough to brace the storms of current challenges and realities of the African world and not of sainthood far removed from coexistence and making a living in homes and communities.

This is what BRP seeks to instill in the mental and social fabric of the continent. All public officeholders work to improve the productivity of the nations or continent and collective identities. This is quite a messianic message, essential but probably may seem a tall order for some but that is what Africa needs to wake up out of present stupor. Great leadership acknowledges that wisdom is not in the head of one person, and the act of accomplishing the common goal can be done both directly or indirectly in various ways with inputs from everyone (regardless of party colors). Being passionate about the mission and the collective interests is also the preserve and a sterling quality of great stewardship.

To reiterate, a key point of BRP, and for that matter Tran-Serve leadership, is that it would require all hands to work toward a common goal of fulfilling needs of society and manifesting the blessings of success for every African. In this case if, for example, military personnel capitalize on popular grievances or leadership and governance failings of civilian administrations to seize power and claim salvation for the populace, it will be clear that such uprisings are premised on falsehood, self-serving, and will only muddy the waters more. Given the African predicament, nothing good will come from any circle of individuals arrogating to themselves whether through sham elections or the barrel of the gun, the power and authority to redeem the people out of their woes and misery without a BRP-motivated system. Africa does not need "create, loot and share" or "bazooka-enabled" governments. Africa's answer lies in a well-thought-through BRP-inspired leadership and governance interventions.

During the colonial days in Africa, the concept of public servants was introduced as the epitome of nascent bureaucracies with a truncated intent and purpose—servants in the sense of serving to enhance exploitation of the African people, resources, and the public purse for the benefit of the former colonial masters and metropolis. This attitude was carried over to the post-independence era whereby many of the emergent nationalist leaders construed the leftover state structures and bureaucracies as avenues of translating public resources into private wealth for families, friends, cronies, so-called middle class, and the elite rulership establishment. Ever since, this situation has continued whereby public servant leadership has not been driven by the motivation to serve others, striving to pursue common goals and aspirations, or nurture, foster, and empower others to flourish, fulfill needs, and manifest the blessings of success for everyone.

The jury is also out there on the efficacy of the application of the servant concept in the context of the widespread activities of international civil servants after the postwar reconstruction of the global economy with the creation of the IMF, World Bank, and the United Nations organizations.

Building rulership institutions with transformational and servant leadership principles would engender "a spiritual culture that creates a caring institution,"[28]; and the motivating influence would enhance workplace spirituality resulting in a more meaningful workplace for followers.[29] These bureaucratic institutions would likely be inspirational, imbued with positive spirit, and evolve to become the glue that binds society with confidence, direction, and group cohesion for pursuing and attaining the established common goal. In this context, rulership institution-building would be shaped by a holistic view of the health and well-being of individuals with the intent of capacitating with high self-esteem ethical behavior,[30] motivation and livelihood satisfaction,[31] and resiliency[32]. Overall, such an approach would possibly decrease burnout at the workplace[33] and improve the general quality of life.[34]

Distinct Profile of Tran-Serve Leadership as the Driver of BRP

From the foregoing, the profile of Tran-Serve leadership can be distinctly constructed as follows:

1. **Tran-Serve Leadership focuses on solutions, builds communities, and creates empowering spaces to uplift voices and mindsets around a common goal.** The concept of BRP connotes sharing of the mandate to rule at the national and local levels to create a formidable solutions-focused leadership structure with the combined traits and tendencies of transformational and servant leadership. From this perspective, an established common goal is the glue which binds the leaders and followers together. With commitment to growth, the head and the body are on the same page of this collective interests. Through inspiration, motivation, encouragement, and better communication, the head leads by example, and the body follows with a conviction of trust, respect, and loyalty. Both are passionate about the mission, putting aside self-serving interests to pursue and attain the collective goal for the benefit of everyone. While caring and concern for individual considerations are not compromised in the

process, all sides are determined to work with dedication, self-efficacy, and confidence to improve outcomes and increase satisfaction and performance regarding achieving the common goal.

2. **Tran-Serve leadership energizes people with improved outcomes, satisfaction, and performance to enhance political participation.** Building communities will create spaces to amplify the voices of the people and induce more commitment from members to recognize as valuable political participation in socioeconomic upliftment. In the process, strong motivation is created to establish community effectiveness, quality of group experience, and positive social relationships. Energizing community members with passion and excitement, persuasion and creative awareness, will likely enhance political participation to achieve the collective goal while reinforcing competence, good relationships, and the autonomy of the individual.

3. **Tran-Serve leadership sets aside self-interests for the transformation of the whole to enable transparent policy decision-making.** Sharing knowledge and power over resource allocations with credible formulas that place the needs of the broader society first and creating the environment for better understanding of the process by the people will increase transparency in policy decision-making. Engaging communities to think outside the box, and conceptualize high-quality stewardship relationships on resource use that set aside self-interest for the betterment of the whole, is certainly remarkable transparency that will decrease conflicting ideas and beliefs for positive development. Furthermore, allowing tolerance of ambiguity, resilience, and attention to details to avoid resource misuse promotes transparent operations execution.

4. **Tran-Serve leadership's underlying value impetus of motivation to serve others is a cardinal driver of accountable stewardship.** Astute behavioral integrity, coupled with measured collaborative-consultative approach for proactive feedback on the practice of ethical leadership where service is rooted in the leadership-follower relationship, will likely increase both horizontal and vertical accountability for situations in the societies. A leadership driven by the motivation to serve others will nurture, foster, and empower the people to ensure that accountability mechanisms and channels are maximally utilized and effective. Such motivating influence will also enhance community spirituality that results in more meaningful accountable communities.

5. **Tran-Serve leadership consideration of every individual's needs and inputs shrinks distance between people and regime in power.** Rulership based on analytical reasoning, strategic thinking, big-picture and proactive approach, and solution-focused mentality that considers everyone's inputs will engender closeness of the regime in power to the people. A regime that is mindful of closing the distance gap will listen, express empathy, and offer healing remedies to confront challenges and fulfill needs. This regime will exhibit high emotional intelligence in its ability to understand

and experience emotions and regulate use of resources toward growth that fosters high-quality relationship with the people.

6. **Tran-Serve leadership construes public service as a vocation to engender economy, efficiency, and effectiveness in the use of societal resources.** Higher levels of Tran-Serve leadership will instill in the public bureaucracy certain attitudes, skills, and domain knowledge for grounding public offices and positions in the tradition of vocation serving the needs of the broader society to ensure administrative efficiency and effectiveness in resource use and management. Public officials will strive to institutionalize meaningful workplaces with the requisite self-governing autonomy and competencies for pursuing and reaching the common goal. Better communication, amplifying creativity, and securing collective identities through empowering the respective workers would produce an administrative culture that creates caring institutional bureaus that exist to fulfill the needs of society and manifest the blessings of success for everyone.

7. **Tran-Serve leadership operates to earn respect and trust voluntarily rather than through real or imagined threat of coercion and force.** Focusing on the whole rather than self-serving narcissistic attitudes inculcates trust, respect, and loyalty toward the overall leadership and governance operational procedures. These attributes are earned and worthy of the honor instead of coerced or exacted with empty political campaign promises and rhetoric. Leadership structures oriented to serve before leading with an underlying recognition that the inner lives of people nourish livelihoods and meaningful communities are trustworthy and respectful of the sanctity of human life and personhood.

8. **Tran-Serve leadership exudes high-level buy-in and a sense of belongingness by its very nature, existential traits, and operational characteristics.** Overall, ensuring stronger collective identities with improved outcomes, increased performance and satisfaction, cohesive communities, sharing unifying experience and lessons will likely lead to high-level feelings of inclusiveness, buy-in, and a sense of belonging among the populace. This, in turn, will enable identifying easily with the leadership and governance arrangements of the society. Tran-Serve leadership operations include continuous learning, openness to change and opportunities, and calculated risk-taking which makes the concept of BRP resilient and robust enough to facilitate effective problem-solving. In sum, the previous outline of traits and tendencies that define Tran-Serve leadership in all contexts and circumstances reinforces the strength of BRP as a commonsensical antidote for the leadership and governance challenges affecting African countries.

Conclusion

Evidence has amplified reasons why BRP remains a commonsense approach to the leadership and governance problematics in Africa. In the past two years, three successful military coups occurred in West Africa.[35] The world is convalescing from the Covid-19 crippling effects. The United States is facing serious internal challenges to the foundations of its democracy practices and together with European Allies (NATO) must grapple with Russia's invasion of Ukraine. The geopolitical balance of power and influence tussle between China and the United States clouds the global atmosphere amid the never-ending missile-related forays of North Korea while the issue of Iran sanctions remains on the radar. Meanwhile, the chickens are home to roost on the climate frontier. Effects of pillaging of the environment and lands across the globe several hundred years ago, and contemporary attempts at replicating this predatory mode of accumulation and consumption processes by the transnational elite consortium, have manifested in serious climate change challenges for the planet Earth.[36]

With all that is happening within the global community simultaneously, nations are increasingly rationalizing "inward retreat" strategies for home-front solutions. Africa can only free itself first from self-inflicted pain before any outside assistance will make a dent on tackling many of the challenges facing the continent. And BRP-inspired leadership and governance arrangement could be the way forward for a continent walloping in distress.

Chapter 8

OPERATIONALIZING BRP

Introduction

This chapter details the necessary steps to operationalize BRP across the continent. The driving task is to ingrain in the collective psyche of Africans and the international community that a systematic building of blended rulership institutions involving so-called formal and informal structures could be the key to the leadership and governance malaise afflicting the continent. An onset reminder is made to revisit the mission, vision of service, and virtues underscoring the overall endeavor of a BRP construct for appropriate directional insights.

A critical mass of BRP champions will not emerge by happenstance. The seeds have to be sown and nurtured to fruition deliberately and proactively. In this regard, essential interventions establishing two basic forefront avant-garde structures—National Task Force on Operationalization (NATFO) and communities of learning and practice (CLP)—are required to propagate and ground the philosophy of service to the mission of building blended resilient and strong rulership institutions.

The ideals and values of Tran-Serve leadership as the driver of service and interactions are required to be learned, imbibed, internalized, and practiced. This undertaking is not a quick-fix, short-term process but a long haul of inspirational motivations and persuasive advocacies penetrating the spirit and soul of the African. The pivotal facilitating thread is grounding the champions of Tran-Serve leadership by encouraging widespread voluntary actions establishing communities of learning and practice at all public facets of society, including state organs, workplaces, schools, churches, villages, and townships.

The National Task Force on Operationalization would oversee the preparation of national command papers, executions of tailored constitutional amendments, a plan of public education, outreach, and sensitization; and well-thought-out capacity enhancement programs for orienting, reforming, strengthening, and adapting the institution of chieftaincy to the expected responsibilities of BRP. The chapter outlines all the concrete steps, actions, and activities to be undertaken including versions of planned constitutional amendment bills, partnerships, and resource mobilization, assigned agency, group or individual responsibilities, duration and completion of assignments, overall timetable, cost implications, likely risks and mitigation options, and sample case-based results framework. With step-by-step guidelines highlighted in this chapter, the seemingly arduous task of operationalizing BRP has been simplified for ease of comprehension and facilitating background efforts.

Mission, Vision of Service, and Traits of African Personhood

Essence of Mission to Build Blended Institutions

Planning to operationalize any proposed initiative requires taking into account the rallying mission for emphasis of right direction and pathway forward. The easier part of a mission is formulation and articulation, and it becomes "unquestionable" once this is done.[1] But the most difficult part remains the process of its occurrence. In this context, how does one ingrain in the collective psyche of Africans and the international community that a systematic building of blended rulership institutions involving so-called formal and informal structures could be the key to the leadership and governance malaise afflicting the continent? Ample evidence pinpoints that neither the Western forms of national institutional leadership arrangements nor the traditional leadership structures by themselves are adequate or capable of handling present-day complexities of serving to fulfill needs and transformation to manifest the blessings of success for every African within the global economy.[2] It is by the combined forces of both leadership sources which can inspire and motivate Africans to develop a deeper sense of the collective and take steps forward toward the articulation and pursuit of the full-blown mission.

This is where service to the mission process—formulation, articulation, and adoption—becomes paramount. It is essential that all possible means must be explored to ensure that Africans can come together and embrace the mission of building blended institutions as the bulwark for fending off adventurisms and uncaringness, and institutionalizing a leadership mentality geared to serve first before leading beyond rhetoric. A critical mass of champions with the requisite tough-mindedness and unflinching zeal to embrace this mission is required as part of the planning and preparing to operationalize BRP in various countries.

Basically, it is blended rulership institutions which will instill and capacitate Africa with regenerative caring societies. Blended leadership institutions are what will forge the mindsets of championing people to embrace the philosophy of serving first before leading. If the institutional practices and services reflect the spirit of the mission, this will have ripple effects on many members of the target societies. People will not have difficulty following and emulating the behaviors of the leaders in respective arenas. Sooner than later, the seeds of champions and enablers will be sown to penetrate the whole fabric of society with the likelihood of a critical mass becoming attracted to this model of leadership. For this fundamental purpose, it is essential to ensure that pragmatic adherence to the philosophy of service to the mission remains the core of widespread planning and preparing to operationalize BRP across the continent.

A critical mass of BRP champions will not emerge by happenstance.[3] The seeds have to be sown and nurtured to fruition deliberately and proactively. As a concept, BRP is about both structurally and intellectually stimulated changes. On the one hand, it calls for changes to the leadership arrangements which have the mandate to lead and govern. On the other hand, it requires reorientation of mindsets, attitudes, and behaviors toward the ideals and values which underlie the need for structural change. In this manner, essential interventions establishing two basic forefront avant-garde structures—National Task Force on Operationalization (NATFO), and communities of learning and practice (CLP)—are required to propagate and ground the philosophy of service to the mission of building blended resilient and strong rulership institutions.

As a first step to operationalize BRP, African countries will have to set up national task forces to oversee actions and ensure coherence and consistency in the widespread embrace, acceptance, and commitment to the mission. As noted earlier, the ideals and values of Tran-Serve leadership are required to be learned, imbibed, internalized, and practiced as the driver of service and interactions. To reiterate, this undertaking is not a quick-fix, short-term process but a long haul of inspirational motivations and persuasive advocacies penetrating the spirit and soul of the African. In essence, the facilitating thread is grounding the champions of Tran-Serve leadership by encouraging widespread voluntary actions. This process will entail establishing communities of learning and practice at all public facets of society, including state organs, workplaces, schools, churches, villages, and townships.

Using a simple model of educating the educators in the ideals and values of Tran-Serve leadership, the communities of learning and practice (CLP) will champion efforts to stimulate society intellectually on the sterling qualities. The CLP will generate public discussions, steer opinions and debates, and provide impetus for individualized learning and practice considerations, as well as shaping and influencing the trajectory of occurrence of the mission almost anywhere in society. For example, schools from the formative stages to tertiary levels would have weekly sessions devoted to civic educating pupils on the ideals and values of BRP. Likewise, church leaders will be encouraged to utilize the pulpits to preach and disseminate the rationale and particularly, the spiritual undergirding elements constituting Tran-Serve leadership.

Some may construe such efforts as indoctrination or proselytization implying unquestionable and passive compliance in conformity with the ideals of BRP. But the critical issue here is judging by the resources available on the continent and what is possible, it has become evidently clear that Africa is now a low-caring continent. Orchestrating high tolerance for changing mindsets with words and not swords to building more caring societies represents a better option. Therefore, it will seem more plausible even if it takes overpowering psychoanalysis of reordering mindsets to convert from uncaring to caring societies, which may give hope and light to future generations given "success and happiness depend on . . . mindset. What you think, you become."[4]

Vision of Blended Institutions Service Provisions

The concept of BRP is a compelling vision of reorienting mindsets and uplifting spirits of people geared at building new forms of societies. In his seminal work on servant leadership, Greenleaf quoted Proverbs 29:18 to reiterate the importance of visioning in a society and without which the people perish.[5] The issue of the youth bulge with its worrisome characteristics of idleness, vulnerability, and joblessness amplifies the yearning by the younger generations for new societies in Africa. And the present generations of mainly geriatric leaders have failed to provide that compelling vision to rally and lead the societies to enable the imagined desired situation by the younger generation. Little wonder that the younger ones always jump at the opportunity of false hopes and promises regardless of the way they are presented. This situation of tidal waves of hopes and promises can be likened to ticking time bombs ready to explode at any given time with little provocations. The present generation of leaders are "simply not giving the maturing help to young people that is well within the means" of the continent.[6]

As noted,

> much like young people all over the world, African youth are bursting with talent and potential, and are looking to have their voices heard. They deserve to make their home countries a place they can be proud of . . . however, more than half of the youth population want to leave the country and never come back. Many have lost hope in political leadership and the possibility of real change, because of blatant corruption and politics that do not truly benefit the people but rather, serve to line the pockets of the higher-ups. This situation is not unique to any one country on the continent.[7]

In the case of gearing BRP to fruition, it is essential to envision the nature of service provisions and delivery for inspiration, motivation, and influence. Such an action is important at the outset to uplift the spirits of particularly the initiating champions and engender their willingness to act constructively and empoweringly. This action will be crucial early steps in increasing the proportion of people especially among the younger generation who will be disposed to the cause of Tran-Serve leadership.

The vision of providing and delivering services under the guiding principle of serving first the needs of others rather than self, family, and friends is certainly a game changer compared to what pertains in the various societies now. It implies a radical change in the image and modalities of how priorities are set and how service providers are organized and oriented to serve. Performance of the respective providers is raised as service delivery outcomes are improved and satisfaction of beneficiaries is increased without any disruptions to the social order. This then will be a true test of the envisaged BRP leadership as its follower base is increased voluntarily and exponentially.

Envisioning service provisions and delivery in a new light will be liberating as the harbinger of idealized BRP leadership arrangements initiating more innovative and better ways ahead in terms of how the needs of society are fulfilled. In this respect, service is undertaken within a framework of ensuring the core beliefs of the vision are not compromised. Those in positions of responsibility will produce based on engendered adaptation capabilities to increase the satisfaction for many beneficiaries and not just selected few or privileged in society. An atmosphere of humility will characterize and becloud service delivery processes as a major distinguishing feature of Tran-Serve leadership. In this regard, operationalizing BRP will be enhanced with tremendous support emanating from many people knowledgeable of the consistent possibilities of service provisions under the envisioned leadership and governance arrangements.

Virtues Underlying the Notion of African Personhood

Furthermore, it is important to consider in this context the unique traits and notion of African personhood given its meaningfulness in relation to the community, and relevance to the spiritual and moral fabric of providers of services. African societies are culturally inherently religious, but a widening gap is now noticeable between the visible practice of religiosity and spirituality on the one hand, and the uncaring mindsets exhibited in public service provisions and delivery on the other hand. Person and community in African philosophical thought are fused, and incorporation of people into the community of persons through designated rites is the process of becoming fully human. Africans believe "personhood is something to be achieved, and is not given simply because one is born of human seed."[8] Instructively, no one is a person because of himself or herself but in relation to others. However, in public service under present-day democracy practice, it seems salt has long lost its saltness. The mentality of economic survival of the fittest and the race is only for the swift and nimble has become the norm. The readiness of service providers to pounce for "a pound of flesh" whenever service (regardless of whether it is public or private) is requested has become pervasive and pronounced across the continent.

The way African public office occupants troop to church and mosque services on Sundays and Fridays respectively, and then throughout the working week, they metamorphose into uncaring ruthless providers of public services to fellow others is unbelievable and totally illogical. This posturing of dual attitudinal character seems an anathema to the quest of building caring societies and would be prominent among feature targets of expected changes in planning to operationalize BRP.

What is instructive of note is the relationship between the meaningfulness of African conception of personhood and the distinct leadership style of Tran-Serve leadership. The meaning and significance of personhood are in relation with others, and a distinct quality of Tran-Serve leadership is serving the needs of others first. In this case, sharing knowledge and demonstrating the inherent power in operationalizing BRP is by "placing the needs of others first and creating an environment for ... growth."[9] Whosoever understands and appreciates personhood in African philosophical thought should not have difficulty grasping the style of leadership that has serving others first as its primary operational principle.

From the foregoing, Tran-Serve leadership is about (a) creating caring societies for everyone to thrive and be successful, (b) serving first the needs of others and not just those of friends, family, and cronies, and (c) nonnegotiable focus on the whole with detailed attention to individualized interests. The moral education here is Africa requires leaders, not saints clothed as paragons of virtues; not "create, loot, and share" leadership style but genuine inherent characteristics of shoving aside narcissistic attitudes, behavior, and mindsets for the betterment of the collective. Therefore, it becomes imperative to have as guidelines from the outset, background reminders of the underlying mission, vision, and virtues in planning and preparing to operationalize the concept of BRP across the continent for the desired results and impact.

Groundbreaking Readiness Actions

National Command Papers

The National Task Force on Operationalization would oversee the preparation of policy documents outlining the concrete steps, actions, and activities to be undertaken, including versions of planned constitutional amendment bills, assigned agency, group or individual responsibilities, duration and completion of assignments, overall timetable, cost implications, likely risks, and mitigation options and alternatives.

A major focus of these documents would cover the structure and functions of the communities of learning and practice (CLP) as the key to implanting the seeds of BRP in the hearts, soul, and spirit of Africans across the continent. CLP would engineer the crucial intellectual stimulation drives, provide emotive inspirations and motivations of the populace, enable considerations of both wholistic and individualized interests in fulfilling needs, and yearn for success by all in society. All this will be done with the general feeling of the desire to give hope, light, and dim doubts in the minds of many.

The CLP would usher learning for all exercises to propagate and internalize the BRP. It will engage in knowledge sharing and exchanges, and peer-to-peer learning with listening loops for feedback-induced course corrections in a bid to improve outcomes, satisfaction, and performance of public service delivery endeavors. With creativity, better communications, interactions, emotional intelligence, the CLP would strive to engender stronger collective identities and more meaningful public workplaces. This engagement should likely change the narrative for many to hope and "aspire to a future of socio-economic security . . . and make some sort of impact in a lifetime."[10]

Now, it will likely be a tall order of convincing with command papers given the "quality of life for many is less than ideal . . . as partisan politics have left the social and economic needs of the citizens at second priority. [For example, in several cases,] nationwide coverage of electricity and potable water is non-existent, with inconsistent supply even when they exist."[11] With persistent persuasive advocacies, the command papers on BRP would be laden with patriotic ideals and dreams geared at eschewing risky behaviors that hinder shared prosperity and success to have major breakthroughs out of existing realities. It is possible to uplift Africa out of the present quagmire, and BRP could prove to be a true game-changer intervention.

In truth, Africa does not need to wait till the perpetrators of acts of horrendous proportions are at their deathbeds and confessing wrongdoings before redeeming itself out of the present squalor.[12] With overhanging debts strangulating almost all countries across the continent, the narrative has been the same and repeating itself within the global community of nations ever since: "There are currently about 34 African countries on the World Bank and IMF's heavily indebted countries' list."[13]

Over the past three decades and counting forward, debt has and will always remain an issue of domination on the part of the lenders and subjugation on the part of the debtors within the global economic system. Debt servicing arrangements have ensured, and continue to ensure, that the debtor countries remain in the grips of the enforcers and guardians of the global economic order (in this case, the World Bank and the IMF). Payments of debt would ensure the lender nations are kept awash with capital gains and returns on lending investments. Rescheduling will replenish the public coffers of the debtor nations and rentier states to continue unceasing spending on sometimes worthless and frivolous trivia to satisfy over-bloated egos and artificial lifestyles of ruling elites. Notwithstanding this foreboding predicament, sooner than later, it is urgent that the shackles of Africa must be broken, and BRP could be a commendable welcome step in the right direction.

Tailored Constitutional Amendments and Enactments

As mentioned earlier, adoption of BRP will trigger constitutional amendments and enactments in the various nations. The specificity of areas and chapters of the constitution will depend on the target respective countries. Generally, the areas and chapters affected will include: (a) Formation and Composition of National Governments and Administrative Structures, (b) Decentralization and Local Government, (c) Composition of Local and National Assemblies, (d) Offices of the lower-level Presiding Heads and Members of Assemblies, and (e) institution of chieftaincy.

The National Task Force on Operationalization (NATFO) will oversee and coordinate the following actions as per local legislative procedures:

1. Prepare submissions on amendments and reviews of relevant articles of the constitutions.
2. Prepare submissions on specified enactments and reviews pertinent to the strengthening of indigenous leadership.
3. Release public statements/communiques on the need for constitutional amendments, enactments, reviews, and reforms.

These actions will be undertaken in conjunction with the overall procedures on the preparation, completion, and release of the national command papers on adoption of BRP.

A Plan of Public Education, Outreach, and Sensitization

NATFO will initiate the execution of comprehensive plans for public education, outreach, and sensitization to culminate in the establishment of communities of learning and practice across various segments including all public workplaces of society. Activities will include but not limited to the following:

1. Develop operational manuals and handouts for public education and sensitization at the district, regional, and national levels for:
   - Roundtable discussions and public lecture series
   - Stakeholder engagement dialogues
   - Citizens' awareness-raising forums

2. Develop guidelines for media engagement on:
   - Script writing, videography, production, and editorial undertakings
   - Creating visibility on the BRP initiative among strategic target groups, opinion leaders, influencers, champions, and the general populace through tailored advocacy campaigns

3. Organize BRP-themed events including goodwill meetings, knowledge exchanges, outreach, planned interviews, bridge-building meetings, information-sharing sessions, expert panel discussions as needed and appropriate.
4. Convene moderated debates, discussions, and pledges on BRP for representatives of functioning political parties.
5. Arrange periodic press releases, article placements, editorial commentaries, and updates for senior editors and journalists at key national publications and private media houses.
6. Develop engaging and news-making virtual conferences and events to project BRP activities among change agents, enterprise associations, businesses, investors, civil service, and the African community at large in the diaspora.

Orienting and Adapting the Institution of Chieftaincy

NATFO will supervise the design and delivery of comprehensive capacity enhancement programs with the objectives of orienting, reforming, strengthening, and adapting the institution of chieftaincy to assume BRP-assigned roles and responsibilities. Detailed needs assessments will entail identifying individual and institutional assets—sterling qualities, coping and adaptive mechanisms, strengths, opportunities, and constraints; outmoded traits and practices;

challenges, weaknesses in relation to present leadership and local governance shortcomings and expectations. The assessments will also identify the providers and facilitators of the requisite capacity enhancement, financial, and other related contributions essential to ensure these pivotal undertakings are executed with the desired outcomes. For example, in the case of Ghana, NATFO coordination efforts will include the following activities:

1. Develop training manual and handouts on the operations of BRP-themed local governance including representation and participation of traditional leaders at the district, municipal, and metropolitan assemblies and other related bodies, service delivery transparency, and accountability of stewardship.
2. Retrofit the structure, composition, and functioning of traditional councils and National and Regional Houses of Chiefs for centrality of gender balance (National and Regional Associations of Queen Mothers, for example); resource support and capacity enhancement to assume the roles and responsibilities of urban, town, area, and zonal councils of the district assemblies.
3. Document for codifications of salient traditional rules, practices, and values necessary to meet the conditions precedent for operationalizing the BRP, including issues of:
   - Representation, Transparency, Accountability, and Participation (RTAP) mechanisms
   - Leadership selection and removal methods
   - Consensus-building and decision-making
   - Rewards for good stewardship
   - Conflict resolution/arbitration
   - Sanctions and disciplinary measures.

4. Organize training workshops for traditional leaders and heads of the public sector departments on the operations of BRP-themed local governance at the district, municipal, and metropolitan levels.

Other Pathway Measures

For ease of rollout and avoidance of setbacks and disruptions, it is strategically perceptive to have in place at the planning stage referral measures for ensuring regularity and reliability of cross-checking along the way to envisaged destinations. Such measures will entail partnerships and resource mobilization targets, possible risks and mitigation options, and sample case-based results frameworks for measuring and capturing expectations, course corrections to improve outcomes, satisfaction levels, and overall performances.

Partnerships and Resource Mobilization Targets

Three main categories of partnerships which should be pursued to mobilize resources in support of BRP interventions are as follows:

1. **Technical:** Engage for expertise, experience, advisory services, and peer-to-peer learning.
2. **Financing:** Engage for funding assistance, goodwill links, advocacy and peer recommendations.
3. **Social influencers/Champions/Local celebrities:** Engage for publicity, education, sensitization, dissemination, lessons sharing, and exchanges.

Likely Risks and Mitigation Measures

Possible risks and corresponding mitigation measures include:

1. Some members of the public would insist on the dogma that the institution of chieftaincy (IoC) has become archaic and outdated, and does not have a role beyond the assigned peripheral position in present-day governance arrangements.

Mitigation measure: Surveys, evaluations, and assessments (ESWs) will be designed to clearly ascertain the efficacy of IoC over current arrangements and the findings used to educate and sensitize citizens about the strength of their own system of governance. Earlier study focused on validating BRP which will be followed by systematic public education, interactions, and media events, all to remove any doubt about the comparative efficacy of indigenous leadership in local administration.

2. The ruling political elites and those with vested interests in the prevailing governance arrangements would resist the adoption of BRP governance as a viable organizing principle of life in Africa.

Mitigation measure: Through focused dialogues and campaigns, the ruling political elites and those with vested interests would understand that BRP is complementary and not antithetical to national and continental aspirations of transformative development. It is worth noting that present-day ruling political elites are quick to adopt and use practices from the indigenous establishment to rationalize certain behaviors and mannerisms if suited to parochial needs and interests. Examples include adoption of lifetime tenures in modern presidencies (Yoweri Museveni of Uganda,[14] Paul Biya of Cameroon,[15] the Eyadema family of Togo,[16] etc.), the Speaker of Parliament of Ghana dressing like a king for an opening address,[17] and the practice of transporting presidential stools and chairs to events in Ghana.[18]

3. Individual denigrating behaviors of some traditional leaders may be used as the lens by some members of the public to undermine the legitimacy and credibility of the institution of chieftaincy.

Mitigating measure: A series of reform actions will be prescribed to make indigenous leadership conform to modern principles. Also, the series of public

Table 1 Sample Results Framework: The Case of Ghana **GOAL:** Enable adoption of BRP to pursue and achieve targeted results as potential pathway to transformative development in Ghana.

Objectives	Activities	Outputs	Outcomes	Milestones	Means of Verification
Increased majority participation in local governance activities from <20% (abysmal) to >75% (excellent)	- Constitutional amendments/Reviews/Enactments - Assessments on the role of female traditional leaders - Preparation and release of position paper on BRP - Suggestions on comparable arrangements for the metropolitan assemblies - Public education and sensitization - Capacity enhancement training - BRP pilot implementation - Rollout of BRP local governance (LG) arrangements - Results monitoring, tracking, evaluation, and development impact assessments	- 100% composition of district and municipal assemblies with traditional leadership - District chief executives (DCEs) and deputies selected by representatives - Male and female as substantive and deputy; vice-versa arrangements - DCE chairs executive committee; and deputy presides over assembly - Traditional councils retrofitted and assume roles/responsibilities of urban, town, zonal, area councils - An applicable variation arrangement for the metropolitan assemblies in place	- Elimination of parallel leadership in LG - High approval ratings of representatives with community-owned selected leadership - Direct leader-to-people communication, mobilization, and organization - Majority response to leadership exercise of local political authority based on voluntarism and consensus and not fear of coercion or reprisal - Over 50% rise in number of people participation in civic duties and forums - Majority perception of civic participation arrangements rated highly satisfactory	- BRP premise revalidation survey in two regions - Submissions on constitutional amendments, reviews, and enactments to appropriate authorities - Commencement of work on respective studies/ESW - Launch of BRP pilot implementation in two designated regions - Launch of public perception of interactions between the rulers and the ruled; and civic participation arrangements	- Pronouncements by government on adoption of BRP-based LG - Action initiated on constitutional amendments submissions - Action initiated on reconfiguration of LG structure and composition - Number of public education and sensitization forums - Number of capacity enhancement training - Pilot of BRP - Number of knowledge exchanges, - Number of peer-to-peer learning forums - Findings and lessons dissemination events

(Continued)

Table 1 (Continued)

Objectives	Activities	Outputs	Outcomes	Milestones	Means of Verification
- Increased demand for accountability of stewardship by the majority at (a) local (from none to 75%) and (b) national levels (from 15 to 65 percent)	Constitutional amendments/ Reviews/Enactments - Assessments on the role of female traditional leaders - Preparation and release of position paper on BRP - Public education and sensitization - Capacity enhancement training - BRP pilot implementation - Rollout of BRP local governance arrangements - Results monitoring, tracking, evaluation, and development impact assessments	- Indigenous channels/spaces of interactions become integral to the structure and composition of LG arrangements - Setup of special advocacy and pressure groups at all levels to ensure persistency of demands and requests for the adoption of BRP - Community mass actions and campaigns on the need for the promulgations of BRP-based reforms	- Majority intimidation eliminated and empowered using familiar and easily understandable language and channels of communications, deliberations, and interactions; and utilize such opportune mechanisms to ensure acceptable behavior from their leaders - Local leadership emboldened collectively through elimination of national executive outreach and patronage to serve as checks on abuse and misuse of power and authority by national leadership - Biannual civic accountability forums as permanent feature of local administration with >75% population participation rate -Majority perception of stewardship accountability arrangements rated highly satisfactory	- BRP premise revalidation survey in two regions - Submissions on constitutional amendments, reviews, and enactments to appropriate authorities - Commencement of work on respective studies/ESW - Launch of community mass actions, special advocacy and pressure groups - Launch of BRP pilot implementation in two designated regions - Launch of public perception of interactions between the rulers and the ruled; and civic participation arrangements	- Quarterly citizens accountability forums - Number of all level advocacy and pressure groups - Number of community mass actions undertaken Number of recorded responses from national leadership relating to specific demands and request emanating from local leadership - Number of knowledge exchanges, - Number of peer-to-peer learning forums - Findings and lessons dissemination events

- Increased transparency in resource allocation, use, and translations into dividends beneficial to the majority at the rate of <15% to >65%

- Constitutional enactments submissions on specified resource areas and mechanisms
- Scan of international protocols on the utilization of indigenous knowledge and leadership and recommend applicable resource allocations arrangements
- Suggestions on comparable arrangements for the metropolitan assemblies
- Capacity enhancement for reforms, adaptation, and strengthening of institution of chieftaincy training
- Results monitoring, tracking, evaluation, and development impact assessments
- Execution of all the aforementioned activities

- Revised formula of referenced resource categories
- A ratio of more equitable resource allocation modalities between national and local government formulated
- Technical heads of applicable public sector departments become members of the executive committee of the assemblies with the right to vote
- Traditional councils retrofitted and assume roles/responsibilities of urban, town, zonal, area councils
- An applicable variation arrangement for the metropolitan assemblies in place

- Acquiescence by government to resource allocation preferences pertinent to strengthening of indigenous leadership
- Concentration of development resources at the center/cities will be curtailed and will be widespread to the hinterlands at the local levels
- Relegation of technical expertise in resource use decisions will be negated
- Majority will shape and influence prioritizations of deployment of available resources and interventions
- Over 50% blockage of leaks in resource use and applications
- Majority perception of leadership resource allocation arrangements rated highly satisfactory

- Submissions on constitutional enactments on specified resource categories
- Reconfiguration of membership of the executive committee
- Commencement of work on scanning international protocols
- Capacity enhancement training on resource allocation formulations
- Launch of public perception of interactions between the rulers and the ruled; and public resource allocation arrangements

- Annual budget appropriations
- Operations formula on referenced resource categories
- Inaugural meeting of the executive committee
- Action initiated on reconfiguration of LG structure and composition
- Number of knowledge exchanges,
- Number of peer-to-peer learning forums
- Findings and lessons dissemination events

(Continued)

Table 1 (Continued)

Objectives	Activities	Outputs	Outcomes	Milestones	Means of Verification
- Deepened closeness of the ruling regime to the majority from a distance gap of <25% to >75% capacity to communicate, mobilize, and organize for collective interventions	- Constitutional amendments/ Reviews/Enactments - BRP premise revalidation - Assessments on the role of female traditional leaders - Preparation and release of position paper on BRP - Public education and sensitization - Capacity enhancement training - BRP pilot implementation - Rollout of BRP local governance arrangements - Results monitoring, tracking, evaluation, and development impact assessments	- 100% composition of district and municipal assemblies with traditional leadership - DCEs and deputies selected by representatives - Male and female as substantive and deputy vice-versa arrangements - DCE chairs executive committee; and deputy presides over assembly - Traditional councils retrofitted and assume roles/ responsibilities of urban, town, zonal, area councils - Indigenous channels/spaces of interactions become integral to the structure and composition of LG arrangements	- Elimination of parallel leadership in LG - High approval rated - Representatives with community-owned selected leadership - Direct leader-to-people communication, mobilization, and organization - Majority response to leadership exercise of local political authority based on voluntarism and consensus, and not fear of coercion or reprisal - Majority intimidation eliminated and empowered through the use of familiar and easily understandable language and channels of communications, deliberations, and interactions; and utilize such opportune mechanisms to ensure acceptable behavior from their leaders - Reduced distance between rulers and ruled rated highly satisfactory	- BRP premise revalidation survey in two regions - Submissions on constitutional amendments, reviews, and enactments to appropriate authorities - Commencement of work on respective studies/ESW - Launch of BRP pilot implementation in two designated regions - Launch of public perceptions of interactions between local rulers and the ruled - Analysis of civic duty response ratings	- Pronouncements by government on adoption of BRP-based LG - Action initiated on constitutional amendments submissions - Action initiated on reconfiguration of LG structure and composition - Number of public education and sensitization forums - Number of capacity enhancement training - Pilot of BRP - Number of knowledge exchanges, - Number of peer-to-peer learning forums - Findings and lessons dissemination events

- Increased administrative efficiency as related to resource use, service delivery, and overall performance record at the rate of <25% to >75%	- Constitutional amendments/Reviews/Enactments - Capacity enhancement for reforms, adaptation, and strengthening of traditional councils; and reconfiguration of the executive committee training - Results monitoring, tracking, evaluation, and development impact assessments - Execution of all the aforementioned activities	- 100% composition of district and municipal assemblies with traditional leadership - DCEs and deputies selected by representatives - Male and female as substantive and deputy vice-versa arrangements - DCE chairs executive committee; and deputy presides over assembly - Technical heads of applicable public sector departments become members of the executive committee of the assemblies with the right to vote and have seats at the decision-making table - Traditional councils retrofitted and assume roles/responsibilities of urban, town, zonal, area councils -	- Service delivery response and quality rated highly satisfactory by beneficiaries - Performance record of the administrative bureaucracy scored satisfactory - Access by the majority to local officials rated very good - Timeliness of interventions related public requests and demands rated satisfactory - Annual revenue generated increased by .>50% - Enforcement of local bye-laws on climate change, environmental behavior, and attitude compliance related matters rated highly satisfactory	- Submissions on constitutional amendments, reviews, and enactments to appropriate authorities - Reconfiguration of membership of the executive committee - Biannual performance scorecard - Administrative efficacy perception index survey	- Action initiated on constitutional amendments submissions - Action initiated on reconfiguration of LG structure and composition - Availability of performance scorecard Number of knowledge exchanges, - Number of peer-to-peer learning forums - Findings and lessons dissemination events

(Continued)

Table 1 (Continued)

Objectives	Activities	Outputs	Outcomes	Milestones	Means of Verification
-Trust and respect for local administration operational procedures increased from <25% to >75%	- Assessments of civic duties responses; local bye-laws compliance and violation occurrence rates, and analysis of majority perceptions of experiences with operational procedures -Conduct of motivation response poll in pilot communities	- As indicated above - Analytical data on leadership motivation capacity, and response rate of community members	- Expectation of all the aforementioned outcomes -More than half of the population expressed high level of trust and respect for the local administration arrangements	- As indicated above - Launch of motivation and response survey	- As indicated above - Motivation gap poll
- Increased sense of belonging toward the local governance arrangement expressed by the majority from <25% to >75%	- Assessments of overall development impact -Conduct enthusiasm poll in pilot communities	- As indicated above - Analytical data on leadership enthusiasm capacity and community members expressions of attachment to the governance arrangements	- Exponential demonstration of pride in being citizens of the local communities - Increased concern for the collective welfare – - Minimized aloofness toward place-based symbols and insignia - More than half of the population expressed strong enthusiasms for the local administration arrangements	- As indicated above - Launch of enthusiasm survey	- As indicated above - Enthusiasm gap poll

lectures and admonishments would reiterate that chieftaincy is an institution with reverently moral responsibility which does not accommodate individual miscreants and provide appropriate severe sanctions to deter repulsive acts.

4. The entrenched custodians of the institution of chieftaincy may oppose the proposed centrality of gender balance in ensuring that female traditional chiefs are accorded equal status and representation in the BRP-based local governance arrangements.

Mitigation measure: The parallel organ for female leaders exists in the indigenous structure. Male chiefs rely on female counterparts (queen mothers) in governance arrangements. The respective assessments will identify ways in which gender balance will be effective as part of the effort to reform indigenous governance for modern administration. Specific activities will be devoted to assessing the centrality of the roles of female traditional chiefs (queen mothers despite some scholarly reservations) in the use of indigenous knowledge, principles, and values for basic service provisions and delivery (health, education, and water) in local communities (Table 1).

Conclusion

In this chapter, a step-by-step approach to operationalize BRP across the continent entails well-thought measures geared at enhancing widespread embrace and adoption of the concept within the global community. As is the case, conceptualizing and articulating a mission is not as rough as the occurrence and realization in practice, which remain the most difficult part of the process. The substantive measures outlined in this chapter are guides and not meant to be prescriptive and have to be followed by the letter and sequentially. "Flexibility" is the watchword, and countries will decide on the mode of adaptation without compromising or truncating the ideals and values which underpin the concept of BRP. It is crucial to uphold concept integrity in the operationalization process for envisioned results and impactful outcomes.

The leadership and governance mess in Africa requires well-coordinated rescue interventions. BRP could provide the certainty of stopping the bleeding and paving way for a momentous redemption. Several cracks noticeable in the edifice of Africa during the 1960s and 1970s have widened and rendered the whole structure complex wobbling and crumbling gradually under the pressure of present-day perennial challenges. Lo and behold, it is largely a BRP-inspired intervention which could provide the resilient and robust foundation for withstanding the onslaught and coming out with a win-win for all.

Chapter 9

CONTINENTAL DIMENSIONS OF BRP

THE AFRICAN TRADITIONAL LEADERSHIP UNION (ATLU)

Introduction

This chapter explores the continental dimensions for boosting the operations of BRP through the prism of an ongoing initiative of the African Traditional Leadership Union (ATLU)[1] with the overarching goal of complementing efforts of the African Union (AU) in building the "Africa We Want"—a continental blueprint and strategic framework for ensuring inclusive growth and sustainable development by 2063 through the pathways of peace, unity, and integration.[2] The thrust of ATLU is restricted in intent and scope than that of BRP. However, both seek to proactively tap the power of communal togetherness inherent in traditional leadership and manifested through peace, love, unity, and development in local communities. BRP is a continental intervention and will utilize the ATLU platform to articulate and disseminate the concept during planning and preparing to adopting and rolling out of the ideals across the various nations to facilitate the pursuit and attainment of the collective objective.

Strategic opportunities afforded by the ATLU platform and the key benefits to the rolling out of the BRP ideals and values including a center of excellence on Tran-Serve leadership at the continental level are highlighted. Also, the propellers of the supranational structure for traditional leadership with the potential to boost the BRP operations are identified and discussed with an end note on the glimmers of lights in the recently launched Africa Continental Free Trade Area (AfCFTA).[3]

The Rationale of ATLU and Synergy with BRP

A framework for the establishment of the ATLU has been proposed in a related work with the overarching goal of complementing efforts of the African Union and the regional economic communities (RECs) in building the "Africa We Want"—a continental blueprint and strategic framework for ensuring inclusive growth and sustainable development by 2063 through the pathways of peace, unity, and integration.[4] Given the centrality of the African traditional leadership under the envisioned mandate of BRP, it is logical to explore and harness potential synergies and accompanying benefits of the continental dimensions. Dovetailing BRP with ATLU in the process of localizing both strategies with mass understanding, involvement, and support for the ideals will fast-track dividends for the vast majority of people in their homes and communities.

From the onset, it is essential to make a clarity of concepts. ATLU is a work in progress and so like the BRP remains a concept. However, the thrust of ATLU is relatively different from that of BRP. On the one hand, the focus of ATLU is to complement the efforts of the African Union by harnessing the developmental contributions and potential capacities of traditional leaders within the prevailing status quo organizational establishment. On the other hand, the BRP ideals are about altering the status quo by sharing the constitutional mandate to lead, rule, and govern at the national and local levels among the currently constituted national and traditional leaders for a Tran-Serve leadership and governance arrangement.

A central position of the ATLU strategy is that African traditional leaders can enhance the outcomes of the AU continental master plan close to the people (the beneficiaries in the "Africa We Want" vision) through their contributions to development administration in localities.[5] Therefore, Africa needs to proactively tap the power of communal togetherness inherent in traditional leadership and manifested through peace, love, unity, and development in local communities. As emphasized, traditional leaders provide the fundamental organization and cultural milieu within which to anchor and complement continental development efforts geared at shared prosperity for everyone.

In the spirit of BRP, the ATLU provides a balancing continental mouthpiece for traditional leaders, just as the African Union creates a conducive platform for current leaders of the nations to articulate and pontificate on the needs of Africans. A continental dimension of BRP could move the needle of closing the gap between normative and empirical practice regarding the existence and utilization of traditional leadership in transformative development in target societies. For example, the effective utilization of the culturally conferred roles of traditional leaders as custodians of the land could help craft suitable adaptation and mitigation measures to combat climate change effects on agriculture, food, land, water, and other dimensions of policy strategy focus in this direction.[6]

African governments have recognized the critical roles of the institution of traditional leadership, and many have enshrined the roles of chiefs in their national constitutions.[7] However, there are no formal supranational traditional leadership structures. This scenario creates a void in harnessing the authority, knowledge, principles, and values of traditional leadership in addressing matters germane to fulfilling needs and manifesting the blessings of success for everyone based on regional and continental unity and integration. BRP is a continental intervention and will utilize the ATLU platform to articulate and disseminate the concept during planning and preparing to adopting and rolling out of the ideals across the various nations to facilitate the pursuit and attainment of the collective objective.

Strategic Opportunity for Enhancing the Ideals of BRP Continentally

The BRP ideals of sharing the mandate to lead, rule, and govern under a Tran-Serve leadership arrangement will have a concrete continental prop under ATLU for inspiring and motivating the African populace around the common goal of fulfilling needs and transforming to manifest the blessings of success for everyone. Efforts to tap and enhance the strength of African traditional leaders in the process of embracing and adopting BRP within localities across the continent could accelerate the realization of the expected outcomes of the AU master plan. In this sense, adopting and rolling out of BRP will proactively entail tapping the power of communal togetherness manifested through peace, love, unity, and development at local and community levels.

As noted earlier, an underlying premise of ATLU is that traditional leaders provide the fundamental organization and cultural milieu within which to anchor and complement continental development efforts geared toward shared prosperity and higher collective purposes. From this perspective, the ATLU concept is formulated with the conviction that the institution of traditional leadership can be relied upon as an agent of development in localities. Over time, the institution has accumulated a deep reservoir of social capital in terms of trust, loyalty, and sense of belonging, which can be harnessed to complement peace, unity, and integration efforts driven at the continental level. Undoubtedly, these characteristics and attributes are essential ingredients which can be catalytic in facilitating widespread adoption and rolling out of BRP in all segments of society across the continent.

Center of Excellence on Tran-Serve Leadership

Under its design of consideration, the ATLU would have an executive body, the African Traditional Leadership Institute (ATLI), similar in operational character as AU and its African Union Commission (AUC). Regarding the BRP efforts of fostering and nurturing communities of learning and practice (CLP), this institute could possibly become a conducive conduit and platform for a center of excellence on communities of learning and practice relating to traditional leadership, governance, development administration, and Tran-Serve leadership in Africa.

Furthermore, the institute would serve both academic and practical purposes, initially carrying out activities that would lead to establishment of the ATLU and thereafter implementing decisions of the union and its governing body. These significant activities could enhance and facilitate crucial BRP-driven reforms energizers for desired outcomes—intellectual stimulation, inspirational motivation, as well as invigorating execution, people, and cognitive skills.

In the same vein, the institute would build partnerships with academic institutions, such as African studies and related programs of universities on the continent and global centers of excellence and practice related to Africa, for example, historically Black colleges and universities (HBCU) and African Studies Association of the US academic community. Such partnerships entail the potential of compounding the effects and impact of idealized influence of BRP in enhancing the image and interests of Africa within the global system.

The institute would also develop a road map for the ATLU to serve as a fulcrum for "Africans Everywhere," providing the basis for stronger ties between African communities and the African diaspora, based on common ancestry, historical links, and philosophy. Through such partnerships and associations or affiliations, the institute would help actualize individual and wholistic considerations in resource decision-making, generate knowledge on traditional leadership systems, and maximize their potential and capabilities for continental development. Also, the ATLI will document and codify indigenous practices showcasing African values at the grassroots level. This will be done in a manner to enable the outcomes of Tran-Serve leadership arrangements be felt by many people in improving and uplifting their standards of living.

In a nutshell, the foregoing reaffirms the relevance and purpose of a continental dimension of BRP utilizing the medium of the ATLU concept to accelerate the adoption and rolling out of the ideals of Tran-Serve leadership under the unification and integration efforts, spearheaded by the African Union and the regional economic communities on the continent.

Key Benefits for the Rollout of BRP

The ATLU would provide tangible benefits for the rollout of the BRP ideals, including the following:

1. Widespread grassroots understanding, popular involvement, and support for BRP-themed interventions at the continental levels geared at uplifting the vast majority out of poverty through implementation of green, resilient, and inclusive growth and sustainable development (i.e., localization of continental BRP-themed green and technology-enabled interventions for combatting the effects of climate change). It is expected that participation of African traditional leadership in implementing the major national, continental, and global frameworks of BRP-induced interventions would facilitate inclusion of people at the grassroots. Through the processes, activities, value chain development, and dividends of such initiatives, the socioeconomic situations of the vast majority will be improved.
2. Better appreciation of the whole BRP-inspired contributions to the entire continental development landscape among stakeholders, political elites, and vested interests to engender constructive dialogues on course-improvement reform pathways carved from positive Tran-Serve leadership ripple effects.
3. Continent-wide Tran-Serve leadership-motivated peer-to-peer experiential learning on forging development with the purpose of inducing a more conducive and enabling environment for doing business, and facilitating trade and investments into rural and local communities across the continent. The spirit of fostering development has always been a major characteristic of communities that are under the rulership of visionary traditional leaders.

Sharing these accumulated experiences among peers on regular basis would be catalytic in pushing the frontiers of the continental blueprint of a BRP construct.

4. Center of excellence as the one and last stop for scholarly research and works on development capabilities of traditional leadership, solutions and remedies for the leadership, and governance malaise hindering continental aspirations.

5. Available strategic frameworks for involving traditional leaders in continental enterprises highlighting their demonstrated superior capability to communicate, mobilize, and organize most of the African people at the grassroots for collective endeavors.

6. Analytical reports on whether a BRP construct would engender continental platforms of a hub with nodes and spokes that are new entities or embedded in targeted, existing, and relevant partner institutions.

7. Mechanisms to interweave and reconcile the complementarities and effects of parallel leadership syndrome of development administration on governance in target societies for deeper, broader, and widespread development dividends.

8. Operationalizing a mandate for reforms to adapt and strengthen the institution of traditional leadership for modern development administration and governance. Efforts will include (i) structural composition and functioning at the continental and regional levels; (ii) consideration of tenure limitations of representation and participation; (iii) delegation of representation in case a community considers a chief not capable of participation; (iv) requirements of retrofitting for centrality of gender balance, resource support, and capacity enhancement to assume the roles and responsibilities which may be engendered by the union; (v) accommodation of suitably balanced integration of female traditional authority counterparts.

9. Building a digital library to include documentation and codification of salient practices of the institution of traditional leadership, detailing principles such as forging togetherness in collective activities, consensus-building, mass participation, accountability for stewardship and transparency in resource management, and conflict resolution.

10. Establishing working relationships backed by Memoranda of Understanding (MoUs) between the ATLU and potential partners and stakeholders, for example, academia, national governments, media, and international organizations relevant to the planning and operational engagements of Tran-Serve leadership arrangements.

11. Knowledge generation and exchanges to enhance the contributions of traditional leadership to overall development of the continent. Relevant activities may include (i) a scan of global practices to determine what has worked elsewhere; (ii) impact that traditional leaders may have had on development efforts in which they participated; (iii) level of composition in local governance arrangements that is likely to lead to superior performance

in a continental union; (iv) aspects of the chieftaincy institution which should be improved for their effective engagement in governance under a BRP construct; (v) articles of national constitutions which could be amended for enhanced contribution of traditional leaders in development; (vi) capacity building to enhance the contribution of traditional leaders in continental affairs; and (vii) resource needs and potential contributors.

12. Creating awareness among African political elites, stakeholders of prevailing national and local development administration and governance arrangements, and the general public on the role of African traditional leadership in regional and continental integration and development.

Supranational Structure for Boosting BRP

Some sterling enabling propellers of a supranational structure for traditional leadership with the potential of boosting the operations of BRP include the following:

The Embodiment of Collective Caring

A platform geared at harnessing for good institutional investiture of safeguarding collective welfare of African societies is a plausible booster for BRP operations. Bringing people together voluntarily for collective action is an essential pull and push factor in transformative development and a cardinal driving force of BRP. African traditional leadership is vested under an ancestral oath the moral obligations to uphold the primacy of collective care and interests.[8] The mechanisms by which African traditional leaders perform this feat of safeguarding the collective over individual acts in local communities would be adapted and strengthened under the operations of Tran-Serve leadership to facilitate gains of a green, resilient, and inclusive growth and sustainable development at the continental level. A few examples will highlight this phenomenal prowess:

1. Annual and periodic festivals under the patronage of traditional leaders are occasions for bringing people from far and wide and across borders together for a common purpose of celebrating heritage, lineage, love, unity, friendships, kinships, and affinities linked to development.[9] As per the universal norms of courtesies, enemies and terrorists are neither invited to the banquets nor provided safe havens to carry out devious plans. These events also double as tourist hotspots for income generation and branding Africa.[10]

2. Community markets enable majority of traders, especially market women, in the informal sector (where the bulk of economic activity including trade occurs) move freely and interact with kinsfolks, consumers, suppliers, producers, and intermediaries across the porous borders; and several of such

interactions are encouraged and facilitated by the established networks of traditional relations and leadership.[11]

3. While the Covid-19 global pandemic exposes the fragility of health systems, poverty, and vulnerabilities across the continent, it also brings to the fore the instrumental roles of traditional leaders in ensuring the security of their people. For example, as public measures went into effect at the onset of the Covid-19 pandemic in Africa with lockdowns, many of the poor in urban communities took drastic measures including breaking mandated restrictions on movement to escape to their rural communities of origin, which they rightly perceived as sanctuaries in times of crisis.[12] Furthermore, health and wellness needs, in general, have highlighted the complementary importance of traditional knowledge. In this notable case, medicinal resources and the essence of community resolve to preserve and conserve herbs, seeds, rare plant species (for their food, nutritional, and ecosystem uses, properties, and values and thus ensuring preservation of genetic diversity of species) play crucial roles in developing future crops in a dynamic climatic function.[13]

4. Ensuring consensual conformity with local norms and practices protects water bodies and streams, which could also help mitigate climate change effects on agroecological zones.

5. Although the roles of traditional leaders as custodians of land in many jurisdictions have been variedly contested, the aspect of facilitating investments and attracting businesses into local communities remains notable for boosting job creation and employment efforts.

6. End-of-life celebrations (funerals) in communities underscore the capacity of traditional leaders to forge togetherness, soothe, and comfort those in stress.

Inducing togetherness for collective actions in community life and existence exemplified in the practices, events, and occasions can serve useful continental purposes for BRP-inspired inclusivity and sustained development. Undoubtedly, whatever is inherent, treasured, and celebrated as "African" is in the domain and custody of African traditional leadership which exudes togetherness.

In fact, the principal attractions for tourism promotion for economic gains in Africa— cultural events and environmental features, among others—are the embodiment of togetherness forged under the patronage of traditional leadership. Even mining and mineral holdings require consensual concessions in harmony with the needs and interests of traditional enclaves to avoid conflict and acrimony during operations. African political leaders and social elites are also the subjects of traditional societies from which they hail and are not excluded in the web of togetherness that bind their respective communities.

Fostering Altruistic Behavior at the Continental Level

The concept of BRP fosters spirituality in a Tran-Serve leadership model that incorporates altruistic love, hope, and faith in serving others first and manifesting the blessings of success for all in society. The spirit of fostering altruistic development has always been a hallmark of communities under visionary traditional leaders across the continent.[14] A large and increasing number of chiefs in Africa are highly qualified professionals and business people with vast experiences in key and strategic sectors in their private lives, which they bring (or could bring) into the local development space. A few examples will elucidate this pertinent development trajectory of traditional leaders:

1. Togbe Afede XIV, the paramount chief of Ho Asogli Traditional Council in Ghana who doubles among several other roles as the chief executive officer of the Strategic African Securities (SAS), led efforts to establish the Sunon-Asogli Power Ltd that built a 200 MW combined-cycle gas-fired plant to help improve electricity generation capacity in the country. Togbe and his Chinese partners also established the Africa World Airlines, which has become pivotal in the domestic aviation market.[15]

2. The immediate past Emir of Kano, Muhammad Sanusi II (a former governor of the Central Bank of Nigeria), launched several development initiatives during his reign, including the sustainable housing pilot projects with the support of Price Waterhouse Coopers (PwC) in West Africa and International Green Structures. This initiative is aimed at building 504 low-cost houses in Kano Nigeria.[16] Muhammad Sanusi II, who served as Governor of the Central Bank of Nigeria in his professional life, also led the SDG Challenge geared at enriching the scope of African education and engaged in partnership with "1Million Teachers" (1MT), a social enterprise to provide access to high-quality teacher education for underserved communities around the world.[17] This particular initiative is very significant with good potential given that "sub-Saharan Africa is the only region where out-of-school children keep increasing."[18]

3. The Kabaka of the Buganda Kingdom in Uganda spearheaded efforts to propel a wide range of tourist attractions, including the Royal Mile (the place for a glimpse sight experience of ancient architectural designs); Nantawetwa Monument (situated within the center of the Royal Mile); the Kabaka's Palace–Twekobe (official residence of all the last six kings of Buganda) declared by UNESCO as one of the World's Heritage sites; Bulange—the Buganda Parliament, among several other attractions.[19]

4. Another epitomizing case highlighted is the leadership of Osahene Katekyi Busumakura II, the Takoradiman-hene of Ghana. Development initiatives in this regard include the Takoradi Institute of Science and Technology (TIST) aimed at offering flagship courses in oil and gas engineering, and biological sciences to meet the demands of the region and the country. Accordingly, the chief is also involved in an aspirational road map to make Takoradi an attractive port city and essential investment center by 2025 through the effective marketing of the city, tailored investments in housing and human capital development, renovation of the Western Regional House of Chiefs and the Kwesimintsim Police Station, among other benevolent contributions to the communities under his rulership.[20]

In a nutshell, these selected cited cases are proofs and testament of the altruistic development orientations and focus of traditional leaders across the continent. Efforts to catalyze and consistently harness such orientations could stimulate a more concerted BRP-centered leadership and boost the continental march toward green, resilient, and inclusive growth and sustainable development.

Energizing Grassroots Enthusiasm

The grassroots penetrative capability of traditional leadership is a tremendous opportunity for BRP-enabled reforms which can be leveraged and multiplied through continental avenues for widespread outcome and impact. As noted, ample evidence abounds that the African traditional leadership system, regardless of its inherent limitations, remains a more cohesive governance and leadership structure at the local level, particularly in rural communities, with symbiotic capability to communicate, mobilize, and organize community members voluntarily for collective development actions. An underlying reason is that the sociocultural realities in rural communities are quite different from urban areas in terms of suitability of arrangements to participate in decision-making and common property resource (CPR) management.[21] Primordial loyalties, social organizations, and structures in existence constitute assets and strength of rural communities.

Majority participation in decision-making is largely linked to the community through council of chiefs (male and female) based on the consciousness of belonging to the "whole." Partly the results of such cohesiveness and togetherness fostered in local communities, some observers noted that although the climate and ecological crises the world is facing are "complex, global problems with multiple causes . . . [they come in their trails] also with multiple solutions." In this context, a pertinent example is the insights and experiences shared on the "power and potential of rural women and community forestry in Cameroon."[22]

ATLU as a Harbinger of Renewed Leap of Faith in Collective Possibilities

The supranational platform constitutes a propitious conduit for reaffirming faith in collective embrace and possibilities. Responsibilities assigned to traditional leadership in Africa under BRP require a new leap of faith and an "audacity of hope"[23] for collective endeavors to tackle the leadership and governance problematics in Africa and turn things around for the better. As noted earlier, irrespective of opinions otherwise, traditional leadership is a powerful mainstay for either transformative or regressive politics and development in African societies and cannot be brushed off as a relic. Rather, this institution remains an underutilized bastion for catalyzing mass participation, transparency in resource management, and accountability of stewardship in fulfilling needs. To reiterate, this home-grown, time-tested leadership institution could be reformed, adapted, and weaned off its anachronistic tendencies so that it can progressively complement the efforts of national leadership to build Tran-Serve rulership institutions across the continent.

The Glitters of Light in the Africa Continental Free Trade Area (AfCFTA)

As part of efforts to forge the "Africa We Want," the AU launched the African Continental Free Trade Area, whose trading regime came into effect on January 1, 2021, considered by many experts in the global community as a very promising undertaking.[24] BRP-induced reforms would bolster efforts across the continent and propel AfCFTA to greater heights by harnessing coherently the enterprising enthusiasm and energy of the people to unify and integrate the continent through targeted trade, business, investments, and development. Adopting and rolling out Tran-Serve leadership arrangements would promote these ideals.

For example, to enhance market integration and bolster commerce on the continent, mechanisms are required to incorporate traditional markets into the formal economy. The traditional markets constitute a critical component of the capital/wealth generation and the cornerstone of commerce regarding socioeconomic accumulation and interactions in sub-Saharan Africa. Regardless of the fact that shopping malls are springing up across the continent, and online (e-commerce) platforms are utilized mainly by the urban middle-class population, these traditional markets will still continue to dominate the commerce landscape, serve as wholesalers to street vendors, create entry points for smallholder farmers, provide employment and income generating opportunities to sellers, and account for almost 65–75 percent sales throughout the region until at least 2030.[25] Above all, these markets place women's access to finance and investments in e-commerce infrastructure, banking, savings, and loan operations at the forefront for policy consideration. As noted earlier, the traditional markets operate under the patronage of the respective traditional leaders of the local communities.

Africa constitutes 17 percent of the world's population but has only 2 percent share of international trade. Intra-Africa trade ranged between 14.4 percent and 18 percent. By comparison, the percentages are between 50 percent and 59 percent for Asia, and 68 percent to 73 percent for Europe. The AfCFTA is expected to turn the scales and boost intra-Africa trade among a total market population of over 1.2 billion consumers to a substantial level.[26]

However, the colonial commercial order of free trade and its compendium of minimal utilization of the complementary development contributions churned out through the representation, participation, and leadership channels and structures of most of African people remain intact. As is the case, the complementary development contributions and potential capabilities of traditional leadership have been minimally utilized in all the post-independence schemes of participatory development administration and governance schemes evolved at the national and continental levels aimed at lifting the vast majority out of abject poverty.

Regardless, through visionary development initiatives, cordial relations, kinships, peaceful coexistence, and population overhangs,[27] traditional leaders across the continent largely have proved capable of reaching most of the people at the grassroots. They continue to surge forward notwithstanding colonial African boundaries that have been maintained and weaponized by an independent African continent. Therein lies the need and wisdom for the continent to now craft a strategy for trading with itself.

Conclusion

Undoubtedly, the Africa we truly want under BRP through peace, unification, and integration would require proactive involvement of traditional leadership beyond what prevails on the continent presently. Peace, unity, and integration as transformational processes require energetic and enthusiastic participation of the masses, transparency, and accountability to meet targeted goals. Mass participation is key to green, resilient, and inclusive development. The involvement of the leadership structure which arguably has superior capability to communicate, mobilize, and organize most of the people at the grassroots for collective actions is fundamental and critical.

Peace, unity, and integration are necessary ingredients for unleashing the continental potentials and capabilities of transforming and uplifting most Africans out of endemic poverty. Many Africans continue to rely more on these so-called unofficial and informal leadership arrangements—a pervasive scenario given the prevalence of entrenched primordial ties, the psychosocial composition of the populace, and the apparent ineffectiveness of the formal structures of development administration to reach the masses. It is essential that the African ruling political class embrace, adopt, and roll out BRP which provides better mechanisms for maximizing the complementary development contributions and potential capabilities of traditional leadership in a Tran-Serve framework at national and continental levels.

Chapter 10

WISDOM ON THE PRACTICE OF DEMOCRACY IN AFRICA

Introduction

In this chapter, carefully selected themes of wisdom which run through the book have been calibrated into enlightening insights on the practice of democracy with the rollout of BRP across the continent. These themes of wisdom collectively reinforce the key message that Africa needs to redesign the foundations of its statehood and democracy practice. The lines of thought which constitute the building blocks of this chapter are as follows:

1. Hopefulness because of the undaunting challenges
2. No saving grace in the status quo
3. Effective participation in democracy reflects the image and realities of society
4. Real transparency inspires trustworthiness
5. Accountability is a mirror of belongingness
6. The youth bulge is an opportune moment for creativity and innovations
7. Food and nutrition are not outsourced products of benevolence
8. Attributes of high-value education are the bedrock of transformation
9. Progress is not clinging to dogmatic ways of doing things.

The amalgam of these wise thoughts underscores the BRP construct geared at pushing for good the practice of democracy across the continent. With this approach of illuminating a topical subject matter for its policy relevance, implications, and consideration, the chapter reiterates the driving narrative of the book that adoption and rollout of BRP will inspire, induce, and instill hope in the outcomes and dividends of democracy practice on the continent.

1. Hopefulness because of the Undaunting Challenges

This means embracing, adoption and rollout of BRP will inspire, induce, and instill hope in the outcomes and dividends of democracy practice on the continent. As noted in earlier chapters, the tangible dividends of the manner of democracy presently practiced in Africa have mainly dimmed hopes on the continent. In reiteration, this situation is succinctly captured in the following observation:

> Authoritarian and semi-authoritarian rulers, mindful of foreign opinion, have dressed their regimes with the forms of democracy, such as regular (if rigged) elections and de jure (not de facto) separation of powers. Presidential term limits, where in place, have been frequently circumvented through so-called constitutional coups.[1]

This situation is such that many of the youth in particular want to leave and not come back. Hopes have been dashed, and dreams become wishful. The grind of eking out a living has taken a tremendous toll on the physique of many. Stunted growth is a common feature of the population. As revealed by the United Nations Children Fund (UNICEF) data, "Africa has the world's highest rate of under-five stunting (33%, compared with a global average of 24 percent) and has made the slowest progress in reducing stunting since 1990."[2]

Service provision and delivery have been erratic. Tales abound of people who are sick but cannot go to hospitals, and those who are fortunate to visit may not see a doctor for proper examination or diagnosis. Some of those requiring admissions must grapple with "no bed" mantra and in such conditions have to utilize the bare floors as sleeping beds.[3] Prescription drugs are more often out of reach as they are mainly available on the shelves of private pharmacies, which operate outside the scope and coverage of any government-mandated health insurance schemes.

Parents complain regularly about the struggles to cope with high school fees and needs regardless of whether there exists in the country a policy of "free education." School infrastructure is inadequate, and the phenomenon of schools under trees occurs in some parts of the societies.[4] The quality of education offered is questionable with the rising trend of eagerness to complete tertiary education abroad among children of parents in positions to afford such ventures. School dropouts roam the streets and swell the army of unemployed at alarming rates. Teenage pregnancies and teachers impregnating pupils are part of social media rumor mills of the communities in some countries.[5]

In homes, some go to bed hungry, and having three meals per day is a luxury several people cannot fathom. The methods of food production and lands for cultivation have not seen any major technological improvements for several decades. With climatic stressors on the rise, yields from the fields are not enough to feed families and generate surplus for sale at the markets for additional income to offset cost of other daily necessities. The homes of many have become empty of regular staples, which will usually enable children to grow and thrive.

Despite the sordid depictions of the extent of deprivations under the practice of so-called democracy, an African journalist once asked a "friend whether or not he believes Africa is a great continent to fulfill one's dreams and his answer was this: Yes, because it is filled with a multitude of problems that need solving."[6] It is worthy of note that many Africans share such sentiments regardless of the numerous episodes of deprivations which can be cited to support the fact why the continent seems bad for dreaming, pursuing, and attaining individual and collective goals.

The embrace of BRP could be construed as a reflection of striving attempts to solve many of the myriad problems and improve the dividends of corresponding democracy practice according to the needs and realities of the continent.

2. No Saving Grace in the Status Quo

This means anyone claiming to have solutions while the established structures of "authoritarianism camouflaged in democracy garbs" remain intact is either out of touch with the realities on the ground or taking the broader populace for a ride on vain and empty promises. The all-powerful executive president is the be-all for every decision. Other structural arms of government, which in real democracy practice in jurisdictions outside the continent are expected to operate as checks on use, misuse, and abuse of power, mainly exist in theory and on paper and function in practice at the behest of His Excellency.[7] Utterances of auxiliaries of the executive president which usually should require clearances and approval from the deliberative chambers become instant policies for implementation.[8] The outcomes of any governance-related matters for adjudication in the courts of law are butts of social media jokes and guesstimates as the discerning public always perceive the weight of the behind-the-scenes invincible influence of the executives in such situations.

Public consensus is more a matter of contestation in terms of whether such a phenomenon exists in practice. The fourth estate practitioners (journalists) are free and vocal in the defense of matters mainly in the interest of ruling regimes and parties. Broadly, public board chairpersons and members, chief executives, and chief directors in charge of the public offices mainly operate either to the attention of the appointments' purse holder, or performances usually are shaped by hierarchical belonging in the ruling party structures. All other functionaries of the democracy setup are considered poodles of the regime in power. A notable expression attributed to former president John Agyekum Kufour of Ghana provides an apt insight into such a scenario: it is better to be a messenger in a ruling party than to be a general secretary of an opposition party.

There are too many charlatans parading under the guise of practicing democracy but perpetuating self-serving interests over the collective goal. Take, for example, recent occurrences in Sudan.[9] The persistent efforts of a broad coalition of concerned citizens toppled a long-serving tyrant only for another to hijack the process and supplant himself at the top. However, after a few days under pressure from the zeal and persevered condemnations by the people, the gentleman caved in to reinstate those who were in charge and summarily dismissed by the adventurism.

Or more perceptive in the case of many Ghanaians who have realized that several promises by the present National Patriotic Party (NPP) ruling regime while in opposition were made in beguilement, and governance by sloganeering has not translated into the "saving graces" envisaged through tweaking of the established structural arrangements.[10] This is not to say things would be better under the charge of any other party that promises change with another branded version of democracy practice while the status quo remains intact. It then brings into the limelight the derision-laden approach that different results can be expected from doing the same things in the same manner repeatedly. Yet the country remains the "beacon of democracy" within the international community regardless of the elusiveness of positive outcomes and dividends.

Africa deserves better particularly under the reversal of so-labeled positive trends of democratization by "a new wave of authoritarianism."[11] Unfortunately, as has been the case, "Governments are becoming less transparent . . . across Africa—leaders ignoring term limits, rigging or postponing elections, exploiting social grievances to gain and maintain power, arresting opposition figures, cracking down on the media, and allowing security services to enforce pandemic restrictions brutally."[12]

All this reinforces the fact that no saving grace of Africa will emerge out of the status quo of the institutionalized brand of democracy currently in practice. The continent should be on alert of oratorical charlatans promising sagacious solutions with the established status quo of leadership and governance arrangements intact and unrefined. In a nutshell, BRP is about cleaning decades of mess veiled in a particular brand of democracy practice choking the breath of many Africans across the continent.

3. Effective Participation in Democracy Reflects the Image and Realities of Society

Under a BRP-inspired arrangement of democracy practice, participation at the local level will be communal, and at the national level, it will be based on multiparty operations. This means that representatives at the local level will be leaders of the communities chosen solely by members based on traditional norms, conventions, and practices for a term limit. Registered competing political parties will present suitable candidates to the communities constituting a constituency, and members of the communities will elect one of them by universal adult suffrage to represent the constituency at the national level. Once a representative is elected, the person becomes a consensual representative for all members of the constituency and not a representative of party members only for those who voted for him or her. The guiding mindset will be allegiance to community which supersedes that of the party, and members of the community will have full rights and control of the power of recall, and not parties deciding the fates of representatives. If community members feel their representative has underperformed, they will exercise the power of recall within the duration of term limits or wait till the end of tenure and vote for another representative.

Leaders of the local assemblies chosen by the community members will select among themselves occupants of the various positions with an important gendered caveat. When a male leader is selected for a substantive position, the deputy will automatically be a female leader and vice versa. Details of these arrangements will be contained in the recommended Constitutional Amendments and Enactments Reports; and also in the Annexes of the guiding National Command Papers on the adoption and rollout of BRP to be released by the respective countries.

Participation under communal and multiparty-based representatives selection principles will principally ensure autonomy of local government institutions and serve as a bastion against leviathan executive overreach and abuse. Decentralization will have real meaning and ceases to be an extension of central government interests at the local level. Corresponding parallel officials at lower levels will no longer exist and operate as poodles of national authorities by the fiats of appointments and dismissals. This manner of participation is geared at providing grounded checks and balancing of individualized and collective interests at both local and national levels.

As community members select their own leaders to constitute local government assembly members and occupants of corresponding offices, they are placed in unhindered positions to exert influence as checks on local performance of duties and responsibilities. This in turn would likely translate into collective strengthening and empowering of local government institutions and catapult them into spheres of influence and pressure to minimize or eliminate impunity at the national level. In this respect, local government will no longer be the weakest link in the ruling national-local partnership value chain in government transactions and operations across the continent.

It is important to note that in certain jurisdictions, local government subpar performance is mistakenly attributed to nonelection and appointment of the heads of the local government institutions by the national executives. However, the crux of the matter is arguably beyond direct election of the heads. Rather, it is a product of the structural arrangements for the exercise of power and authority under the practice of democracy in a manner unreflective of societal needs and realities. The problem lies more in national minority elite aspirations to organize societies similar to what pertains elsewhere and which reflects borrowed truncated images.

Another striking feature of participation under communal and multiparty-based representatives selection principles is securing independence of ruling institutions. This is likely an era which will usher in true separation of powers as attained in other jurisdictions. Participation in this manner is geared to avoid rubber stamp legislatures or cabinets and ensure independence of the judiciary. The hovering character and trait of executive influence lurking in the shadows of the operations of other ruling institutions will be tamed. Following this trail will be guaranteed free media and a professional public service which will be objective in its operations guided by the principles of economy, efficiency, and effectiveness in the management of public resources.

The quality of participation under a BRP-inspired practice of democracy will be genuine and authentic in terms of voluntarism, energy, and enthusiasm. Participation will neither be "rental" nor "bussed" and induced by T-shirts, caps, or related party paraphernalia. In a word, the manner of participation will not be orchestrated by monetary, jobs, or gifts incentives. Such is the narrative of participation now that the term has lost its currency and credibility in the practice of democracy in Africa. In fact, in one of his usual rants in the South African parliament, Honorable Julius Malema, for example, has been recorded lamenting that the youth does not understand the essence of participation in a functioning democracy and will mainly engage unless materially induced.[13]

BRP is crafted to invigorate participation in the practice of democracy across the continent. In this regard, BRP offers a form of participation, which is markedly different from, and arguably superior to, the concept of participation practiced presently under so-called democracy in Africa. At the lower levels, BRP-induced form of participation will bring in vogue institutions, which are intrinsically linked to the communities, and revitalize the spirit of people who will cease seeing themselves "as self-regarding atomized beings in essentially competitive and potentially conflicting interaction with others. Rather, their consciousness is directed toward belonging to an organic whole."[14]

As a matter of strategic survival and relevance within the global community of nations, Africa needs to redesign the foundations of its democracy practice along the lines noted whereby

> people participate not because they are individuals whose interests are different and need to be asserted. but because they are part of an interconnected whole. Participation rests not on the assumption of individualism and conflicting interests, but on the social nature of human beings. . . . Participation is as much a matter of taking part as of sharing the rewards and burdens of community membership. It does not simply enjoin abstract rights but secures concrete benefits.[15]

In this sense, BRP-inspired participation in democracy practice includes an inbuilt process of groundings in traditional practice unlike the wholesale Western notion of the "occasional opportunity to choose, affirm or dissent." Participation under BRP focuses on the active involvement in a process of setting goals and making decisions. It is involvement in the process rather than the acceptability of the end decision that satisfies the need to participate.

4. *Real Transparency Inspires Trustworthiness*

Transparency in future democracy practice will be knowledge-driven and wheeled by expertise. In the extractive sphere, for example, Africa's educational institutions will be paramount in shaping brains and mindsets to promote and protect the collective interests. African expertise would be at the forefront of technological exploration and prospecting feasibilities in the determination of concessions' values and investment viability. Collaborative investment partnerships would be forged to avoid relegation as rear spectators in the process of exploiting resources endowed by nature. Scans of global practices will be undertaken to put in place appropriate formula-based value for money allocations which honor in deeds community royalties and usufructuary rights.

What pertains now whereby extractive policies are most often derived from data generated by external prospectors, and African expert role in the value chain portrayed as secondary is not a good motivator of value for money in the collective interests of the continent. For decades, the extractive sector has been operating to keep afloat transnational investment interests. Coalitions and partnerships are constructed in a manner that often proscribes the positions of African nations as willing facilitators of exploitative approaches which chart away resources outside the continent. Africans are signatories to agreements in fine prints, which guarantee returns and gains for owners of investment capital without much benefit for the millions of masses whose dwelling places are the extractive spaces.

This state of affairs is possible because African leaders have failed to lead and rather delegate the extractive spaces to outside forces based on flimsy excuses of knowledge dearth and absence of investment capital. Such excuses are unacceptable ruses because similar and related jurisdictions have demonstrated that natural resources can be gainfully extracted to securitize and promote collective interests. Since independence, African leaders have established institutions of higher learning for harnessing resources without the accompanying strategies of ensuring that expert mindsets are produced in critical mass to lead this effort. Many graduates largely become employees of transnational companies who work to safeguard interests of corporate capital. In the process, neighborhood developmental interests become secondary and negated as backbench afterthoughts.

More often the extractive spaces are the same locations for meeting livelihood needs of the people who reside in these areas, and many find themselves displaced and removed from their ancestral land, and are unable to subsist at the new places.[16] Extractive operations leave in their trail environmental challenges with monumental consequences for the communities in the operational areas. With increased climatic stressors, leaders are obliged to lead and manage public resources in the manner of substantive contributions to fulfill collective needs and manifest blessings of success for everyone.

Transparency under future practice of democracy would enable administrative efficiency by ensuring effective public service provisions and delivery. A closer look at utility services provisions in several countries across the continent would reveal that effectiveness is more of a function of mindsets, attitudes, and behaviors of people at the forefront of the delivery value chain. Having a core staff or responders on the same page as management and with the conviction and belief in the paramountcy of the collective goal is central to ensuring ease of access to services in terms of quality, sufficiency, and convenience.

Privatizing the management of hitherto large publicly owned service delivery agency while notions and ethics of work and professionalism are burrowed in antique nostalgia of public ownership is not a good policy strategy. The delivery processes of such approaches are not laden with hope capable of upliftment and endearing ruling institutions to targeted beneficiaries. Management in private hands must be accompanied by a level of proactiveness that inculcates mindsets of safeguarding collective interests in fulfilling clients' needs. It is such delivery approaches which would enable effectiveness to be institutionalized and move the ruling regimes in power closer to people who would feel and acknowledge the presence of leadership in their lives. The prevailing systems of service delivery in many countries across the continent push people far away from the ruling regimes and depict images of incompetency, sabotage, and sloppiness as characteristics of service providers.

A major impact of service delivery is on efforts to build solid political cultures—an essential phenomenon undergirding democracy dispensations beyond intermittent and sporadic enthused responses during sporting events which pitch national figures against others from other nations on the continent. In real-world life, respect and loyalty to national emblems are earned through leadership reputations as earnest hardworking and consistent quality service providers. Leadership performance is key to nurturing impactful needle-moving political cultures, which would motivate people with intentions to do good with an underlying knowledge that security of the polity is ensured in great hands.

Strong political cultures are instruments of institutional robustness and resilience equipping nations with adaptive and coping strategies for tackling common challenges which emanate from coexistence. Given historical experiences, Africa has incipient political cultures to be forged into fortresses of power, authority, and influence at home and on the international stage. Transparency in leadership and governance transactions across the continent will enable great entry points for this phenomenon to materialize. Africans can only make this happen by themselves because it will not be given out by anyone or drop like the biblical manner from the heavens. BRP seems the surest guarantee of solid political cultures in Africa.

A further insight into transparency regarding the performance of roles and responsibilities by public officials under the future practice of democracy is that measures will be in place to sharpen the execution skills of management and frontline officials. On-the-job capacity enhancement schemes will instill tolerance of diverse opinions, ambiguities, and conscientiousness. Also, such schemes will enable paying attention to details and critical elements of specific delivery requirements to meet the satisfaction of clients without compromising on quality and timelines. Officials will be motivated with incentives to improve orientations to serving clients which have been appalling in certain situations. Individual workplace mobility considerations will be shaped by proactive feedback of satisfied clients for professional growth and development. Furthermore, these tailored measures would deepen cognitive skills with big-picture strategic thinking, analytical reasoning, collaborative and consultative approaches for inculcating solution-focused mentality.[17]

5. *Accountability is a Mirror of Belongingness*

The approach to accountability for good stewardship under a BRP-inspired future practice of democracy will be strengthened by maximal utilization of the target societies' guardrail channels and avenues. Accountability will not be once in a term event at the ballot box but applying and adhering to the underlying principles of the pathways more often. It will be an obligatory responsibility-enforced mechanism underlying the mandate to rule with an assurance of good stewardship. Accountability under a Tran-Serve leadership will reaffirm confidence in stewardship by ensuring both vertical and horizontal actions requiring all public officeholders to be held accountable regularly for misbehavior and underperformance regarding expectations and trust reposed in respective public positions.

Likely measures to maximally utilize the guardrail channels of accountability would certainly include actions to rein in executive overreach regarding mandates and commitments. From the outset, there would be four-level intensive civic education curriculum on the entire BRP-induced leadership and governance arrangements. The curriculum would entail middle, secondary, tertiary, and adult/lifelong-learning integrated designs for both formal and informal civic education targeting various segments of the population.

Chapters on the electoral processes and procedures would highlight the underlying accountability, essence, and the accompanying civic obligations requiring informed choices from all eligible and capable citizens when choosing leaders and representatives. Choices would be construed as essential civic responsibility which should be made based neither on vain promises from the highest bidder nor on rhetorical prowess. The formal schools, churches, mosques, and community-tailored events would be the visible and proactive platforms for immersing the population in the dynamics of real leadership and governance in an empowering manner. This will generate an outcome of putting the necessary brakes on runaway democracy as experienced now across the continent.

In several instances, Africa has experienced the conflictual vested interests of disrespecting term limits.[18] Some African leaders have surreptitiously carried over to their national positions the traditional notion and practice of lifelong tenure leadership and proclaim themselves as "fathers of the nations." Such scenarios are anathema under Tran-Serve leadership guiding expectations which will not be countenanced. Arrangements are in place for a two-term tenure limitation on traditional leadership while retaining and respecting prevailing mandates at the national level. For the purpose of serving in local government, the institution of traditional leadership will factor tenure limitations into requisite adaptation reforms with the provisions of serving on advisory councils and chief emeritus title for leaders who complete terms satisfactorily. An advisory council comprising former leader-occupants of service stewardship positions would constitute potent accountability instruments for preventing misuse and abuse of power and privileges of public office.

The constitutional mandate of preparing and delivering "State of the Nation" addresses as accountability channels will be sharpened with broad-based realistic content consultation mechanisms. Quite often, the general populace drift in amazement over the content of these addresses and question aloud whether they are true reflections of the numerous challenges of making a living in the societies. The inbuilt feedback loop of civic education curriculum will be utilized to gather views and opinions of the populace geared at ensuring the content elements of the annual addresses are realistic reflections of what pertains on the ground. Ruling regime and partisan coloring of the content will be minimized in a manner enabling several people to recognize, identify, and acknowledge situations highlighted in the addresses without doubts and speculations of hidden agendas.

The elements of budgeting as an accountability mechanism have been overshadowed by the endless and recurring anxieties on the part of the populace associated with the preparation, reading, approval, and releasing of budgets by ruling governments. Too many people have resigned to the perspective of budgets as statements and announcements of price increases, vexatious taxation, inflationary debauchery, increments in costs of quality living, and throwing crumbs from trickle-down economic tables to the masses. Budgets have become miracle statements where projections are often made to spend more and way above envisaged revenues in a particular fiscal year. Explanations are often not given regarding how the deficits and gaps in projected revenues and expenses will be reconciled, thereby continuing deepening the mythical thoughts on budgets.

Balancing budgets are uncompromising underpinning measure of Tran-Serve leadership, which will operate as preventive fortress against overspending, frivolous allocations, artificial copy-cat-borrowing-based standards of living. Budgets will no longer be synonymous with the dreaded disease of price increases. Rather, cordial relationships and understanding inculcated in the governing arrangements at all levels will enable better and more appreciative reactions to an essential unavoidable instrument of good stewardship in society.

Revenue generation and taxation obligations are also muddied in the leadership and governance unresponsiveness and overburdening narratives, which dominate economic management operations across the continent. In other words, if ruling regimes are not responsive to the needs of the populace, why should the latter be burdened with obligations which only serve to prop up the predatory interests of the former? In this regard, the more objective issues of capability and affordability which define substance, scope, and limits of taxation are lost in the construct of perceived belongingness in a viable polity.

Across the continent, ruling regimes have been unable to grow the economies into prosperity and thus are often met with resentment whenever attempts are made to exercise the mandates of generating revenue and exacting reciprocal obligations from the population.[19] The crux of the matter is the critical factor of sense of belongingness as a lens of good stewardship is yet to take roots in several societies. Several people think whether rightly or erroneously that proceeds from natural and related resources are not utilized judiciously by those in charge and attempts to extend sharing of the governance burden in terms of taxations are misplaced and unjustifiable. In this regard, taxation and revenue generation as veritable channels of accountability have been misunderstood and unable to serve intended purposes in such directions.

A BRP-inspired democracy will ensure that revenue generation and taxation obligations are construed and operated as channels of accountability, whereby value for money audits will be front and center of managing the public purse. The integrity of all public officials responsible for the allocation and use of funds will be measured by the extent of adherence to internal measures in place at the workplace for accountable service in the respective office. Above-the-fray performance will become normal practice which will grow the economy to enable shared prosperity across all segments of society. Sectors hitherto untouched by public service will be reengineered in ways which will enable target beneficiaries understand reciprocal obligatory responsibilities toward justifiable taxation demands and requests. Open revolts and resentments toward taxes will be minimal and, in some cases, extinct because a measure of belongingness has roots in the minds, attitudes, and behavior of a large section of the populace.

Public press briefings have often become glorified propaganda spewing routines, lies, and falsehoods rather than serving as measures of accounting for stewardship. In recent times, the proliferation of social media platforms has switched government briefings from being one-way traffic. Constant attempts to fact-checking government statements with what prevails or common trends in social media have become the norm. No longer are people gullible in imbibing whatever emerges from government machines. At times, internet trolls are utilized to reveal and make mockery whenever there are noticeable gaps, or an agency becomes too economical with the truth. Exaggerations and embellishments continue to punctuate government briefings. The practice of democracy under a BRP-inspired leadership and governance arrangements will operate to minimize such tendencies. Furthermore, it will encourage the preponderance of feedback from numerous social media sources to enhance regular government press briefings as effective tools of accountable stewardship.

Many are of the opinion that the Office of the Auditor General (AG) has been transformed by ruling regimes into "revelatory barking watchdog" given several instances of failure on the part of the authorities to act on malfeasance by public officials unearthed in AG's annual reports. In fact, whole audit services of nations are perceived as tools of the elite establishment to sanitize and reaffirm milking of the public purse. There is a running joke among high schoolers that whenever corresponding dining halls receive facelifts toward the end of a fiscal year, it means auditors are on campus to examine records on administration and management of the education outfit. It is a commonly held view that auditors are wined and dined, and rained with lavish gifts, by school authorities for glorified reports. And these reports are always ridden with gaping holes depicting utterly different scenarios from on-the-ground realities.

Some ruling regimes perceive the fact-finding agency's report as sensational and antagonistic, thereby impugning the credibility of its products as not neutral and professionally objective. Attempts are made to sideline the office through direct sabotage by either suffocating with delays in releasing budgetary resources or withholding other essential support services if considered and labeled as such. This preposterous position only deepens the decadence usually encountered in the management of the public purse. Rather than embracing and empowering the office with swift and timely actions regarding recommendations contained in reports, the narratives have been tilted to stifling accountability purposefulness and rather highlighting real or imagined confrontational posture of the accountability agency.

A BRP-inspired practice of democracy will be relentless in resourcing adequately the office of the AG to execute its assigned mandate without fear or favor, and ensuring that corresponding actions and sanctions are applied swiftly where appropriate. Tran-Serve leadership will restore confidence in the office by getting rid of sleaze and corruptibility with measures imbued with incentives, rewards, and meritocracy. The AG's reports will be accorded due respect and reverence deserving of the offices. Proactive efforts geared at revamping and equipping the entire audit services will be in place to enable efficient and effective execution of corresponding mandatory accountability roles and responsibilities.

Specialized Commissions and Task Forces designated for purposes of enhancing management of public services will not experience still-births after inauguration and respective tangible products negated to gathering dust in offices. Instead, assigned teams for the execution of recommendations and suggestions will be regular features of the accountability value chain for safeguarding good stewardship. Similarly, revelations of administrative reviews will be integrated into masterplans to shape and influence reforms or restructuring efforts geared at improving the operational procedures in the use of public resources. Furthermore, support for the Office of the Comptroller and Accountant General will be extended and coordinated to provide well-focused and supervised technical assistance for meeting delivery expectations of mandatory public services thresholds.

Enabling environments for smooth operations of autonomous civil society organizations (CSOs), nongovernmental organizations (NGOs), and think-and-do tanks will be forged to enable frank, open, and unfettered discussions of public policy directions as vehicles for trustworthy inputs and views of an engaged public. No matter the unpleasantness of opinions, ample opportunities will be created for gathering constructive criticisms, and high-level tolerance becoming the epitome of government interactions and dealings with the public. Striving for a rigorous pursuit of flourishing politics of words and not swords devoid of public office occupants' arrogance and impudence will be the standard yardsticks for utilizing such channels as accountability mouthpieces for good stewardship.

Parliamentary brakes and controls in Africa will mainly be meaningful with hands-free executive branches and not constrained constitutionally to appoint a percentage of ministers and cabinet members from the deliberative chambers. Given unique cultural dispositions, a clean slate of separation between both branches is required for parliament to play its expected role of acting as effective checks on executive actions and behavior. This prevailing situation in certain jurisdictions across the continent only serves to deprive the populace of merits associated with balanced branches of governments with the overall debilitative effects of sapping energy out of democracy practice. In societies struggling to have grounded democracies, such crippling arrangements only tend to amplify voices of sycophancy and bootlicking in ruling regimes.

A Tran-Serve leadership arrangement will encourage situations of balanced relationships and interactions and avoid giving undue advantage to one branch of government over the other in order to minimize compromising behaviors, mindsets, and attitudes on the part of representatives chosen under blended principle's selection procedures. A situation of role-playing to the gallery of executives for ministerial appointments by elected representatives not only promotes self-serving vested interests but tends to deprive communities of the saliency of representation, which will facilitate fulfillment of needs and manifest the blessings of success with ease.

Of course, the whole gamut of BRP-induced local governance structures and operations will engender influential actions for horizontal accountability measures which collectively will fertilize opportune moments for ensuring vertical accountability of stewardship at the national levels. In fact, the ideals enshrined in BRP are prime enablers of institutionalizing accountability in the mandate to lead, rule, govern, and manage resources in trust of the owners within a polity. Thus, the practice of democracy under such leadership and governance arrangements will shun impunity, and provide regular, periodic, and predictable moments for holding officeholders accountable for exercising the rights to serve the people.

Officials in charge of government service provisions and delivery will be preoccupied with the quality and quantity satisfaction of the target beneficiaries as the motivating operational values. Also, the officials will be aware of the consequences of dereliction of responsibilities in the discharge of assigned duties. Impunity will be minimized or eliminated, and beneficiaries will develop a deeper sense of belonging to communities through their willing attestations of benefiting from public services at open grassroots forums and events. It is in this regard government will then qualify as for the people, of the people, and by the people.

6. The Youth bulge is an Opportune Moment for Creativity and Innovations

Africa is currently experiencing a situation where a large share of the population is comprised of children and young adults, and it seems the leadership has placed both arms on the head and resigned to the fate of dejection and hopelessness. Although the proportion of the youth outnumbering the rest of the population is a critical challenge of economic management, this phenomenon is construed under a Tran-Serve system of rulership as a moment of creativity and innovations, which would increase and expand the productive capacity of the economies. In this context, windows of opportunities enabled through increased acquisition of digital skills, green and technology-enabled investments, and an accessible and affordable child- and elder care sectors could contribute immensely to ushering in an Africa of shared responsibilities, wealth, and prosperity based on strategies for green, resilient, and inclusive growth and sustainable development.

Policy openings likely to provide pathways to the labor market for the youth and other able bodies are in terms of skills for just energy transition (JET), digital market integration for robust retail value chain and commerce, and reduction of emissions with less dependence on fossils fuels, from deforestation and degradation, renewable energy products of solar and wind. Available opportunities will also be in the domain of feeding, clothing, sheltering, health and wellness, protection and guidance, education, and peer-to-peer training and learning schemes. Each opening is an industrial boom for productive capacity, purchasing power, accumulation, and consumerism raining potential benefits on the economies that may not have existed before in adequate magnitude. These opportunity outlets are avenues for substantial entrepreneurship, wealth creation, financing engineering, capital accumulation, as well as credible sources of inspirations and motivations in any society. It is worthwhile to buttress such notions of possibilities with lessons of advanced economies that have, for example, "affordable, accessible child- and elder care sectors, [and are at the forefront of finding suitable solutions to the climate change effects within the global community,] and those economies have higher participation rates of the very people we're talking about."[20] It takes leadership visions, peoples' mindsets, attitudes, and behaviors to marshal societal energy, and mold and direct toward creative and innovative solutions for tackling a particular challenge of a moment.

Tran-Serve leadership will formulate policies geared at communicating, mobilizing, and organizing society to tackle the effects of climate change; feed, clothe, and shelter the youth as well as others across the continent. This fundamental task will neither be outsourced to any entity nor based on handouts—a crucial leadership responsibility integral to the mandate to serve, lead, and govern in any polity. Climate change solutions as per the requirements under the Paris Agreement,[21] children and young adults' health and wellness policies, like those of other segments of the global community, will make available and affordable preventive and curative measures, options, and alternatives to enable less worrisome choices among the patronizing public. Policies to educate, train, and impart skills will be tailored and deployed to the doorsteps in ways which will facilitate coverage, access, and usage among the population where need is highly required and necessary.

There will be proactive planning for growth and responsibility, and no free-range, "breed, go, and grow" mentality countenanced. Formal and informal education strategies will specifically target climate change adaptation, resilient and mitigation measures, child care facility and kindergarten operations. All these measures will ensure that the requisite needs of reaching zero carbon levels, early childhood and related businesses are carefully considered, catered, and legislated where appropriate. Provisions will be made that enable and encourage freewill compliance and compulsory public elementary and secondary schooling for all and sundry so no household will ever have excuses for non-basic education of members.

Backing legislation will be operationally enforced by monitors and neighborhood associations empowered to report any possible case of neglect, abuse, and noncompliance. It will be an acceptable norm of societal existence that, for example, every child will complete the minimum education of secondary schooling and whosoever does that will be able to read, write, compute, and solve basic mathematical problems. This will be the minimum standard yardstick for government, parents, schools, and society at large commitments. Conformity will be strictly enforced and not compromised to ensure that every child born into society will have a foothold in life and placed on a pathway for fending for self as an adult.

Policies for higher learning, training, and knowledge acquisition will be in vogue. The enabling environment with opportune assistance for vocational, technical, undergraduate, and graduate education will be created. Avenues for volunteering, mentoring, internships, and extra-curricular activities for tapping youthful enthusiasm and energy into more productive ventures will be abundant and access awareness not limited or restricted to the privileged few. Children will be prepared and proactively encouraged to develop the mentality for higher achievement motivations, embrace, and enroll in higher learning endeavors. Ideally, a child will enter the workforce well-equipped with either vocational, technical, graduate skills, certifications, or diplomas. In this respect, no child will be left off the hook to roam the streets naively and ignorantly and become a burden on society later in life.

Simultaneously, corresponding manufacturing, production, and business strategy policies with underlying supportive financing engineering will be in place to cover needs and demands in the various spheres and developmental stages of human and societal growth. This will be guided by the firm belief that increasing the economic supply side through investments in public goods to handle the need requirements of the youth will expand the productive capacity for job opportunities in the longer term, which will ease some of the burden and pressures faced by families in homes and communities.

A true test of tackling the youth bulge and eliminating youth idleness, vulnerability, and frustration which currently pervade Africa's existence will lie in the robust responsiveness of the various sectors policy solutions crafted out of the creativity and innovativeness to be unleashed under Tran-Serve leadership practice of democracy. Furthermore, goods distribution and marketing outlets will provide the reinforcing convenience for employment and job creation to handle numerous and competing labor market-related generational needs, demands, and pressures. Strategic measures crafted will ensure the services are tailored and customized for specific entities, and are available and affordable in public or private domains.

In a nutshell, a society that cannot provide to satisfy the requisite needs of its children and young adult population will be on the verge of exploding with conflictual interests. This scenario is likely especially if the youthful population feel neglected and sidelined by the elder folk generations in the sharing of dividends or proceeds from what is considered as God-given resources. The youth are in want of fair share of the continental cake, and if they perceive unfair treatment, as alluded in previous pages, then the continent will continue to be magnets for avoidable troubles; hence, the situation requires redress to upturn the scale. Africa cannot avoid such potential situations of volatility with the status quo practice of democracy.

7. Food and Nutrition are Not Outsourced Products of Benevolence

A cardinal feature of a thriving self-sustaining nation lies in the capacity to feed itself and assuring adherence to nutritional guidance for better quality living. It is beyond comprehension that Africa cannot feed itself and food imports dominate the budgets of all countries. Growing an economy to be capable of feeding itself is a nonnegotiable responsibility of leadership. A future practice of democracy under Tran-Serve leadership will engineer enterprises of seed-to-plate agriculture (StP). This will be manifested largely through systematic transformation of small-scale agriculture into highly attractive and profitable businesses covering the entire value chain of maximizing production, use, and consumption of food crops, fruits, fisheries, and livestock to handle the food and nutrition requirements of the continent.

As a concept, the StP agriculture lens means that social enterprise business service facilities (BSFs) will be created to assist spanning from "Cape to Cairo" in the case of food crops, for example, for seed lots, land preparation, tilling and nurturing, makeshift irrigation, harvesting, storage, digitalization, processing, packaging, marketing, and distribution for widespread internal uses and export. The same goes with the other product categories. The smallholder farmer in the various agriculture zones are the targets to be supported to maximize productivity in the products of choice within the agroecological space of cultivation. The compendium skills, tools, and equipment upgrade, retooling, and automation regarding productivity capacity enhancement support services in the value chain will create myriad jobs and employment opportunities for the many youths and young adults able and willing to be engaged as private social enterprise business owners and partners, and/or formal employees of business services entities.

The StP agriculture products and services targeted would guarantee high payoffs due to access to wider markets as well as benefiting from digital extensions of regional value chains to the informal, micro- and small-scale enterprises. Investment interventions would be tailored for extensions to the goods that are produced primarily in rural areas and other informal, micro- and small enterprise settings and which can enter into the African Continental Free Trade Area (AfCFTA) trading regime.

First and foremost, the StP agriculture activities will benefit from the trading regime of the AfCFTA agreement. Second, these activities are tailored to support communities to provide numerous jobs/employment opportunities for the many idle and vulnerable youths and young adults domiciled mainly in the domains, where traditional leadership is highly effective.

Meeting the food and nutrition-related needs of Africa "is the world's supreme development challenge, and growing the agricultural sector is key to achieving a transformational impact. The agricultural economy employs 65–70 percent of Africa's labor force and typically accounts for 30–40 percent of GDP. More than

70 percent of the continent's poor live in rural areas, and agriculture is their most important economic activity."[22]

Agriculture is therefore appropriately one of the sectors that experts advise the AfCFTA should focus on for regional value chain development and industrialization for Africa. The potential of AfCFTA in enhancing food market integration and boosting intra-African food trade has been touted.[23] Experts have pointed out that the AfCFTA commitments on harmonization of food trade rules, policies, and tariff and non-tariff barriers and coordinating policies across the regional economic communities could promote a vibrant intra-African food trade and market integration and help turn agri-food trade into a catalyst for economic growth and structural transformation.

While an absolute value may be difficult to obtain, it is generally agreed that the value added in agriculture in Africa is low. Most experts emphasize that more value added can be obtained by more processing, digitalizing the retail supply chain, commerce, and market integration. The space exists for more processing in Africa given that a large proportion of agricultural exports from Africa are primary products and raw materials. Steering regional social enterprises with a focus on boosting agricultural sector productivity, processing, value addition, and intra-Africa trade would certainly be a step in the right direction.

The continent's agriculture and agribusiness industry are expected to reach US$ 1 trillion by 2030, that is, more than threefold the 2010 value, potentially creating opportunities to boost intra-African trade in food and non-food agricultural commodities and services; enhance food security; and with regional integration, open new market opportunities for farmers and other economic operators.

That the AfCFTA should focus on the agriculture sector is also in line with the commitment of African Heads of State and Government in 2014 to triple intra-African trade in agricultural commodities and services by 2025 as part of the Malabo Declaration.[24] And much of the efforts will occur in the domains where African traditional leadership is most vibrant and effective. Therefore, routing some of the catalytic investments through BRP-inspired leadership arrangements will be well-informed and intentioned.

In sum, social enterprises in StP agriculture with a regional lens would likely provide opportunities for maximizing socioeconomic benefits for a large segment of the population while maximizing profit for dividends in support of operations under a BRP-driven practice of democracy.

Key Elements of the Seed-to-Plate (StP) Agriculture

Food production (increasing productivity per acreage of smallholder producers)
1. Farming tools and implements improvement measures (hoes and cutlasses are not attractive and will not work the deal – Investments in small and medium-type cultivation tools machine shop businesses – manufacturing, sales, repairs, and servicing)
2. Land preparation support to all farmers (dedicated enterprises to assume responsibility on a contractual basis)

3. Seeds (provide weather and drought-resistant seeds for local edible crops and vegetables, and if possible, adopt no-till techniques)
4. Dig wells on all farms as makeshift irrigation measure (rain-fed food production is not attractive and will not cut the deal; provide opportunities for farmers to engage in all year-round production; investments in small and medium enterprises with the technological know-how to provide this service)
5. Harvest assistance, buying and purchasing of farm products at farm gates, and storage facilities (make investments in medium and small-scale businesses responsible for providing reliable and regular services, guarantee fair prices and incomes for farmers, prevent post-harvest losses and market glut due to increased yield and productivity and bumper harvests)
6. Processing, packaging, distribution, and marketing facilities and channels (dedicated small- and medium-scale businesses to provide services)
7. Extension, advisory, and maintenance services; training and skills acquisition initiatives (market value chain development, agriculture water management, soil nutrient management, pest and disease control, etc.)

Fruit Trees Plantation and Agri-Forestation
1. Fruit trees seedling lots ventures (involving all locally known and grown fruits—(make an inventory)
2. Fruit tree farms and plantations with corresponding farm help services—tools, seedlings, wells, and so on (cooperatives, individuals, and small/medium companies)
3. Fruit harvesting, purchase, storage, processing, distribution, and marketing facilities and outlets

Livestock and Fish/Mushroom Farming
1. Livestock feed production and processing businesses (cultivation, packaging, and distribution services)
2. Livestock and fish farms (poultry, goats, cattle, tilapia, etc.; ventures—(current practice where goats, sheep, chicken, and other domestic birds are part of households is not good and attractive and moreover unhygienic)
3. Livestock and fish products purchasing, processing, packaging, distribution, and marketing facilities (dedicated ventures)

Targeted Artisan Labor Force Program
• Revamping, retooling, and reorganization of the local apprenticeship systems—farmwork, building construction and related public works, carpentry, clothing design and dressmaking, hospitality and restaurant operations, wholesaling and retailing trading businesses, and so on.

Stimulating the focus of Tran-Serve leadership on social enterprises in StP agriculture as a major concentration to meeting the food and nutrition requirements of the continent will be timely and well-placed. Elements of the StP agriculture exhibit tremendous promises of engaging and providing the idle and vulnerable youth with decent job opportunities and uplifting the mass of Africa's population out of misery and poverty. With the glitters of hope in the trails of AfCFTA, the StP agriculture is bound to be a game changer if implemented as envisaged and in its entirety under BRP-inspired leadership and governance regimes.

8. Attributes of High-Value Education are the Bedrock of Transformation

Presently, it seems the sense of care particularly for the commons, duty, and responsibility has been interred with the bones of some early independence struggle leaders. Thenceforth, things continue to spiral downwards out of control, and the leadership of the continent has clung to a type of democracy practice which has been galloping fast to the gallows to hang itself. Africa is now practicing a runaway democracy partly attributable to an established post-independence education system, which churns out more self-serving mindsets that glorify other peoples' creative possessions and superintend over the hyper-exploitation of what belongs to them. The inherent wisdom in the adage of everyone showcases pride in ownership of his or her own belonging has long been thrown into the dustbin.

After the immediate independence struggles, many among the generation of leaders who assumed the reins of governing the continent lost touch with the grassroots, and never imbibed the virtues of public caring and embracing the onus of responsibility to uplift the continent for fulfilling needs and transforming to manifest the blessings of success for everyone. This debilitating mindset and attitude toward the public interests has been transplanted into future generations with reckless alacrity leading to a mentality of instant gratification taking hold among present generation.

A pivotal feature of democracy practice under a Tran-Serve leadership will be dedicated efforts of inspiring and motivating widespread consciousness and stimulation of generational responsibility for public goods and welfare in several dimensions of education, coexistence, growth, and development. Several approaches, initiatives, and programs specifically for this purpose will be in place to restore trust, cohesion, and togetherness for public interest goods. For example, Beyond Certifications Programs (BCP) could be instrumental in the formal and informal education sector. Such tailored initiatives would ensure that formal and informal knowledge acquisition will go beyond certifications, diploma requirements accolades, and institutionalize pathways imbued with a curriculum of moral education on the collective, public sense of concern, care, and duty. Graduands of the formal school systems will be motivated to participate voluntarily in civic duties and regular neighborhood communal labor engagement practices. Involvement in these encounters will likely be an integral part of the established education systems curricula, and corresponding incentivized activities well-coordinated, organized, and communicated as appropriate to the target population in respective locations.

An admirable resolve test of BRP-inspired education will be the extent and degree of deepening ingrained grassroots political culture without compulsive national legislation. Here initiatives under the broad-brush banner of "Deepening Political Culture" will be in the right direction. Widespread consciousness of self-motivation to embrace the cause of liberation from deprivation amid abundance or unfair and unequal sharing of resource proceeds will be the focus and norm. The pride of place and heritage will define generational outlook and responses to the challenges of the moments. Lyrics of national anthems, pledges, homeland songs, and music will not be perfunctory stale and ritualistic words to be recited for oratory impressions but elements of wisdom and virtues by which moral character and patriotic aspirational standards are construed. Physical expressions of attachment will go beyond sporting teams, competitions, and entertainment events that extol common ancestry, identity, and symbols. The spirit of oneness vividly on display during the height of the early independence struggles will be rekindled in flames of trustworthiness and willingness of the older generations to always think about the consequences of actions or footprints in terms of legacy and caring for the successor generations.

Talent Access Programs (TAP) entailing hand-holding, mentoring, experiential guidance, and directions would lace the processes of socialization, interactions, and networking credentials and portfolio of the younger generation. This will constitute integral core elements of operational performance evaluations requirements of all senior public officials enforced with urgency annually within the public service. As part of mandatory expectations, representatives at the local and national levels will enable systematic identification, nurturing, and support of all talents in the localities, communities, and constituencies. The realization that not all and sundry will be able to go through the formal schooling system successfully will ensure that provisions are in place preventing such occurrences becoming impediments. Responding and accounting to the needs of every individual talent regardless of background and societal connections will be assured pathways by which the critical consciousness of intergenerational sense of care, duty, and responsibility are intertwined with the socialization processes of various societies across the continent.

Presently, many of the younger generation are frustrated and consider the older folks as insensitive, uncaring, patronizing, and self-serving. The unwillingness among the young to go the extra length and sacrifice for the land of heritage is evidently alarming and frightening for nation-building. Something more proactive must be done to change the course of frustration and desperation if the youth would still be admonished and guided by hope, hard work, dreams, and dedication as the future of the continent. The spirit of instant gratification and get-rich-quick attitude and mentality meticulously acquired and learned from the older generation as the norm of politics under ongoing dispensation of democracy practice across the continent is a scar on the consciousness of reckless global order and coexistence. It is for a reversal of such scenarios that regimes of Tran-Serve leadership are crucial in Africa.

Successful grounding of deepened sense of intergenerational care, duty, and responsibility in Africa requires dramatic reconstruction of the logic of international development theory, particularly its emphasis on trade and its historical application to developing countries in the present era. Technological advancements in the industrialized countries have unleashed an unsustainable pattern of production, consumption, distribution, investments, and capital appropriation. The long-held economic view of participation at the global marketplace based on the principles of comparative advantage and specializations in the production of unprocessed raw materials must be permanently revised with deeds and actions.

A vivid figurative illustration of the outcome for Africa of such mode of participation can be gleaned from "visualizing the $94 Trillion World economy in one chart."[25] On this chart, forty-eight African countries combined for $1.01 trillion whereas the United States and China, for example, have $22.94 trillion and 16.86 trillion respectively. In this context of global coexistence, why will anyone blame the youth of Africa if they refuse to consign themselves to derogatory pittance amid abundant resources and yearn to move out of the continent to seek greener pastures elsewhere and never return? A trading system of mainly contributing as major raw materials producer has partly spelt doom and disaster for the continent. For centuries, this distorted mode of engagement in the global economy has been a synonym for perpetual bondage which no one else except Africans themselves can change with caring leadership and governance.

This trading pattern is what, to a large extent, the continental initiative of AfCFTA seeks to redress so that the countries can add value to their products, increase trading among themselves, and act collectively as dominant factor in the global economic system. As alluded in earlier pages, AfCFTA will thrive more swiftly and dynamically under Tran-Serve leadership arrangements given the underlying motives and synergy of both interventions, which are intrinsically aligned to the progress and upliftment of the entire continent. The duty and responsibility of intergenerational care underpinning Tran-Serve leadership will likely pivot AfCFTA with value-added goods and products in the global economic system to engender shared prosperity dividends in Africa.

Furthermore, it is emerging more difficult in Africa to inculcate and instill a sense of care, duty, and responsibility towards the environment, and address effectively the compendium tentacle of climate change with the continuous separation of Nature from God and people in harnessing resources for the marketplace. Instructively, African societies cannot be divorced from God and expected to exist solely for the individual pursuits of profits because several members of the communities are inherently religious and do not see themselves in that light.[26] Therefore, positive environmental adaptation and transformation necessary to tackle climatic stressors effectively would entail a reinterpretation of the relations between humans, nature, and God at least in the operations of the international market forces in Africa.

It is demonstrative of some attitudes among Africans that continuous use of herbal medicine is maintained as have been done for several centuries. This practice signifies inclinations to preserve known plant species for medicinal properties. Thus, in the various communities. it is common to see forests and groves set aside and enshrouded in myths that they are the dwelling places of the spirits and gods which should be left untouched. Taboos are used to set some days aside in the week that prevent anyone from tilling the land; nobody farms on that particular day. Communal vigilance and discipline are applied to regulate access to natural forest resources.

Together, the myths, taboos, and tales about forest protection constitute ecological management regimes, which have been practiced for generations. With population growth and expansion of settlement patterns, as well as rural-urban migration trends, some of the taboos have lost their regulatory potency. This is especially so because of the subordinate position the indigenous leadership arrangements have been occupying under the present-day reorganization of the communities. Erosion of power to exercise political authority implies erosion of authority to enforce ecological and environmental resource regulations effectively because the mechanisms are rooted in the sanctity and wholeness of indigenous leadership arrangements. Tapping some of these traditionally conventional practices to instill the consciousness of caring for nature and the environment would be regular features of attempts to tackle climatic change stressors effectively under Tran-Serve leadership practice of democracy in Africa.

The continuous relevance of the indigenous arrangements for promoting ecological harmony and addressing some present-day climate change challenges has been widely recognized and calls made to utilize these management strategies. Accordingly,

> in a number of African countries indigenous institutions are already available, such as chieftainship and village councils charged with responsibility for conservation activities. . . . The unique elements of the systems are solidarity, responsibility, accountability, collaboration, and initiative. [These elements] form the core of social organization of the [African] and can be used as a basis for institutionalization of land use planning and management of the village territory. . . . To be successful, projects at community or village level should involve indigenous management structures (e.g., representatives of each clan, elders, etc.) from the start, and the project planning should be in accordance with local decision-making and local labor planning practices. These institutions—where they exist—need to be strengthened. Where they have become defunct, they should be reestablished, and where they have never existed, some other form of local opinion should be encouraged.[27]

9. Progress is not Clinging to Dogmatic Ways of Doing Things

Africa has endured and continue to endure its share of tragic woes within the global community. From its battered image, global stigmatization and anti-blackness, flawed development paradigm embedded with colossal and rapacious looting of resources to the present-day minimal trust and faith by the vast majority in the capability of leadership to uplift them out of the carnage and mess they find themselves,—all these occurrences have taken a tremendous toll and unleashed untold hardships and fragility by depleting the reservoir of coping and adaptive resources. The continent needs replenishing coping and adaptive resources for building and sustaining strong institutional resiliency in all facets of organizational coexistence—political, economic, social, cultural, and ecological.

In the sense of Tran-Serve arrangements of democracy practice, political institutional resiliency will derive roots from engendering governance into an endogenous enterprise for self-government, proactive empowerment, majority participation in decision-making and problem-solving in society—This will be an enterprise providing ample opportunities for the deliberate involvement of all citizens partaking in the administration and management of resources upon which depend their existence. And this feat can mainly be pursued and accomplished by BRP-inspired leadership arrangements capable of mobilizing and organizing human interactions in an orderly and peaceful manner. Tran-Serve leadership will operationally be spurred by the driving philosophy of peace, security, and prevention of conflicts which might arise as a result of exclusion in the resource management and distribution processes. It is by such a process of endogenizing governance that institutional resiliency will be grounded to withstand any salvos hurled at the continent from all corners within the global community.

It is worth noting the salient elements underpinning the essence of endogenizing governance:

> [governance] involves reciprocity in the relationship between those who govern and those who are governed. It imposes constraints upon the exercise of power: in the process of being legitimized, power is necessarily limited. Governance is a social technology—"know-how" for problem-solving. In this sense, governance involves first and foremost citizen's empowerment to make meaningful and responsible choices. This process of empowerment is the practice of wisdom [relating to grounding institutional resilience in Africa].[28]

The implication of these prerequisites of grounded institutional resilience is that decision-making under a Tran-Serve leadership will never be the prerogative of a few handpicked elites, and the ideals of democracy in terms of freedom for peaceful coexistence are not the creations or the postulations of one axis of thought and power within the global community. As indicated in prior pages, decision-making in post-independence Africa has increasingly become the preserve and prerogatives of a few handpicked elites in transnational relationship with external financiers.

In a sense, counteracting the previous observations means refraining from imposing one form of democratic values and principles on all nations without regard to the respective needs and realities of life of target societies. Such a perspective should induce democratic practices based on the cultural orientations of the majority of the people in any particular society within the global economy. It is in this direction that a BRP-inspired leadership arrangement will strive toward revamping Africa's fragile coping and adaptive resources and build sustained robust institutional resiliency across the continent.

Building economic institutional resilience now will require efforts toward addressing the seeming phenomenon of Sino-Western development financing engagement approaches and influence in Africa given the conceivable fact that monetary issues are incidentally power struggles within the global community. For centuries, Africa has been immersed with the Western conventional model, and over the "past two decades China and Africa have dramatically expanded their political and economic ties. . . . Unlike Western donors, China doesn't condition its assistance on political agendas such as the promotion of democracy and human rights."[29] Central concern issues about both models pivotal to building economic institutional resilience remain political influence, economic power, deprivation, debt, and subsistence. A key query of relevance here is whether both models have leveled income differences, made the "have not" noticeably happier, and satisfied the basic needs of the continent's poorest? The jury is out there on this crucial question particularly given that both models have generated serious geopolitical-economic thought provocations.[30]

For our purpose, outsourcing financing of the continent's development, growth, and prosperity to both pathways should be of utmost concern which does not augur well for endogenous efforts to build institutional resilience, fulfill needs, transform, and manifest the blessings of success for everyone. It is an important priority and nonnegotiable task a Tran-Serve leadership arrangement would tackle with diplomacy, sensitivity, and dexterity for peaceful coexistence and interactions within the global community. This situation of Sino-Western development financing trapping is neither a proclivity toward a particular form of societal organization—multiparty democracy or one-party authoritarianism. Rather, the quest of a BRP evolvement of an Afrocentric grounded form of rulership is to thrive on judicious utilization of the continent's endowed resources for the betterment of all and sundry.

The debate about the proportion of labor cost in relation to the amount of investment capital required to create decent jobs and reduce unemployment to appreciable levels is central to building social institutional resilience in Africa.[31] Very high levels of unemployment, jobless growth, low wages, incomes, revenues, and purchasing power, coupled with inflationary trends, mainly tend to deepen labor disorganization, weakened strength, and disunity.

In many cases, such characteristics of diminished position of labor are correlated to retaining abysmal profit margins and rate of returns on capital investments at the global marketplace. This scenario, augmented with the Sino-Western development financing engagement trappings, has made it practically impossible in Africa to consider national or community reforms based on cultural perceptions of what is "good." Such a scenario mainly exudes the notion that people of some cultures are incapable of devising coherent, need-oriented and genuine democratic programs without external interference and direction. In truth, Africa can be classified as congenitally poor but not full of all-embracing unintelligent peoples. BRP operations are imbued with the countervailing capacity to dispel such a notion as myth and enable a surge forward to restore adequate investment incentives capable of jobs creation at levels that would balance profits not at the expense of labor.

As noted earlier, while forests, energy sources, minerals such as gold and cobalt, and related resources are depleted in Africa to service debts at the global marketplace, human beings are conceptually separated from nature in the process. In reiteration, the materialist philosophy and manner of living negate the values, principles, and beliefs of communities that consider themselves as part of nature and thus have in place resource management modalities aimed at ensuring ecological institutional integrity and resilience. These communities are subjected to constant contempt at the international marketplace and their cultural practices occasionally labeled as inferior by some foreign and domestic experts. As a matter of fact, positive social and ecological institutional resilience cannot be attained with the idea that aspects of African culture are infantile, primitive, and archaic in the context of problem-solving, conflict resolution, and resource management within the global community.

To attain institutional resilience in Africa, a Tran-Serve leadership arrangement would strive for conceited efforts to adopt integrated and collective strategies for tackling the lingering associated problems of engagements at the global marketplace. The practice of paying attention to one dimension and neglecting others compounds the problems. Robust institutional resilience in Africa certainly requires alternative ways of thinking, management of human relations peaceful co-exitence within the international community.

Conclusion

This chapter utilizes an amalgam of wise thoughts to underscore the way in which BRP-inspired leadership and governance arrangements can be crafted to invigorate for good the practice of democracy across the continent. Each line reveals the current state of play and expatiates options and alternatives, which will facilitate the march to fulfilling needs and transforming to manifest the blessings of success for everyone across the continent. This approach of illuminating a topical subject matter for policy relevance, implications, and consideration enables cogent reiteration of the driving narrative of the book that adoption and rollout of BRP will inspire, induce, and instill audacious hope in the dividends of democracy practice on the continent. The message is loud and clear: either redesign the foundations of democracy practice with BRP-laden reforms without further delay or risk deepening unpalatable responses to elusive dividends of prevailing bogus and shambolic democracy practices on the continent.

EPILOGUE

AN ALTERNATE SOLUTIONS PATHWAY

Introduction

This chapter serves as a final note on the BRP concept as an invaluable solutions pathway to conclude the in-depth discussions on potent solutions for the leadership and governance problems in Africa. A reiteration of some key inconvenient truths about the design and shape of statehood in Africa ends the journey with corresponding parting thoughts on the moral lessons in the practical utility of a BRP construct. The key inconvenient truths are:

1. Democracy practices can mainly flourish when derived from the needs, aspirations, and realities of the target societies.
2. African structures of statehood are not designed and shaped to exert influence and pressure on each other and ensure accountability in the use of the public purse.
3. The institution of chieftaincy in Africa is pivotal to the spirit of togetherness of constituent communities and cannot be marginalized in ensuring robust democracy practices on the continent.

The corresponding practical lessons of such inconvenient truths are as follows:

1. The gains of democracy practice can be firmly anchored with BRP.
2. Empty political promise destructs the spirit and soul of society.
3. Multiparty politics is not the glue that binds Africa together; rather, it is the institution of chieftaincy.
4. Voluntarism is the supreme sustainer of compliance.
5. Acts of impunity regarding management of the public purse will be rare under a BRP-inspired regime.
6. A child does not soil the laps of a parent and is cleaned with a knife.

All these moral lessons double down on the inherent healing prowess of BRP as a suitable cure for the leadership and governance ailments on the continent.

Practical Lesson One: Anchoring the Gains of Democracy Practice in Africa

There is an urgent need for mechanisms of consolidating democracy practice with subnational administration reforms in Africa. Consolidation of democracy in a nation is partly a function and result of two interrelated measures: robust electoral process and grounded state-level structures, institutions, and relationships, which contribute immensely to institutionalize the principles of representation, participation, transparency, and accountability for good stewardship in the use and management of public resources. However, elections, particularly in Africa, are mainly followed by claims of rigging. For example, Ghana completed its eighth elections under the fourth republic constitution albeit followed by Supreme Court petitions filed by the opposition parties.[1] Likewise, Kenya elections 2022 was successfully completed amid claims by the opposition that the results sheets were altered.[2]

By and large, elections are periodic events for holding elected leaders accountable for public resources held in trust and managed on behalf of the populace. However, accountability for stewardship of the public purse is not a periodic event or a one-time act. Instead, it is a continuous process of participatory relations with the electorate embedded in the operations of state governance structures and institutional practices responsible for the management of public resources. The efficacy and effectiveness of these state structures and institutions at various levels in terms of involving the people in managing public resources would largely influence and determine the development prospects and transformation of lives in the nation.

The high voter turnout recorded in completed elections (almost 80 percent) on the continent does not mean or translate to high level of participation by the majority in the development governance of the nations. In other words, high-level participation of the people is more or less restricted to elections and not in the aftermath of development governance. This is a serious anomaly which tends to retard efforts and progress toward transformational development. There is a fundamental lesson worthy of note in this situation: democracy does mean not only participating in elections but also partaking in the dividends of the aftermath development benefits which elections of leaders should engender in a nation.

Practical Lesson Two: State Structures of Governance
Restricts Participation in Development

State structures of governance in Africa are not configured to exert influence and pressure on each other. This undermines the prospects of effective participation, transparency, and accountability of stewardship in the use of public resources. Lower-level structures are the weakest links between the central-regional-local structure nexus. Such a scenario severely affects the participation of citizens in development governance decision-making with serious implications for deploying both vertical and horizontal accountability mechanisms to consolidate the dividends of democracy in the nation. Prevailing scenario translates into disconnect and distance (or at best tenuous/artificial relations) between citizens and the structures of statehood. This phenomenon undermines the effectiveness of applying the principles of participation, transparency, and accountability to ensure that public resources are utilized efficiently by elected officials for the delivery of services and improvement of development outcomes.

Participation of the vast majority in development decision-making is a key ingredient in the success of any targeted effort to reduce poverty. Participation for desired results and outcomes requires trustworthy and respectable leadership structures capable of being utilized for communicating, mobilizing, and organizing, as well as the principles and rules of engaging people. For effective participation, the people must be pivotal in creating the leadership structures, be familiar and comfortable with the principles and rules of engagement, and understand the corresponding uses for intended purposes. And such structures must be rooted in their belief systems and ways of life. Ownership, understanding, familiarity, and ease of usage of the participation structures are thus the linchpins of responsive governance which strive to ensure that leaders are transparent and held accountable for the stewardship of public resources in a society.

If the participation apparatus is neither understood by ordinary people nor are they familiar and comfortable with their effective usages, alienation, marginalization, and aloofness toward the behaviors and actions of leaders in terms of accountability for public stewardship ensue. The effective participation of the poor in efforts to find collective solutions to problems of poverty would therefore be predicated on the leadership structures, principles, and rules of engagement established and operated by the people themselves. It is by such arrangements and organizational frameworks within which the poor and the silent majority would be enabled to unleash their creative energies toward concerted and sustained involvement in improving governance and stewardship of public resources.

Practical Lesson Three: Foundation of Responsive Designs of Statehood Is Traditional Leadership

Weak local governance structures based on prevailing constructs are retarding development efforts on the continent. A move to the next stage of the nations' transformation process requires serious rethinking and fundamental subnational administration reforms. Africa needs to craft a system of local governance based on a blend of the existing traditional institutions and prevailing official national structures for managing public resources and delivery of services to the people. It is largely by this means that Africa could consolidate democracy in terms of ensuring high level of participation at both fronts—during elections and continuous involvement in the aftermath more important development process.

Africa needs to make better use of its traditional leadership institutions for development purposes beyond what currently pertains. Due to historical experiences, there is no country in Africa that still has its traditional institutions intact in pristine forms and involved in how several people make living in homes and communities. The relative peace countries such as Ghana enjoy in a sub-region riddled with turmoil is arguably attributable to ways and means the traditional leadership institutions have been kept intact and utilized albeit at times for parochial purposes. Unfortunately, these institutions sometimes are perceived in current democratic practices mainly as veritable sources of access to votes and exploited for self-serving purposes during election campaigns to boost vote-grabbing efforts and voter turnouts.

The usual popular refrain on reforming current local government systems (LGS) in Ghana, for example, is about electing the district chief executives (DCEs). As stated earlier, the critical issue of local government is beyond the elections of DCEs. The existing local governance structures, unlike democratic governance arrangements elsewhere, are not designed to function as checks on national state structures or influence and shape behavior and actions of national state officeholders. This phenomenon deprives the national structures of the foundations upon which cohesive institutions would thrive to inspire and rally citizens around a common sense of purpose, vision of development, and transformation of lives.

Africa could redesign the shape of statehood to incorporate the principles of leadership, organization, and participation many citizens utilize to subsist and manage common resources upon which existence and livelihoods depend as sources of fundamental operational strength. This could entail considerations of having a first tier of administrative leadership in districts as local leadership councils (LLCs) comprising of male and female traditional leaders the people themselves have nominated, selected, and elected in their localities. Such a policy action would be an accessible leadership structure influenced by ordinary people in terms of participation in decision-making, organization, and mobilization to rally around a common cause and purpose.

Members of such local leadership council would select among themselves on rotational basis for a determined period a presiding member as head of the council. The local leadership council would be supported by the existing technical and clerical staff in the administration and management of the district affairs. This arrangement would be based on creative adaptation of the positive elements of the existing traditional governance arrangements which hold the communities intact in most cases and blended with Western principles and systems of administration.

Efficiency and effectiveness in the management of public resources for development purposes within districts could be enamored with participatory methods of planning, prioritization, budgeting, program implementation, monitoring and evaluation, and performance impact assessments. In a sense, this would be local governance arrangements grounded in African cultural values and belief systems which would be capable of:

1. bringing government closer to ordinary people;
2. having in place efficient, value for money administrative structures for resource management;
3. institutionalizing operational procedures and transactions which command the respect, trust, and loyalty of the people, and

4. inculcating in the people a sense of belonging and buy-in of the overall governance process of the nations.

Of course, the views expressed here is not to glorify or be nostalgic about the traditional leadership institutions. It is also not to be oblivious of the fact that such institutions exhibit certain negative traits and features which do not conform to the representation nuances of present-day society. What this means is to undertake strategic critical reviews and assessments to identify the positive traits and features, which would constitute the cornerstone of a viable and unique democratic arrangement for robust development governance at local grassroots levels.

In practice, the call for subnational administration reforms would mean some of the intractable issues pivotal to the institutions of chieftaincy such as tenure, succession, and land management arrangements are subjected to critical and realistic reviews in order to codify and adapt the positive aspects to strengthen and consolidate democracy on the continent. The time for such a reform is now as it has the potential to move the continent to a higher level in its development transformation trajectory. To recap, a BRP construct can firmly anchor the gains of democracy practice in Africa and strengthen togetherness of constituent communities.

Practical Lesson Four: Multiparty Politics Is Not the Glue That Binds Africa Together

The enterprise of nations in many parts of Africa evolved fortuitously to be anchored presently on the institution of chieftaincy instead of the intentioned founding tenets of multiparty politics. Indisputably, the relative peace in many countries of Africa could be attributable to the community-binding groundings of the institution of chieftaincy and not the partisan-driven organizing prowess of the nation-states. All such countries have similar traditional institutions, and these heritage-based community-binding features have been utilized to forge national identities in the name of state and country. In this regard, attempts at undermining the institution of chieftaincy which at times emanate from some elements of the axis of state power and authority could mainly signal the beginning of the end of the nation's enterprise and must be avoided at all cost.

The statehoods of Africa are pillared on the tenets of multiparty politics as the principal means by which communities within the continental territorial boundaries coexist, organize, and make a living. Regardless of the disruptive historical experiences, the tradition of multiparty politics prevails albeit with the burden of incessant individualism, divisive, and acrimonious tendencies associated with the practice which have strangulated families and communities to become wary and suspicious of each other based on party affiliations.

What has sustained the enterprise of African statehood in many countries is the uniqueness of the institution of chieftaincy regardless of inherent flaws. Wherever appropriate, these leadership institutions have remained the more cohesive governance and leadership structures particularly at local levels with symbiotic capability to communicate, mobilize, and organize community members for collective development actions. It is mainly for such reasons that the establishment of the African Traditional Leadership Union has been proposed to complement efforts of the African Union in building the "Africa We Want."

Practical Lesson Five: Empty Political Promise Destructs the Spirit and Soul of Society

The fundamental antidote to politics of lies, dishonesty, and first-guessing in Africa is BRP of governance. Arguably today in Africa, the politics of lies, dishonesty, and first-guessing is prevalent and on the ascendancy.[3] A fundamental grassroots solutions search will include a layer of long-range lens in social media parlance as #AdoptBRP. Adopting BRP of governance in Africa will mean an autonomous local government under adeptly revamped traditional authorities and national government under multiparty-based elected officials. It will also mean a balance of head and body in sync to constitute formidable institutional checks on preventing politics of impunity, winner knows it all posturing, and leaders can get away with any utterances attitude across the continent.

BRP has an inherent preventive bastion with appalling consequences for, among many errors and missteps, leadership plagiarized speeches, family, clan, and friends-driven appointments, and naïve politicking with exchange rate matters while the production structures of the country remain intact ever since created. Rulers and representatives will be subjected to continuous assessments, and citizens' sense of having the power to effect desired changes will not have to be manifested in a four-year timeframe of exercising this right of recall and empowerment.

Under BRP, leaders will not have the audacity to take citizens for granted and make statements later to be verified as inaccurate and reduce the nation to ridicule and trolls at the international public space. In the span of several weeks, citizens had to embrace the reality that some important statements emanating from the seats of government were false. It may seem even pooh-poohing statements have become the new normal regarding reporting on the Covid cases in many countries in Africa.[4]

Now in Ghana, for example, there is serious first-guessing ongoing regarding the intentions of the seat of government, the Electoral Commission (EC), National Identification Authority (NIA), and some of the opposition parties.[5] The act of first-guessing occurs when there are grounded convictions of intent. Some ruling elites parade themselves as ostriches when politics is reduced to a zero-sum, winner-takes-all game. At the end of such intransigence, ordinary folks are always caught up in the resultant melee.

Africa has enough resources—natural and technical to operate governing systems responsive to the needs of all and sundry. With a bit of tweaking under the banner of BRP, the continent can avoid the infamy visited on its image with the prevailing politics of lies, deception, and first-guessing.

Practical Lesson Six: Volunteerism Is the Supreme Sustainer of Compliance

The Covid-19 pandemic is another reason for adopting BRP of governance in Africa. The pandemic has exposed the frailty of the administrative state in Africa. This situation has reaffirmed the "hanging" character of the governing structures whereby the corresponding "head" and "body" are not in sync for education, sensitization, and ensuring compliance to abate the ravages of the disease.

To stem the spread of Covid-19 requires extensive public education, sensitization, and ensuring compliance with the protocols of lockdown, social distancing, contact tracing, isolation, treatment, and adherence to hand-washing and related hygiene regimen. Ideally, communities must be penetrated with the right information and understanding that allows compliance with the requisite protocols. Communities must be sensitized that noncompliance exposes individual and society to very high risks. However, national executive reach is limited and can mainly be extended through a robust local government. Ensuing incidents in some parts of the lockdown areas have tested the penetration capacity of both the national and local leadership, and revealed concerns for citizens-leaders power and authority relations.

Some residents flocking to the beaches[6] and traditional authorities embarking on purifying rites while openly flouting lockdown directives speak volume of the mindset and the psychosocial relations of citizens and leaders.[7] Furthermore, the images of able-bodied and vulnerable young men dashing across the street for free food wherever such could be found without regard to any social distancing protocols mainly caused heads to spiral in disbelief about the lurking time bomb uncovered by the pandemic. The broader approach of distributing food to the vulnerable only muddied waters and rendered questionable the essence of local governance across the continent.

Nowhere in the annals of many parts of the continent has been faced with the stark realities of the proportion of the population without toilet facilities, potable water, and related essentials necessary for lockdown compliance. Citizens have been consigned to hailing token offers and crumbs from the leaders. However, all the token prevention facilities out there represent a scar on the consciousness of the elites and visible reminder of past policy failures. Covid-19 will be overcome and society will ease back to normality. However, Africa is urged to consider BRP for better-aligned leadership structures to the needs, aspirations, and realities of the people in order to handle the ramifications more effectively.

Practical Lesson Seven: Acts of Impunity would be Rare Under BRP-inspired Regime

Reportedly, there were worrisome meanings of different data sets in Ghana's 2018 and 2019 Budget Statements and IMF (the International Monetary Fund) Covid-19 loan document, as well as utterances on the state of the economy afterwards. The revelation that government shared different macroeconomic data with Ghanaians and IMF placed the country at a crossroad of falsifying concern.[8] Three worrisome meanings in the realm of policy and decision-making can be construed from this palpable action as related to issues of:

1. credibility, integrity, and authenticity;
2. transparency, accountability, and participation; and
3. inherent frailty and hanging character of the administrative state.

The downsides of these factors tend to expose the inherent hypocritical diplomacy of the status quo levers of power within the global community and reassert the urgency of autonomous local government based on BRP of governance in Africa. Indicators of fiscal deficits, primary account balance, gross international reserves, among others, speak volumes of the health of any economy. At any point, sharing two different data sets on these vital elements automatically subjects the country policy statements to the test of credibility, integrity, and authenticity. And if found wanting, then the critical tenets of trust and respect for the governing operational procedures are thrown into the dustbin. The question remains which of these data set is right and accurate, and what else of government pronouncements is false. Not only does this action feeds into the negative narratives and corridor jokes of the twin Bretton Woods institutions that data from African countries are susceptible to "falsehood." Such an action ultimately undermines the reservoir of goodwill toward the continent within the international community.

Presenting a set of facts on the economy to citizens and thereafter the same set of facts presented differently to another audience means there is lack of transparency in dealings between the rulers and the ruled. The rulers are enamored to engage in such distortions by the absence or weak mechanism of accountability usually manifested in lack of autonomous local government acting as institutional checks on national executive official behavior. Such an act may also be driven by the calculation that citizen participation in governance is mainly active in periodic elections devoid of systematic scrutiny of macroeconomic data by the broader public.

Government officials mainly get away with flagrant display of opaque actions because the administrative state is inherently frail and hanging. This situation is an albatross on the necks of Africans as the nation-states have been constructed and operated in response to the needs of the privileged educated few—a situation which requires urgent change to accommodate the needs of the majority. It is to induce such a change in the governing structures that the adoption and implementation of BRP in Africa have been the thrust of this book.

Practical Lesson Eight: A Child's Soil on the Lap is never Cleaned with a Knife

In the same vein, pronouncements that exogenous factors are mainly responsible for Ghana's sordid economic situation reinforce prior IMF clarification on claims of misreporting figures in budget statement and loan documents as commonplace international diplomacy relations dealings. That the IMF maintained the same script in opinion does not deviate from the norms and ethics of international diplomacy. Nonetheless, projecting adherence to computational methods of standard practice contrary to visible impact and outcomes of government practices experienced among target population has the tendency of leaving an asterisk on existence of forthrightness in dealings with citizens within the global economic system.

As the "guardian" of the global economic system, the IMF by virtue of its Article IV consultations was aware of the occurrences in the economy but could not give up on its "high-performing member" country and reveal publicly that such "alternative" facts and figures do not reflect the true nature of the country's fiscal situation. It is up to agencies like Fact Check Ghana to pinpoint the discrepancies and draw the attention of ordinary citizens to the misreporting by government. To some observers, it is a dereliction of responsibility on the part of IMF to allow such a distortion without publicly insisting on appropriateness and reconciliation of records.

Furthermore, on the issue of gross international reserves, the government chose to include in its computation methods "Oil fund, Heritage and Stabilization Funds" against standard global practices. Usually, many countries refrain from using reserved funds as "piggy banks" and only fall on such stocks as a measure of last resort. It is partly for such reasons that standard computation of current gross international reserve excludes at first instance intergenerational investments. However, Ghanaians in this case have become witnesses to the government's penchant for reaching out to the oil and related funds with the least hint of imbalance in economic projections. No wonder, widespread resentful sentiments have been expressed regarding such comments from the IMF boss that "the current difficulties in Ghana are not due to the government bad policies but due to the COVID-19 pandemic and the Russia-Ukraine war."[9] Something must change in the way governance is executed under the banner of prevailing partisan winner-takes-all politics practiced in Africa. And that something has heightened the urgency of autonomous local government in the genre of BRP leadership and governance.

A Revolution of the Mind

Embracing, adopting, and operationalizing BRP construct as solutions for the leadership and governance problematics on the continent require a revolution of the mind both within and outside Africa. BRP is evidence-based, commonsense solutions pathway for transformational development in Africa. Tran-Serve leadership is an attitude of a mindset committed to long-term creativity and innovation for integrated plans capable of solving practical problems of life.

Deep-seated deprivations, plundering of the public purse, the privatization of public wealth, friends, family, sycophants, and bootlickers' regimes of control; internecine conflicts, senseless killings, forced displacement, deliberate creation of refugees, and the malaise of poverty which have become the development trajectory of Africa revolve around the post-independence operations of the so-called modern state leadership and governance mismanagement.

The African majority needs real independence. Independence from colonial rule has been half-baked and silver-coated for the minority educated elites— civilian and military. A real independence is needed to free many Africans from their own internal ruling elites and external collaborators and financiers—that is, independence from the neocolonial arrangements presided over by African elites as part of the strategy to safeguard the interests of the major beneficiaries of the prevailing world order.

A revolution of the mind is about ideas, knowledge generation, integration, and innovation for collective wisdom to solve problems. African intellectuals need to awaken, become conscious of their fundamental obligations to their people, and strive to bring about far-reaching and drastic changes necessary to cure the ills of leadership and governance on the continent.

NOTES

Chapter 1

1 Tran-Serve leadership is discussed in detail in Chapter 6, "The Concept of BRP."

2 The constituent countries of the West can be gleaned from: Fabricus, P. (2022), "Time for Africa Strategies on the Big Powers," *ISS Today*, September 9, www.issafrica.org. RT News (2022), "West Destroying Its Own Privileges—Lavrov," September 21, www.rt.com.

3 See Campbell, J. and N. Quinn (2021), "What Is Happening to Democracy in Africa?" in *Council on Foreign Relations*, May 26, http://www.cfr.org.

4 The designation of "district assemblies" refers to the present context of Ghana. Usually, there are four main types of local governance structures—counties, municipalities, (cities and towns), special districts, and school districts. Although varied labels and designations of these structures exist across the continent, they basically refer and mean the same structural arrangements of local government anywhere in the world. For details, see The Cities Alliance (November 2018, 3rd Edition, United Cities and Local Governments of Africa (UCLG), Cities Alliance), *Assessing the Institutional Environment of Local Governments in Africa, United Cities and Local Governments of Africa*, November, www.citiesalliance.org.

5 For insights, see Ebert, R. (2022), "The Woman King Movie Review and Film Summary," September 16, www.rogerebert.com.

6 Landell-Mills, P. (1992), "Governance, Cultural Change and Empowerment," *The Journal of Modern African Studies* 31 (4): 543–4.

7 Ayittey, G. (1990), "Guns, Idiots. Screams," *New Internationalist*, June, 8, www.jstor .org.

8 Mikell, G. (1991), "Equity Issues in Ghana's Rural Development," in D. Rothchild (ed.), *Ghana: The Political Economy of Recovery*, 85–100, Boulder: Lynne Rienner.

9 Ibid., 89.

10 Arhin, K. (1985), *Traditional Rule in Ghana: Past and Present*, Accra: Sedco, www .worldcat.org.

11 Vaughan, O. (1995), "Assessing Grassroots Politics and Community Development in Nigeria," *African Affairs* 94 (77): 501–18, www.jstor.org.

12 WhatsApp post. Origin and date unknown.

13 See Ghanaweb (2022), "Our Governance System Needs Retuning and Fine-Tuning—Kyei-Mensah-Bonsu," October 2, www.ghanaweb.com.

14 Vaughan, O. (1995), "Assessing Grassroots Politics and Community Development," 518.

15 While this list is by no means an exhaustive mention of all the significant post-independence episodes on the African development landscape spanning over six decades, it depicts a context of unceasing supply efforts of righting wrongs within the global community and provides insights into why the continent remains hopeful despite the litany of problems and challenges—a theme which pervades the book.

16 Campbell, J. and N. Quinn (2021), "What Is Happening to Democracy in Africa?."

17   Ibid., Yamson, I. (2022), "Our Problem Is Bad Leadership Corruption," *Ghanaweb*, September 23, www.ghanaweb.com.

18   Kpandu is a semi-urban town in the Volta Region of Ghana.

19   Remarks by President Obama to the Ghanaian Parliament, July 11, 2009, www .obamawhitehouse.archives.gov.

20   Ashun-Sarpy, A. (2021), "Ghana's Youth: Resilience Despite the Odds," *NewAfrican*, November 8, http://www.newafricanmagazine.com.

21   UNICEF (2018), report on reducing stunting in Africa, November 28, http://www .unicef.org. Skoufias, E. (2018), "All Hands on Deck: Halting the Vicious Circle of Stunting in Sub-Saharan Africa," November 28, http://www.blogs.worldbank .org. CGTN News (2020), "58.5 Million Children in Africa Suffering from Stunted Growth," February 10, http://www.newsaf.cgtn.com. Nshimyiryo, A., B. Hedt-Gauthier, and Z. El-Khatib (2019), "Risk Factors for Stunting among Children under Five Years: A Cross-Sectional Population-based Study in Rwanda Using the 2015 Demographic and Health Survey," *BMC Public Health* 19 (75), February 11, http://www.bmcpublichealth.biomedcentral.com.

22   Campbell, J. and N. Quinn (2021), "What Is Happening to Democracy in Africa?."

23   See Songwe, V. (2022), "Strategies for Financing Africa's Health Sector," *Brookings Institute Foresight Africa*, February 3, http://www.brookings.edu. Ghana News Agency—GNA (2022), "Stick to Commitment to Reallocate SDR $100 billion to Africa—President to G20 Leaders," *Ghanaweb*, February 7, http://www.mobile .ghanaweb.com.

24   See Fox, L. and S. Jayne Thomas (2020), "Unpacking the Misconceptions about Africa's Food Imports," *Brookings Institute*, December 14, http://www.brookings.edu.

25   See Agbor, J., O. Taiwo, and J. Smith (2012), "Sub-Saharan Africa's Youth Bulge: A Demographic Dividend or Disaster?," *Brookings Institute, Africa Growth Initiative. Foresight Africa: Top Priorities for the Continent in 2012*, http://www.brookings.edu.

26   Onukwue, A. (2022), "Microsoft Is Leading Big Tech's Push to Relocate African Developers to North America," *Quartz Africa*, August 19, http://www.qz.com.

27   Politico Staff (2021), "The Man behind Bidenomics," *Politico*, December 17, http:// www.politico.com.

28   See Global Witness Briefing Document (2009), "Natural Resource Exploitation and Human Rights in the DRC, 1993-2003," December 17, http://www.globalwitness.org. Henning, M. (2019), "Has the Relationship Between Namibia and Germany Sunk to a New Low?," *The Conversation*, August 4, http://www.theconversation.org.

29   Amalric, F. (1998), "Sustainable Livelihoods: Entrepreneurship, Political Strategies and Governance," *Development* 4 (3): 31–4, http://www.jstor.org.

30   The politics of sustainable livelihoods is about opening constructive spaces for engagement and interactions regarding identifying societal problems and organizing to solve them. For details, see Anani, K. V. (1999), "The Pursuit of Politics of Sustainable Livelihoods: Focus on Governance in Ghana," unpublished PhD dissertation, Guelph, Canada: University of Guelph.

31   Edinger, S. (2021), "Good Leaders Know You Can't Fight Reality," *Harvard Business Review*, October 8, http://www.hbr.org.

32   Reference is made here to the African Union—AU (2013), pronouncements on "Agenda 2063: The Africa We Want." For details, see www.au.int.

33   Diop, M. (2022), "Africa's Pandemic Recovery Requires Investments that Build the Foundation for the Region's Future," *Brookings Institute Foresight Africa: Top Priorities for Africa in 2022*, January, http://www.brookings.edu.

34 Credit for the idea of an African Traditional Leadership Union (ATLU) goes to Togbe Afede XIV, paramount chief of Ho Asogli State, the immediate past president of the Ghana National House of Chiefs, and the CEO of Strategic African Securities (SAS). This idea, expounded by the author in collaboration with Dr. John C. Afele, is a focus of an ongoing continental initiative convened by Togbe Afede XIV and counterpart traditional leaders in Benin, Zambia, Botswana, and so on. See Ghanaweb (2022), "Togbe Afede XIV to Establish African Traditional Leadership Institute," September 8, www.ghanaweb.com.

35 African Union (2013), "Agenda 2063: The Africa We Want."

36 Ibid., African Continental Free Trade Area (AfCFTA), http://www.au.int.

Chapter 2

1 The politics of sustainable livelihoods is about opening constructive spaces for engagement and interactions regarding identifying societal problems and organizing to solve them. For details, see Anani, K. V. (1999), "The Pursuit of Politics of Sustainable Livelihoods."

2 Harcourt, W. (1998), "Editorial- Sustainable Livelihoods and Governance: Our Role as Intermediaries," *Development* 41 (3): 3–5, www.jstor.org.

3 Amalric, F. (1998), "Sustainable Livelihoods: Entrepreneurship, Political Strategies and Governance."

4 See Rostow, W. W. (1960), *The Stages of Economic Growth: A Non-Communist Manifesto*, Cambridge: Cambridge University Press. Amin, S. (1972), "Underdevelopment and Dependency in Black Africa: Origins and Contemporary Forms," *The Journal of Modern African Studies* 10 (4): 503–24, www.jstor.org. Rodney, W. (1972), *How Europe Underdeveloped Africa*, Dar es Salaam: Tanzania Publishing House. Wallerstein, I. (1974), *The Modern World System Vol. 1*, New York: Academic Press.

5 See Hayter, T. (1981), *The Creation of World Poverty*, London: Pluto. George, S. (1988), *A Fate Worse than Debt: A Radical New Analysis of the Third World Debt Crisis*, London: Penguin. Stallings, B. (1978), *Class Conflict and Economic Development in Chile. 1958-1973*, Stanford: Stanford University Press. Rau, B. (1991), *From Feast to Famine*, London: Zed Books Ltd.

6 Fanon, F. (1963), *The Wretched of the Earth*, New York: Grove Press Inc.

7 See Chambers, R. (1983), "Rural Development: Putting the Last First," in R. Chambers (ed.), *Rural Development: Whose Knowledge Counts?*, Special issue of IDS Bulletin, University of Sussex, Institute of Development Studies, 10 (2), New York: Longman.

8 Mennasemay, M. (1982), "Political Theory, Political Science and African Development," *Canadian Journal of African Studies* 16 (2): 223–44.

9 Bobbio, N. (1989), "The Upturned Utopia," *New Left Review* 177: 37–9.

10 See Herman, E. S. and N. Chomsky (1988), *Manufacturing Consent: The Political Economy of the Mass Media*, New York: Pantheon Books.

11 Landell-Mills, P. (1992), "Governance, Cultural Change and Empowerment," 543–67.

12 See Anani, K. (1999), *The Pursuit of Politics of Sustainable Livelihoods*.

13 Harcourt, W. (1998), "Editorial- Sustainable Livelihoods and Governance: Our Role as Intermediaries," 4.

14 Landell-Mills, P. (1992), "Governance, Cultural Change and Empowerment," 543.

15 Wignaraja, P. (1984), "Towards a Theory and Practice of Rural Development," *Development* 2: 3-11, www.jstor.org.
16 Achebe, C. (1958), *Things Fall Apart*, Oxford: Heinemann.
17 Almaric, F. (1998), "Sustainable Livelihoods: Entrepreneurship, Political Strategies and Governance."
18 Wignaraja, P. (1984), "Towards a Theory and Practice of Rural Development," 7.
19 Landell-Mills, P. (1992), "Governance, Cultural Change and Empowerment," 567.
20 P. Landell-Mills, P. and I. Serageldin (1991), "Governance and the External Factor," World Bank's *Annual Conference on Development Economics*, Washington, DC, April 25–6.
21 See Dia, M. (1991), "Development and Cultural Values in Sub-Saharan Africa," *Finance and Development*, 10–13, December, Washington, DC.
22 Dzobo, N. K. (1997), *African Proverbs: The Moral Value of Ewe Proverbs. Guide to Conduct Vol. II*, vii, Accra: Bureau for Ghana Languages.
23 Ayittey, G. (1991), *Indigenous African Institutions*, New York: Transnational Publishers.
24 Olowu, D. and J. Erero (1996), "Governance of Nigeria's Villages and Cities through Indigenous Institutions," *African Rural and Urban Studies* 3 (1): 99–121, 115.
25 Owusu, M. (1992), "Democracy and Africa: A View from the Village," *The Journal of Modern African Studies* 30 (3): 369–96.
26 Lewis, W. A. (1965), *Politics in West Africa*, 69, London: Oxford University Press.
27 Ake, C. (1997), "The Unique Case of African Democracy," *Africa World Review*, November 1997–March 1998, 42–5.
28 Ndue, P. (1998), "Best Practices in Institutional Reform," *Development Policy Studies* 4 (3): 16–22.
29 Ayittey, G. (1990), "Guns, Idiots. Screams," 8.
30 Owusu, M. (1992), "Democracy and Africa: A View from the Village," 378–80.
31 Landell-Mills, P. (1992), "Governance, Cultural Change and Empowerment," 543–4.
32 Ayittey, G. (1990), "Guns, Idiots. Screams," 9.
33 Mikell, G. (1991), "Equity Issues in Ghana's Rural Development," 85–100.
34 Ibid., 89.
35 Arhin, K. (1985), *Traditional Rule in Ghana: Past and Present*.
36 Vaughan, O. (1995), "Assessing Grassroots Politics and Community Development," 501–18.
37 Ibid., 518.
38 See *The Globe and Mail, Toronto, Canada, April 16, 1998:16*, www.theglobeandmail.com.
39 Woode, S. N. (1997), *Values, Standards and Practices in Ghanaian Organizational Life*, Accra: Asempah Publishers.
40 Ibid., 1–2.
41 Ibid., 4.
42 Achebe, C. (1974), *Arrow of God*, 17, Oxford: Heinemann.

Chapter 3

1 Edinger, S. (2021), "Good Leaders Know You Can't Fight Reality."
2 Bob Marley in the legendary and powerful lyrics of "Redemption Song" urging the downtrodden listening audience to "emancipate yourself from mental slavery . . .

none but ourselves can free our minds." Excerpted from the *Uprising* album released June 10, 1980.

3 Although the alleged infamous address of Lord Thomas Babington Macauly to the British Parliament on 2 February 1835 has been proven by scholars in India to be a hoax, the sentiments expressed in the following lines are profound in terms of the manifested assault on the culture and heritage of Africa and other colonial establishments: "I do not think we would ever conquer this country unless we break the very backbone of this nation, which is her spiritual and cultural heritage and therefore I propose that we replace her old and ancient education system, her culture, for if the Africans think that all that is foreign and English is good and greater than her own, they will lose their self-esteem, their native culture and they will become what we want them, a truly dominated nation." Whoever penned these lines understood *how* to make the quest of colonialism feasible because "breaking the backbone" of the colonized societies was indeed what took place. The mental enslavement syndrome of Africa, for example, can be partly attributed to the outcome of this calculated method revealed in these lines. See Aniban Mitra, "The Infamous Macauley Speech That Never Was," February 19, 2017, www.thewire.in.

4 See Associated Press and Charetta Bellamy, "US Museums Return African Bronzes Stolen in 19th Century," *NBC News*, October 13, 2022, www.nbcnews.com.

5 See, for example, Mark Curtis in *HuffingtonPostUK, 2019* cited by Jefferey Asiedu, "LSE Controls US$1 Trillion Worth of Africa's Resources in Just 5 Commodities," www.ghanafinancialmarket.org.

6 The Rhodes Scholarship is a classic example. Established in 1903, this is an international postgraduate award to students to study at the University of Oxford. However, this was the man considered by many historians such as Basil Davidson as a plunderer who took with both hands what did not belong to him. Several publications of Basil Davidson pointed to the direction of carnage and massive plundering under the expeditions of Rhodes and peers. See "The Colonial and Post-Colonial State in Africa," https://www.jstor.org; Stelios Michalopoulos and Elias Papaioannou, "Historical Legacies and African Development," March 2019, www .voxdev.org.

7 Reference is made here to the many African leaders of the decolonization struggles, some of whom would be turning in their graves at the present conditions of the continent they valiantly fought for with their lives.

8 See Tih, F. and J. Tasamba (2019), "8 African Nations to Withdraw Cash Reserves from France," November 15, www.aa.com.fr. Samba Sylla, N. (2017), "The CFA Franc: French Monetary Imperialism in Africa," July 12, www.blogs.lse.ac.uk. Signe, L. (2019), "How the France-backed African CFA Franc Works as an Enabler and Barrier to Development," December 7, www.brookings.edu.

9 Keita, M. and A. Gladstein (2021), "Macron Isn't So Post-Colonial After All," August 3, www.foreignpolicy.com.

10 Some pertinent scholarly studies highlighting the polarized categorizations include Benjamin, N. and A. Aly Mbaye (2020), "The Informal Sector in Francophone Africa: The Other Side of Weak Structural Transformation," July 7, www.brookings.edu. Ninsin, K. (1991), *The Informal Sector in Ghana's Political Economy*, Accra: Freedom Publications. Adeleye, I. (2011), "Theorizing Human Resource Management in Africa: Beyond Cultural Relativism," *African Journal of Business Management* 5 (6): 2028–39. Izugbara, C. O., M. O. Obiyan, T. T. Degfie, and A. Bhati (2020), "Correlates of Intimate Partner Violence among Urban Women in sub-Saharan Africa," *PloS one*

15 (3): e0230508. Abor, J. and P. Quartey (2010), "Issues in SME Development in Ghana and South Africa," *International Research Journal of Finance and Economics* 39 (6): 215–28. Dungy, T. N. and H. Achidi Ndofor (2019), "A Dialogue on the Informal Economy in Africa," *Africa Journal of Management* 5 (4): 401–7. Mbaye, A., S. Golub, and F. Gueye (2020), "Formal and Informal Enterprises in Francophone Africa: Moving toward a Vibrant Private Sector," July 10, www.brookings.edu.

11 See, for example, Jackson, T. (2016), "Why the Voice of Africa's Informal Economy Should be Heard," January 21, www.theconversation.com.

12 Landell-Mills, P. (1992), "Governance, Cultural Change and Empowerment," *The Journal of Modern African Studies* 31 (4): 543–67. Signe, L. and A. Gurib-Fakim (2019), "Africa Is an Opportunity for the World: Overlooked Progress in Governance and Human Development," January 25, www.brookings.edu.

13 Muller-Crepon, C. (2021), *State Reach and Development in Africa since the 1960s: New Data and Analysis*, Cambridge: Cambridge University Press.

14 Kodero, C. U. (2020), "Review—Authoritarian Africa: Repression, Resistance and the Power of Ideas," August 30, www.e-ir.info.

15 Krawczyk, K. A. and J. Sweet-Cushman (2016), "Understanding Political Participation in West Africa: The Relationship between Good Governance and Local Citizen Engagement," *International Review of Administrative Sciences*, April 7, www.journals.sagepub.com.

16 Onyinkwa, B. (2017), "The Nature of Political Parties in Africa: What Is the Role of Political Parties in a Democratic Process?" December 14, www.papers.ssrn.com.

17 Britannica, The Editors of Encyclopaedia (2018), "African Religions," February 23, www.britannica.com. Assessed January 12. Ranger, T. O. (1986), "Religious Movements and Politics in Sub-Saharan Africa," *African Studies Review* 29 (2): 1–69, www.jstor.org.

18 James, P., J. Wardie, and J. Adams (2018), "Traditional, Complementary and Alternative Medicine use in Sub-Saharan Africa: A Systematic Review," *BMJ Publishing Group*, August 27, www.ncbi.nlm.nih.gov.

19 See Traub, L., E. Mabaya, and W. Sihlobo (2022), "What It Will Take for Africa's Agri-food Systems to Thrive," January 11, www.theconversation.com. Rukuni, M. (2002), "Africa: Addressing Growing Threats to Food Security," *The Journal of Nutrition* 132 (11): 34435–85. AFSA (2019), "Towards a Food Policy for Africa," May 29, www.afsafrica.org. Ehui, S., H. Kray, and E. Mghenyi (2020), "Policy Priorities for Achieving Food and Nutrition Security in Africa by 2030," *World Bank Blogs*, January 22. United Nations (2021), "Policy Brief: Africa and Food Security," October, www.un.org. Ghins, L. and J. Bouscarat (2021), "How Should We Understand Sustainable Food Systems in West Africa," May 13, www.blogs.lse.ac.uk. APET Secretariat (2020), "Is Africa Addressing the Food Security Dilemma Through Modern Agriculture Technologies," December 18, www.nepad.org. Staatz, J. and F. Hollinger (2016), "West African Food Systems and Changing Consumer Demands, FAO and OECD," www.wathi.org.

20 See Sommers, M. (2011), "Governance, Security and Culture: Assessing Africa's Youth Bulge," *International Journal of Conflict and Violence (IJCV)* 5 (2): 292–303. El Ouassif, A. (2021), "The Challenge of the Youth Bulge in Africa and the Middle East: Migration and the Brain Drain," January 29, www.africaportal.org. Fabricius, P. (2020), "Africa's Youth Bulge Alone Won't Deliver Economic Growth," March 19, www.issafrica.org. Mampilly, Z. (2021), "The Promise of Africa's 'Youth Bulge'," July 7, www.foreignaffairs.com. Saldinger, A. (2020), "How Can the US Help Address

Africa's Youth Bulge?," February 17, www.devex.com. Thurlow, J. and V. Mueller (2020), "Does Rural Africa Have a 'Youth Problem'?," February, www.theafricareportt.com.

21 This is a theme explored extensively throughout this book for the conceptual groundings of the blended representation principle (BRP). For a fuller account, see Greenleaf, R. K. (1998), *The Power of Servant Leadership*, ed. Larry C. Spears, Berrett-Koehler Publishers Incorporated, September.

22 Chan, S. (2017), "Africa's Elderly Leaders Get No Prizes for Hanging On," *SOAS, University of London*, March 3. The Economist (2017), "Africa's Ageing Leaders Don't Know When to Quit," December 7, www.economist.com. Ibrahim, M. and Special to CNN (2013), "Africa's Elderly Leaders 'Risk More Revolutions'," September 17, www.cnn.com.

23 Mishera, A. (2021), "Coups Are Making a Comeback in Africa, but What's Driving Them?," November 1, www.orfonline.org. Munshi, N. and A. Schipani (2021), "Failure of Democracy?: Why Are Coups on the Rise in Africa," *Financial Times*, November 14, www.ft.com. Campbell, J. (2021), "Coups Are Back in West Africa," September 8, www.cfr.org. CNN (2021), "Why Are Coups Making a Comeback in Africa?," September 13, www.cnn.com; Loanes, E. (2022), "How to Understand the Recent Coups in Africa," February 5, www.vox.com.

24 Some examples of graduate attitudes are contained in Nwagwu, N. A. (1976), "African Students' Attitudes Towards School Teaching as a Career," *Educational Review* 29 (1): 47–57. Silvey, J. (1969), "Unwillingly from School: The Occupational Attitudes of Secondary School Leavers in Uganda," *Unemployment Research in Africa* 2 (1): 2–16, www.jstor.org/stable/43390826.

25 Woode, S. N. (1997), *Values, Standards and Practices in Ghanaian Organizational Life*, Accra: Asempah Publishers.

26 This is a scheme describing practices in public office popularized by the Ghanaian Supreme Court justice Jones Dotse during the NPP election petition trial of 2012. For related comments on the scheme, see Badu, K. (2020), "Ghana: Why Did an Eminent JSC Label NDC 'Create, Loot and Share?'," October 13, www.ghanaweb.com. Darko, K. (2021), "Empower Citizenry, Not Create-Loot-and-Share Schemes Disguised as Investments—Sam Jonah," April 25, www.myjoyonline.com. MyNewsGh (2021), "Create, Loot & Share: How Weeks Old Company Won GHc518 Million Govt. Laptop Contract on Sole-Sourcing," November 21, www.mynewsgh.com. Mikdad, M. (2013), "A Modest Proposal: Create! Loot! Share!," December 5, www.modernghana.com.

27 See Mbaku, J. M. (1996), "Bureaucratic Corruption in Africa: The Futility of Cleanups," 16 (1), www.dlib.indiana.edu; Public Service Commission (2008), "Report on the Management of Gifts in the Public Service—South Africa," March, www.gov.za. Levy, B. Hirsch, V. Naidoo, and M. Nxele (2021), "When Strong Institutions and Massive Inequalities Collide," March 18, www.carnegieendowment.org.

28 See Boldexpert (2021), "Rethinking Higher Education in Africa—21st Century Skills," February 4, www.bold.expert.com. Watkins, K. (2013), "Too Little Access, Not Enough Learning: Africa's Twin Deficit in Education," January 16, www.brookings.edu. Malatji, K. (2016), "Moving Away from Rote Learning in the University Classroom: The Use of Cooperative Learning to Maximize Students' Critical Thinking in a Rural University of South Africa," *Journal of Communication* 7 (1): 34–42, July.

29 See Ninsin, K. (1991), *The Informal Sector in Ghana's Political Economy*.

30 "The term big man syndrome within the context of political science refers to corrupt, autocratic and often totalitarian rule of countries by a single person," www.en.m

.wikipedia.org. See also reference to "accumulating wealth and business opportunities are tied to controlling the state, Houeland, C. and S. Jacobs (2018), "The 'Big Man' Syndrome in Africa," March 11, www.africascountry.com.

31 See Signe, L. (2018), "Accountability and Demand for Democracy Drive Leadership Changes in Africa," June14, www.brookings.edu. Bratton, M. and C. Logan (2006), "Voters But Not Yet Citizens: The Weak Demand for Political Accountability in Africa's Unclaimed Democracies," *Working Paper* No.63, September, www.afrobarometer.org. Kessy, A. (2020), "The Demand and Supply Sides of Accountability in Local Government Authorities in Tanzania," *Public Integrity* 22 (1): 1–20, March, www.researchgate.net.

32 Fredua-Kwarteng, E. (2020), "In Africa, University Proliferation Is Not an Unqualified Good," April 27, www.timeshighereducation.com. Nsereko, N. (2018), "Proliferation of University Institutions in Africa: Student Academic Life and Mental Health Challenges," October 3, www.researchgate.net.

33 See Diane, A. (2011), "Education in Africa Is Failing Its People," August 9, www.newafricanmagazine.com. Khwaja, M. (2014), "Jack in the Box: The Failure of Education in Sub-Saharan Africa," September 25, www.fairobserver.com.

34 Collin, D., M. Kirchberger, and D. Lagakos (2017), "Measuring Living Standards in African Cities and Rural Areas," October 2, www.voxdev.org. Campbell, J. (2018), "Rural Poverty in Sub-Saharan Africa," December 28, www.cfr.org. Gastineau, B. and V. Golaz (2016), "Being Young in Rural Africa," *Afrique Contemporaine* 259 (3): 9–22, www.cairn-int.info. Ogunkola, I., Y. Adebisi, and D. E. Lucero-Prisno (2021), "Rural Communities in Africa Should Not be Forgotten in Responses to COVID-19," *The International Journal of Health and Management*, July 10, www.ncbi.nim.nih.gov.

35 See Adam, S., D. Adom, and A. Bediako (2016), "The Major Factors That Influence Basic School Dropout in Rural Ghana," *Journal of Education and Practice* 7 (28): 1–8; Inoue, K. (2015), "Why Do Sub-Saharan African Youth Drop Out of School?," April, www.elibrary.worldbank.org. The World Bank (2015), "Half of Youth in Sub-Saharan Africa Are Out of School," July 15, www.worldbank.org.

36 See Atta Mills, C. (2018), "Politics, Policy, and Implementation: 'The Ghanaian Paradox'," July 18, www.brookings.edu.

37 This is an expression associated with the perennially high cost of living associated with all the economies of Africa.

38 See Zwane, T. (2021), "Jobless Growth Stymies SA," December 5, City Press, www.news24.com; Smit, S. (2021), "GDP Stats: Economy Grows, But Not Enough to Secure Jobs and Long Term Recovery," September 7, www.mg.co.za.

39 The African Continental Free Trade Area (AfCFTA) is the strategic framework for delivering on Africa's goal for inclusive and sustainable development, www.au.int.

40 The Punch (2021), "Nothing to Celebrate at 61, Poverty, Insecurity, Poor Leadership Still Thrive—Nigerians Living Abroad," October 2.

41 See, for example, Kauppi, N. and M. Madsen (2013), "Transnational Power Elite: The New Professionals of Governance, Law and Security," *Transnational Power Elites*, 12–26, www.taylorfrancis.com. Graz, J.-C. (2003), "How Powerful Are Transnational Elite Clubs? The Social Myth of the World Economic Forum," *New Political Economy* 8 (3): 321–40. Koh, A. and J. Kenway (2012), "Cultivating National Leaders in an Elite School: Deploying the Transnational in the National Interest," *International Studies in Sociology of Education* 22 (4): 333–51. Aviles, W. (2008), "US Intervention in Columbia: The Role of Transnational Relations," *Bulletin of Latin American Research* 27 (3): 410–29.

42 Cross, H. (2015), "Divisive Democracy and Popular Struggle in Africa," *Review of African Political Economy* 42 (143): 1–6; Suleiman, M. and S. Maiangwa (2021), "History of Divisive Ethnic Identities Shows It's Time: Nigeria Admits Its Role in Enforcing Them," February 24, www.theconversation.com. DW Africa (2017), "In Kenya Politics Split on Ethnic Divide," October 26, www.amp.dw.com. Lancaster, A. (2012), "The Divisive Nature of Ethnicity in Ugandan Politics, Before and After Independence," May 25, www.e-ir.info.

43 Reference to the Washington-based multilateral agencies, the World Bank Group and the International Monetary Fund (IMF).

44 Malpass, D. (2021), "World Bank Chief Calls for Comprehensive Debt Relief for Poor Countries," October 11, www.moneycontrol.com.

45 See Fitzgibbon, W. and D. Cenziper (2021), "American Lawmakers Denounce South Dakota, Other US States as Hubs for Financial Secrecy," *Pandora Papers*, December 8, www.icij.org.

46 Culled from Bob Marley and the Wailers (1983), "Lyrics of 'Stiff-Necked Fools,'" *Confrontation Album*.

47 See Beckman, B. and G. Adeoti, eds. (2006), *Pretensions and Resistance in African Politics (Africa in the New Millennium*, October 1, www.bloomsbury.com.

48 See Hayes, A. (2020), *Comparative Advantage*, updated October 26, www .investopedia.com.

49 Nef, J. (1989), "Development Processes: Contradictions Between Theory and Practice," *Worldscape* 3 (1): 3–4.

50 See Tih, F. and J. Tasamba (2019), "8 African Nations to Withdraw Cash Reserves from France," November 15, www.aa.com.fr. Sylla, N. (2017), "The CFA Franc: French Monetary Imperialism in Africa," July 12, www.blogs.lse.ac.uk. Signe, L. (2019), "How the France-backed African CFA Franc Works as an Enabler and Barrier to Development," December 7, www.brookings.edu.

51 Business Financial Times (2021), "Cedi Sinks Further Against Dollar Despite Strong Buffers," October 11, www.mobile.ghanaweb.com.

52 Park, A. and S. Vercillo (2021), "African Agriculture without African Farmers," October 9, www.Aljazeera.com.

53 See, for example, World Vision (2021), "Seven Million People at Risk of Starvation across Six Countries in East Africa,", April 1, Nairobi, www.worldvision.org.

Chapter 4

1 See Gumede, V. (2016), "Leadership for Africa's Development: Revisiting Indigenous African Leadership and Setting the Agenda for Political Leadership," *Journal of Black Studies*, November 21, www.journals.sagepub.com. Acheng, R. (2014), "A Moral Consciousness: A Leadership Approach for a New Africa?," *Journal of African Union Studies* 3: 115–32. Asante, M. (2017), *An Afrocentric Manifesto: Toward an African Renaissance*, Cambridge: Polity Press. Wa Thiong'o, N. (1993), *Moving the Center: The Struggle for Cultural Freedoms*, London: James Curry. de Vries, D. (2020), "A Classical Grounded Theory Study of How Heads of State in Africa Lead: A New Theory of Political Leadership," Eastern University ProQuest Dissertations Publishing Well-Grounded, Leadership Development, www.well-grounded.org. Bongila, J.-P. K. (2012), "Grounding Leadership Ethics in African Diaspora and Election Rights," *Journal of Third World Studies* 29 (1): 263–86.

2   See Leatt, J., T. Kneifel, and K. Numberger (1987), "Contending Ideologies in South
    Africa," *International Journal on World Peace* 4 (2): 181–4. McCain, J. A. (1975),
    "Ideology in Africa: Some Perceptual Types," *African Studies Review* 18 (1): 61–87.
    Hendrickson, J. and H. Zaki (2013), "Modern African Ideologies," in M. Freeden and
    M. Stears (eds.), *The Oxford Handbook of Political Ideologies Online*, December, www
    .oxfordhandbooks.com.
3   Chulu, J. (2015), "Africa Is Largely Influenced by Foreign Culture Especially Western
    Culture. Has Africa Now Sacrificed Her Own Culture on the Altar of Expediency?,"
    October 13, www.papers.ssrn.com.
4   Reference is made here to the African Union, Agenda 2063—the blueprint and
    masterplan for transforming Africa into the global powerhouse of the future.
5   See Sibani, C. M. (2016), "Impact of Western Culture on Traditional African Society:
    Problems and Prospects," *Journal of Religion and Human Relations* 10 (1), www.ajol
    .info. Chulu, J. (2015), "Africa Is Largely Influenced by Foreign Culture Especially
    Western Culture."
6   See Felter, C. (2021), "Africa's 'Leaders for Life,'" July 30, www.cfr.org. McClean, R.
    (2020), "With Elections Ahead, Some African Presidents Try Engineering Results,"
    October 11, www.nytimes.com. Siegle, J. and C. Cook (2020), "Assessing Africa's
    2020 Elections," November 3, www.africacenter.org.
7   See Angai, C. K. (2016), "West Africa's 'Promise' Trackers Hold Politicians to Their
    Word," November 4, www.openfoundations.org. Turi, G. C. (2020), "Kenyan Voters
    Need Leaders Focused on Equity and Inclusivity," October 6, www.issafrica.org;
    Managa, A. (2012), "Unfulfilled Promises and Their Consequences: A Reflection on
    Local Government Performance and the Critical Issue of Poor Service Delivery in
    South Africa," May 1, www.africaportal.org.
8   Hayzlett, J. (2019), "4 Principles of Servant Leadership," October 16, www
    .entrepreneur.com.
9   Athal, K. (2021), "Why Servant Leadership Is Becoming the Leadership Style of the
    Future," October 2, www.entrepreneur.com.
10 See Chihuri, S. (2014), "Sycophantic Praises and Bootlicking: The Curse of African
    Politics," March 6, www.newzimbabew.com. Thomas, A. R. (2018), "When Leaders
    Tolerate Sycophants—The Nation Perishes," November 18, www.thesierraleonet
    elegraph.com. Daily Champion Lagos, Nigeria (2002), "Sycophancy Is an Art," May
    28, www.allafrica.com. Ojiakor, I. C. (2012), "Sycophancy and Objective Journalism,"
    Advances in Applied Sociology 2 (3): 159–66.
11 Atta Mills, C. (2018), "Politics, Policy, and Implementation."
12 Athal (2021), "Why Servant Leadership Is Becoming the Leadership Style of the
    Future."
13 See Signe, L. (2018), "Accountable Leadership: The Key to Africa's Successful
    Transformation," January 5, www.brookings.edu.
14 A perceptive analogy made by Chinua Achebe in his numerous literary works. For
    details, see Wikipedia profile, www.en.m.wikipedia.org;
15 See Ezra (2021), "Where Sycophancy Thrives, Innovation Dies," June 8, www
    .helloezra.com.
16 See Adams, S. and B. Mengistu (2008), "The Political Economy of Privatization
    in Sub-Saharan Africa," *Social Science Quarterly* 89 (1): 78–94. Nellis J. (2005),
    "Privatization in Africa: What Has Happened? What Is to Be Done?," January, www
    .researchgate.net. Bennell, P. (1997), "Privatization in Sub-Saharan Africa: Progress
    and Prospects during the 1990s," *World Development* 25 (11): 1785–801, November.

17 Lodge, T. (1998), "Political Corruption in South Africa," *African Affairs* 97 (387): 157–87. Utas, M. (2012), "African Conflicts and Informal Power: Big Men and Networks," *DiVA Portal*, www.uu.diva-portal.org. United Nations (2001), *Public Service Ethics in Africa, Volume 1*, New York, www.administration.un.org. OECD (2005), "Managing Conflict of Interest in the Public Sector," www.oecd.org.

18 A play on the commonly referenced phrase "Sword of Damocles," which is "an allusion to the imminent and ever-present peril faced by those in positions of power." For details, see www.en.m.wikipedia.org.

19 Athal (2021), "Why Servant Leadership Is Becoming the Leadership Style of the Future."

20 Ibid.

21 See Opalo, K. (2021), "It's Time to Democratize Public Finance Management Systems in African States," *Finance and Development Special Series*, IMF, www.imf.org. Basheka, B. C. and K. Phago (2014), "What Constrains Effective Public Financial Management in African Democracies?," *Africa Insight* 43, no. 4 (March): 1–14. Peterson, S. (2011), "Reforming Public Financial Management in Africa," January 11, www.hks.harvard.edu. Andrews, M. (2010), "How Far Have Public Financial Management Reforms Come in Africa," *HKS Faculty Research Working Paper Series, John F; Kennedy School of Government, Harvard University*. PEFA 2016 Framework, Public Expenditure and Financial Accountability, www.pefa.org.

22 See World Bank, Country Assistance Strategy—World Bank Group, www.worldbank .org.

23 For details, see PEFA 2016 Framework, Public Expenditure and Financial Accountability, www.pefa.org.

24 World Bank, Country Assistance Strategy—World Bank Group.

25 Corrigen, C. C. (2014), "Breaking the Resource Curse: Transparency in the Natural Resource Sector and the Extractive Industries Transparency Initiative," *Resources Policy* 40: 17–30.

26 Ejiogu, A., C. Ejiogu, and A. Ambituuni (2019), "The Dark Side of Transparency: Does the Nigeria Extractive Industries Transparency Initiative Help or Hinder Accountability and Corruption Control?," *The British Accounting Review* 51 (5): 100811.

27 Van Alstine, J. (2017), "Critical Reflections on 15 Years of the Extractive Industries Transparency Initiative—EITI," *The Extractive Industries and Society* 4 (4): 766–70.

28 For details on investment woes, see Bawelle, E. B. G. (2022), "Ghana: Is the Preferred Investment Destination Becoming Africa's Fading Star?," January 18, www .thefricareport.com.

29 Hayzlett, J. (2019), "4 Principles of Servant Leadership."

30 See Chikerema, A. F. and O. Nzewi (2020), "Succession Politics and State Administration in Africa: The Case of Zimbabwe," www.eisa.org; Lodge, T. (2013), "Alternation and Leadership Succession in African Democracies," *Irish Studies in International Affairs* 24 (1): 21–40. Ighobor, K. (2013), "Politics of Succession: Coping When Leaders Die," *Africa Renewal*, January, www.un.org.

31 See Alemazung, A. (2011), "Leadership Flaws and Fallibilities Impacting Democratization Processes, Governance and Functional Statehood in Africa," *African Journal of Political Science and International Relations* 5 (1): 30–41. van Wyk, J.-A. (2007), "Political Leaders in Africa: Presidents, Patrons or Profiteers?," *Accord*, 2 (1): 1–38. Songwe, V. (2013), "The Mandela Rule—A Legacy to African Leaders," December 6, www.brookings.edu. Sackey, F. G. (2021), "Impact of African Leaders'

Characteristics and Regime Transitions on Economic Growth in Africa: A Dynamic Model Approach," *Social Sciences and Humanities Open, 4* (1): 1–10.

32   See Bratton, M. and C. Logan (2006), "Voters But Not Yet Citizens," Afrobarometer Working Paper 63, www.afrobarometer.org. Thompson, L. (2014), "Examining Government and Public Officials' Accountability and Responsiveness," *Afrobarometer Briefing Papers* 13, www.afrobarometer.org. Cho, W. (2010), "Citizens' Perceptions of Government Responsiveness in Africa: Do Electoral Systems and Ethnic Diversity Matter?," *Comparative Political Studies*, June 28, www.journals .sagepub.com.

33   ACCA (2020), "New Report, Accountability in Africa," December 10, www.account abilitycounsel.org. Signe, L. (2018), "Accountability and Demand for Democracy Drive Leadership Changes in Africa." McNeil, M. (2010), "Demanding Good Governance: Lessons from Social Accountability Initiatives in Africa," *Open Knowledge Depository*, www.worldbank.org.

34   See Adibe, C. E. (2020), "Accountability in Africa and the International Community," in *Social Research, From Impunity to Accountability in Africa's Development in the 21st Century* 77 (4): 1241–80, www.jstor.org.

35   Chirwa, D. M. and L. Nijzink, eds. (2012), *Accountable Government in Africa: Perspectives from Public Law and Political Studies*, United Nations University, www .unu.edu.

36   Ibid.

37   See Baker, B. (2004), "Twilight of Impunity for Africa's Presidential Criminals," *Third World Quarterly* 25 (8): 1487–99, www.jstor.org; Amnesty International (2015), "Impunity vs Immunity: Africa and the ICC," June 24, www.amnesty.org. Crisis Group (2009), "The Politics of Ending Impunity," *Aegis Trust*, February, www .crisisgroup.org.

38   Luna, J. (2015), "Constituency Service in Ghana—Scholars at Harvard," August 20, www.scholar.harvard.edu. Economist (2021), "Pricey Politics: Why Does It Cost So Much to be an African MP?," February 27, www.economist.com. Davies, J. (2009), "Parliamentarians and Corruption in Africa: The Challenge of Leadership and the Practice of Politics," *The Parliamentary Centre, Ottawa*.

39   Chirwa, D. M. and L. Nijzink, eds. (2012), "Accountable Government in Africa."

40   Cross, H. (2015), "Divisive Democracy and Popular Struggle in Africa." Olewe, D. (2019), "Is Africa Going Backwards on Democracy?," *BBC News*, February 22, www .bbc.com. Boone, C. (2009), "Electoral Populism Where Property Rights Are Weak: Land Politics," *Contemporary Sub-Saharan Africa* 41 (2): 183–201, www.jstor.org.

41   See Lauer, H. (2007), "Depreciating African Political Culture," *Journal of Black Studies* 38 (2): 288–307, www.jstor.org. Ani, K. (2013), "Globalization and Its Impact on African Political Culture," *World Affairs: The Journal of International Issues* 17 (2): 44–61, www.jstor.org.

42   International Peace Institute (IPI) (2011), "Elections in Africa: Challenges and Opportunities," September, www.ipinst.org. Lindberg, S. I. (2006), "The Surprising Significance of African Elections," *GSDRC Applied Knowledge Series*, www.gsdrc.org.

43   See Moosa, F. (2018), "Understanding the 'Spirit, Purport and Objects' of South Africa's Bill of Rights," *Journal of Forensic Legal & Investigative Sciences, Herald*, December 26, www.heraldopenacess.us. Nisihara, H. N. (2001), "The Significance of Constitutional Values," www.ajol.info.

44   Resnick, D. and D. Casale (2011), "The Political Participation of Africa's Youth: Turnout, Partisanship Protest," www.gsdrc.org.

45 Afrobarometer (2021), "Women's Political Participation," March 18, www.idea.int.

46 Isaksson, A.-S. (2014), "Political Participation in Africa: The Role of Individual Resources," *Electoral Studies* 34: 244–60, June, www.sciencedirect.com.

47 Mbaku, J. M. (2021), "Entrenching Democracy in African Countries: Policy Imperatives for Leaders in 2021," March 18, www.brookings.edu.

48 Campbell, J. and N. Quinn (2021), "What Is Happening to Democracy in Africa?."

49 Gyimah-Boadi, E. (2021), "Good Governance: Building Trust between People and Their Leaders," January 21, www.brookings.edu.

50 Ibid.

51 Al Jazeera Staff (2021), October 12, www.aljazeera.com.

52 See Collins, T. (2022), "Economic Outlook 2022: Africa Faces Rickety Rebound," *African Business*, January 10, www.african.business. African Development Bank (2021), "African Economic Outlook 2021, From Debt Resolution to Growth: The Road Ahead for Africa," www.afdb.org. Deloitte Insights (2021), "Africa Economic Outlook," December 2, www.deloitte.com.

53 Majambere, S. (2021), "Ending Malaria in Africa Needs to Focus on Poverty: Quick Fixes Won't Cut It," October 14, www.theconversation.com.

54 Ibid.

55 World Bank (2021), "Ensuring a Strong Recovery for Developing Countries," October 15, www.worldbank.org.

56 Ibid.

57 See Zulu, A. (2020), "Prosperity Gospel: Excusing Poverty and Its True Causes in Africa," January13, www.premiumtimesng.com.

58 See Collins, T. (2022), "Economic Outlook 2022"; International Monetary Fund (IMF) (2022), "Tackling the Global Food Crisis: Impact, Policy Response and the Role of IMF," September 29, Washington, DC,, 1–98.

59 Pandey, K. (2021), "Sub-Saharan Africa's Debt Burden Increased to Record $702 Billion in 2020—Highest in a Decade," October 14, www.downtoearth.org.in.

60 Ibid.

61 See The Infrastructure Consortium for Africa (ICA), ICT Financing Needs and Trends, www.icafrica.org. David, O. O. and W. Grobler (2020), "Information and Communication Technology Penetration Level as an Impetus for Economic Growth in Africa," *Economic Research* 33 (1): 1394–418, May 2, www.tandfonline .com.

62 Faria, J. (2021), "Internet Penetration Rate in Africa 2021 by Region," *Statista*, March 12, www.statista.com.

63 Cropley, E. (2021), "Africa's Digital Payments Race Becomes a Scramble," *Reuters*, May 5, www.reuters.com. Parekh, N. and A. Hare (2020), "The Rise of Mobile Money in sub-Saharan Africa: Has This Digital Technology Lived Up to Its Promises?," *J-PAL*, October 22, www.povertyactionlab.org.

64 Gbadegesin, J. and L. Marais (2020), "The State of Housing Policy Research in Africa," *International Journal of Housing Policy Research* 20 (4): 474–90, www .tandfonline.com. Kroeker-Falconi, C., R. C. Kettle, ACT-es, G. Sumeghy, ed. (2021), "Compendium of Best Practices for Housing in Africa," February, www.habitat.org.

65 Neophytou, N. (2021), "'okayafrica,' Quoting Actor, H. Gerima on the Need for African Filmmakers to Reflect on a Continent That Lost Its Mind," October 4, www .okayafrica.com.

66 The Punch (2021), "Nothing to Celebrate at 61."

67 Ibid.

Chapter 5

1   Diop, M. (2022), "Africa's Pandemic Recovery Requires Investments that Build the Foundation for the Region's Future."

2   See Haque, S. (2017), "Greatness of a Nation," May 26, www.fredericknewspost .com. Ryan, P. H. (2019), "What Is National Greatness," Winter, www.nationalaffairs .com.

3   For details, see Clementi, J. (2021), "Greatness Is Not Primarily a Matter of Circumstances," January 9, www.joeclementi.com. Ng, J. (2021), "What Is Greatness? (What You Must Comprehend)," January 20, www.worldscientific.com.

4   See Finch, A. M. (2021), "How Belongingness Can Drive Business Success," August 18, www.unleash.ai. Baldoni, J. (2017), "Fostering the Sense of Belonging Promotes Success," January 22, www.forbes.com.

5   Carr, E. W., A. Reece, G. R. Kellerman, and A. Robichaux, (2019), "The Value of Belonging at Work," December 16, www.hbr.org. Mellon, D., Y. V. Durme, and M. Hauptmann (2020), "Belonging: From Comfort to Connection to Contribution," May 15, www.deloitte.com. Wiles, J. (2020), "Build a Sense of Belonging in the Workplace," August 4, www.gartner,com.

6   See Brown, C. (2014), "If You Want Your Brand to Succeed, Make It Aspirational, Not Inspirational," December 4, www.fastcompany.com.

7   Pew Research Center (2021), "Beliefs & Practices," December 21, www .pewresearchcenter.org. Zed, R. (2017), "Faith Forum: What Should be the Role of Religion in Society?," February 24, www.amp.rgj.com.

8   Scott, R. G. "The Transforming Power of Faith and Character," www .churchofjesuschrist.org. Lickonia, T. (2000), "A Comprehensive Approach to Character Building in Catholic Schools," *Catholic Education: A Journal of Inquiry and Practice* 4 (2): 259–71.

9   Weber, M. (1864–1920) affirmed this notion in his Protestant Ethic Thesis, where he argued that "Protestantism was the seedbed of character traits and values that under-girded modern capitalism." For details, see www.eh.net.

10 Zulu, A. (2020), "Prosperity Gospel: Excusing Poverty and Its True Causes in Africa."

11 See Anani, K. V. (1999), "The Pursuit of Politics of Sustainable Livelihoods."

12 Kolko, J. (1988), *Restructuring the World Economy*, New York: Pantheon Books.

13 See Signe, L. and A. Gurib-Fakim (2019), "Africa Is an Opportunity for the World." Agyeman, O. (1988), "Setbacks to Political Institutionalization by Praetorianism in Africa," *The Journal of Modern African Studies* 26 (3): 403–35, www.jstor.org.

14 Observations here double down, reinforce, and expand earlier analysis on the fundamentals of the leadership and governance conundrum in the previous chapter.

15 Prah, K. K. "Multi-Party Democracy and Its Relevance in Africa," *Center for Advanced Studies of African Societies*, www.elections.org.za. Makinda, S. M. (1996), "Democracy and Multi-Party Politics in Africa," *The Journal of Modern African Studies* 34 (4): 555–73, www.jstor.org.

16 Olewe, D. (2019), "Is Africa Going Backwards on Democracy?," *BBC News*, February 22, www.bbc.com.

17 Wignaraja, P. (1998), "Revisiting the Grassroots Initiatives and Strategies Program (GRIS) of the Society for International Development," *Development* 41 (3): 6–11, www.jstor.org.

18 Afrobarometer (2018), "Africans Increasingly Support Multiparty Democracy, but Trust in Political Parties Remains Low," June 14, www.afrobarometer.org.

19 Adibe, C. E. (2020), "Accountability in Africa and the International Community." IDEA Policy Brief (2016), "Democratic Accountability in Service Delivery—Lessons from Africa," *International IDEA*, www.idea.int. Bratton, M. (2006), "Voters but Not Yet Citizens."

20 For example, during the 2020–21 CAR general elections held on December 27, 2020, turnout among registered voters was 76.3 percent. For details, see Wikipedia, www.enm.wikipedia.org.

21 See the themes of existing realities an African must battle with at the global marketplace in Chapter 2. African Studies Center (2016), "African Constitutions," *Leiden,* October 14, www.ascleiden.nl.

22 Ndulo, M. (2019), "Constitutions and Constitutional Reforms in African Politics," July 29, www.oxfordre.com.

23 See Bawelle, E. B. G. (2022), "Ghana: Is the Preferred Investment Destination Becoming Africa's Fading Star?." Ezra (2021), "Where Sycophancy Thrives, Innovation Dies."

24 See Diop, M. B. (2021), "The Role of African Elites in West African Countries," July 7, www.afropolicy.com. Mbeki, M. (2021), "How South Africa's Elites Are Stunting the Economy and Democracy," July 29, www.theafricareport.com.

25 See World Bank (2012), "Africa Can Feed Itself, Earn Billions and Avoid Food Crises by Unblocking Regional Food Trade" for insights on Africa's food situation, October 24, www.worldbank.org.

26 See Aremu, A. O. (2022), "Africa Is a Treasure Trove of Medicinal Plants: Here are Seven That Are Popular," July 13, www.thisisafrica.me.

27 Sindiga, I. (1994), "Indigenous (Medical) Knowledge of the Masai," *Indigenous Knowledge Monitor* 2 (1), www.jstor.com. Riley, M. (1993), "Indigenous Resources in a Ghanaian Town: Potential for Health Education," *The Howard Journal of Communications* 4 (3): 249–64.

28 Africa Developer Ecosystem, 2021.

29 See Onukwue, A. (2022), "Microsoft Is Leading Big Tech's Push to Relocate African Developers to North America."

30 Zulu, A. (2020), "Prosperity Gospel: Excusing Poverty and Its True Causes in Africa."

31 WhatsApp post. Author unknown.

32 Diop, M. (2022), "Africa's Pandemic Recovery Requires Investments That Build the Foundation for the Region's Future."

33 Ibid.

Chapter 6

1 The Africa Leadership Forum is a nonprofit organization involved in leadership development, capacity building, enterprise development, and economic empowerment. For details, see www.africaleadership.org.

2 The Global Knowledge Partnership (GKP) is the world's first multi-stakeholder network geared at promoting innovation and advancement in knowledge and ICT for development. See https://m.facebook.com.

3   For details, see www.imf.org; and www.worldbank.org.

4   See Campbell, J. and N. Quinn (2021), "What Is Happening to Democracy in Africa?."

5   Ibid.

6   The Young African Leadership Initiative is supposedly the United States' significant effort to invest in the next generation of African leaders. For details, see www.yali .state.gov.

7   See Baloyi, T. B. (2016), "The Role of Traditional Leadership in Local Government," A research report submitted to the Faculty of Commerce, Law and Management, *University of Witwatersrand* in partial fulfilment of the requirement for the Master of Management in the Field of Public Management and Development degree, January.

8   See Constitute Project (2021), "Ghana's Constitution of 1992 with Amendments through 1996," August 26, www.constituteproject.org.

9   Pulse (2019), "Referendum: Otumfuo Slams Neglect of Chiefs in Local Government Reforms," November 23.

10 Ghana News Agency (2019), "Okyenhene Calls for Inclusion of Chiefs in Local Governance," December 4.

11 Graphic Online (2019), "What Nana SKB Asante told National House of Chiefs on December 17 Referendum," January 19.

12 The theme of involving traditional leadership more in the broader development of the country and the continent has been central to the reign of Togbe Afede XIV, paramount chief of Ho Asogli State and the immediate past president of the Ghana National House of Chiefs, 2016–20.

13 Ghanaweb (2022), "Togbe Afede XIV to Establish African Traditional Leadership Institute."

14 See Asokorehene, Graphic Online (2019), "What Nana SKB Asante Told National House of Chiefs on December 17 Referendum."

15 Ibid.

16 Ibid.

17 As noted earlier, the designation of "district assemblies" refers to the present context of Ghana. Usually, there are four main types of local government structures— counties, municipalities, (cities and towns), special districts, and school districts. Although varied labels and designations of these structures exist across the continent, they basically refer and mean the same structural arrangements of local government anywhere in the world. For details, see The Cities Alliance (2013), *Assessing the Institutional Environment of Local Governments in Africa, United Cities and Local Governments of Africa.*

18 See Ebert, R. (2022), "The Woman King Movie Review and Film Summary."

19 For example, shared responsibility, nonpartisan elections of the mayors, specific sector responsibility assigned to traditional authorities.

20 Chiefs would continue to have traditional lifelong tenure on respective stools but would have term limitations at the DAs with the conferred title of Chief Emeritus for those who participated and completed tenures.

21 See Atuoye, K. N. and F. S. Odame (2013), "Queenmother Concept in the Upper West Region of Ghana: Is This Advancement or an Emerging Conflict with Tradition in a Patriarchal Society?," *European Scientific Journal* 9 (35), December, www.eujournal.org.

22 See Ghanaweb (2022), "Asantehemaa Stops Election of New Kumasi City Market Leaders," October 14, www.ghanaweb.com.

Chapter 7

1   See, for example, Ghanaweb (2022), "Odenho Kwafo Akoto III Calls for Reforms to Reclaim Respect for Chieftaincy Institution," October 21, www.ghanaweb.com.
2   See Brookings Africa Growth Initiative, Foresight Africa (2022).
3   Ayee, J. A. (2016), "Ghana Continues to be a Beacon for Democracy in Africa," December 12, www.blogs.lse.ac.uk. Cheeseman, N. (2019), "Democracy in Africa: Success Stories That Have Defied Odds," July 28, www.theconversation.com. Obeng-Akrofi, E. I. (2020), "Will Ghana Shine Once More as a Beacon of Democracy in Africa," April 12, www.blogging.africa. Mohammad, S. (2019), "A Beacon of Democracy in Africa, Ghana's Campaign: An Election That Western Nations Would Envy?," January 14, www.macleans.ca.
4   This observation revealed earlier in critical analysis of local governance subperformance in Ghana is restated here to buttress the seriousness of the situation.
5   See in the case of Ghana, Ghanaweb (2022), "Mahama, Godfried Dame Face Off in Stiff Fight," September 13, www.ghanaweb.com.
6   Faucon, B., S. Said, and J. Parkinson (2021), "Military Coups in Africa at Highest Level since End of Colonialism," *Wall Street Journal*, November 3.
7   See Ndaba, V. (2021), "Sub-Saharan Africa to See Mixed Economic Recovery into 2022," *Reuters*, October 27. Fitch Ratings (2021), "Ghana to Opt for IMF Financing If Liquidity Strains Mounts," November 2, www.norvanreports.com.
8   See Fredua-Kwarteng, E. (2020), "In Africa, University Proliferation Is Not an Unqualified Good." Nsereko, N. D. (2018), "Proliferation of University Institutions in Africa: Student Academic Life and Mental Health Challenges," *European Journal of Counselling Theory, Research and Practice* 2 (4): 1–6. Akinwumi, F. S. (2010), "Proliferation of Higher Education in Nigeria; Implications for Quality Education," June, www.researchgate.net.
9   The Democratic Alliance (2018), "#Healthcarecollapse: Public Hospitals Have Become a Death-Trap for the Poor. Time for Action," June, www.da.org.za. Sanders, D. M., C. Todd, and M. Chopra (2005), "Confronting Africa's Health Crisis: More of the Same Will Not be Enough," www.ncbi.nim.nih.gov. United Nations (2016), "Health Care Systems: Time for a Rethink," *Africa Renewal* 30 (10), December 2016–March 2017, www.un.org. Pulse (2017), "Have Ghana's Foremost Hospitals Become Death Traps?," *Business Insider Africa*, February 15, www.pulse.com.gh.
10 See Zulu, A. (2020), "Prosperity Gospel: Excusing Poverty and Its True Causes in Africa."
11 See Institute of Local Government Studies (ILGS) and Friedrich Ebert Stiftung (2016), "A Guide to District Assemblies in Ghana."
12 Woode, S. N. (1997), *Values, Standards and Practices in Ghanaian Organizational Life.*
13 See Hurndall, S. (2021), "Transformational Leadership and Its Benefits to Your Business," November, www.breathehr.com. Patterson, R. (2021), "9 Reasons to Invest in Transformational Leadership," March 25, www.lifeintelligence.io. LeHane, M. (2020), '4 Characteristics of Transformational Leadership," December 9, www.mileslehane.com. Yukl, G. (1999), "An Evaluation of Conceptual Weaknesses in Transformational and Charismatic Leadership Theories," *Leadership Quarterly* 10: 285–305. Langston University, *Transformational Leadership—Booklet*, www.langston.edu. Smarp Blogs (2020), "Transformational Leadership: The Secret to Organizational Success," November 17, www.blog.smarp.com.

14 Bass, B. and R. E. Riggio (1998), "Transformational Leadership: A Comprehensive Review of Theory," www.goodreads.com. Zeinab, N. B., H. M. Khorasan, and F. A. Eskandani (2019), "Investigating the Effect of Transformational Leadership on Employees' Communicational Performance," *Revista Orbis* 14 (42): 40–52.

15 Paterson, R. (2021), "9 Reasons to Invest in Transformational Leadership."

16 Ibid.

17 Greenleaf, R. (2002), *Servant Leadership: A Journey into the Nature of Legitimate Power and Greatness (25th anniversary ed.)*, Paulist Press. Hesse, H. (2003), *The Journey to the East (H. Rosen Translations)*, Picador (original work published 1932).

18 Maglione, J. L. and K. Neville (2021), "Servant Leadership and Spirituality Among Undergraduate and Graduate Nursing Students," *Journal of Religion and Health* 60: 4435–45.

19 Ibid.

20 Ficht, A. and M. Ponton (2015), "Identifying Primary Characteristics of Servant Leadership: Delphi Study," *International Journal of Leadership Studies* 9 (1): 44–61, Google Scholar.

21 Kefgan, K. (2021), "The Myth of Crisis Leadership," May 1, www.forbes.org.

22 Ibid.

23 Ibid.

24 Ibid.

25 Reddy, A. V. (2019), "Servant Leadership and Spirituality at Workplace: A Critical Review," *International Journal on Leadership* 7 (1): 8–12, Google Scholar. Khan, S. E., K. E. Khan, and A. J. Chaudhry (2015), "Impact of Servant Leadership on Workplace Spirituality: Moderating Role of Involvement Culture," *Pakistan Journal of Science* 67 (1): 109–13, Google Scholar. Nelms, L. W., E. Hutchins, D. Hutchis, and R. J. Pursley (2007), "Spirituality and the Health of College Students," *Journal of Religion and Health* 46 (2): 249–65, Google Scholar.

26 Ashmos, D. and D. Duchos (2002), "Spirituality at Work," *Journal of Management Inquiry* 9 (2): 134–45, Google Scholar.

27 These are legendary leaders whose combined ideas and styles of rule are admired by many and needed to capacitate solutions pathways for tackling the leadership and governance ills in Africa.

28 Reddy, A. V. (2019), "Servant Leadership and Spirituality at Workplace: A Critical Review."

29 Khan, S. E. et al. (2015), "Impact of Servant Leadership on Workplace Spirituality."

30 Ozawa, C., T. Suzuki, Y. Mizuno, R. Tarumi, K. Yoshida, K. Fudjii, J. Hirano, H. Tani, E. B. Rubinstein, M. Mimura, and H. Uchida (2017), "Resilience and Spirituality in Patients with Depression and Their Family Members: A Cross-sectional Study," *Comprehensive Psychiatry*, 77: 53–9, Google Scholar. Naseer, S., F. Syed, S. Nauman, T. Fatima, I. Jameel, and N. Riaz (2020), "Understanding How Leaders' Humility Promotes Followers' Emotions and Ethical Behaviors," *Journal of Positive Psychology* 15 (3): 407–19, Google Scholar.

31 Rahmati, A., M. Sajjadi, and A. Negarestani (2018), "A Spiritual Approach to Satisfaction and Motivation among Special Education Teachers," *Health, Spirituality and Medical Ethics Journal* 5 (3): 29–35, Google Scholar.

32 . Almazon, J. U., J. P. Cruz, M. S. Alamri, J. S. M. Alotaibi, A. S. B. Albougami, R. Gravoso, F. Aboceejo, K. Allen, and G. Bishwajit (2019), "Predicting Patterns of Disaster-Related Resiliency among Older Adult Typhoon Haiyan Survivors," *Geriatric Nursing* 39 (6): 629–34, Google Scholar.

33 Wu, X., M. Hayter, A. J. Lee, Y. Yuan, S. Li, Y. Bi, L. Zhang, CI. Cao, W. Gong, and Y. Zhang (2020), "Positive Spiritual Climate Supports Transformational Leadership as a Means to Reduce Nursing Burnout and Intent to Leave," *Journal of Nursing Management* 28 (4): 804–13, Google Scholar.

34 Roming, S. and K. Howard (2019), "Coping with Stress in College: An Examination of Spirituality, Social Support, and Quality of Life," *Mental Health, Religion, and Culture* 22 (8): 832–43, Google Scholar.

35 Ghanaweb News (2020), "Where Ghana Stands in the Middle of the 4 Coup Countries," January26, www.ghanaweb.com.

36 See Ghosh, A. (2022), "European Colonialism Helped Create a Planet in Crisis," *The Guardian*, January 14, www.theguardian.com. Mire, S. (2022), "Africa's Heritage Is Humanity—and It's Been Overlooked for So Long," The *Guardian*, January 3, www.theguardian.com.

Chapter 8

1 Vaill, P. B. (1998), "Foreword," Robert Greenleaf, *The Power of Servant Leadership*, ed. Larry C. Spears, Berrett-Koehler Publishers, Inc: ix-xxiii.

2 See Cascade (2012), "Leadership Structure: The African Experience," April 2, www.cascade.org. Adeyemi, S. (2017), "Africa Doesn't Need Charity, It Needs Good Leadership," *World Economic Forum*, May 4, www.weforum.org. van Wyk, J. A. (2007), "Political Leaders in Africa: Presidents, Patrons or Profiteers?," *GSDRC Applied Knowledge Services*, www.gsdrc.org. Abebe, M. A., A. G. Tekleab, and A. A. Lado (2020), "Multilevel Perspectives on Leadership in the African Context," *Journal of Management* 6 (3): 145–60, July 15.

3 See White, M. and M. Robson (2014), "The 'Critical Mass' Initiative—Helping Promote an International New Understanding in Arts in Health," *Journal of Applied Arts and Health* 5 (3), December. Brown, S. (2014), "Sustaining Change by Achieving Critical Mass," *TidalShift*, www.tidalshift.ca.

4 See Razzetti, G. (2019), "How to Upgrade Your Mindset to Succeed in Life," November 12, www.psychologytoday.com. Paunesku, D. (2019), "5 Strategies for Changing Mindsets," May 30, www.medium.com.

5 Greenleaf, R. K. (1998), *The Power of Servant Leadership*.

6 Ibid., 25.

7 Ashun-Sarpy, A. (2021), "Ghana's Youth: Resilience Despite the Odds."

8 Menkiti, I. A. (1984), "Person and Community in African Traditional Thought," in R. A. Wright (ed.), *African Philosophy: An Introduction*, Lanham: University Press of America.

9 Maglione, J. I. and K. Neville (2021), "Servant Leadership and Spirituality Among Undergraduate and Graduate Nursing Students."

10 Ashun-Sarpy, A. (2021), "Ghana's Youth: Resilience Despite the Odds."

11 Ibid.

12 See Reuters (2021), "Africa, Text of de Klerk's Video Message to South Africa," November 11, www.reuters.com.

13 Africa Business Insider (2021), "Ghana, Tanzania, Ethiopia and 30 Others Are on the World Bank's Heavily Indebted Poor Countries' List," November 12, www.africa.businessinsder.com.

14 In power since January 29, 1986.

15 In power since November 6, 1982.
16 The patriarch of the family, Gnassingbe ruled from 1979 to 2005. After his death, his son, Faure, has been installed ever since with no end in sight.
17 See Pratt, K. (2022), "Bagbin Is Not a 'King' in Parliament," January 27, www.mobile .ghanaweb.com.
18 BBC News (2022), "Why Ghana Government Assign Toyota V8 Vehicle Which Dey Transport Prez Akuffo-Addo Office Chair Everywhere," January 11, www.bbc.com.

Chapter 9

1 See Akumatey, S. (2022), "Togbe Afede XIV to Establish African Leadership Institute," *Ghana News Agency (GNA)*, September 9, www.gna.org.gh.
2 African Union (2013), "Agenda 2063: The Africa We Want."
3 AfCFTA (2013), "African Continental Free Trade Area."
4 African Union (2013), "Agenda 2063: The Africa We Want."
5 Nutakor, P. (2013), "Traditional Leadership and Development in Contemporary Ghana," Feature Article, *Modern Ghana*, March 21, www.modernghana.com.
6 See The World Bank Group (2021), "Climate Change Action Plan 2021-2025, Supporting Green Resilient and Inclusive Development," Washington, www .worldbank.org,
7 Baloyi, T. B. (2016), "The Role of Traditional Leadership in Local Government."
8 See, for example, Ghanaweb (2022), "All Mining Concessions Should be Granted with Consent of Paramount Chiefs—Akufo-Addo Orders," October 14, www.ghanweb .com.
9 See Ogbenika, G. E. (2020), "Festivals in Africa and Social Mobilization," *International Journal of Research and Innovation in Social Science* 4 (3): 291–5, March, www.rsisinternational.org. Akintan, O. A. (2013), "Traditional Religious Festivals and Modernity: A Case Study of Female-Oriented Cults Annual Festivals in Ijebuland of South Western Nigeria," *International Journal of Humanities and Social Science* 3 (9): 267–76, May, www.ijhssnet.com. Ayesu, S. M., M. A. Osei, C. A. Chichi, and R. Acquaye (2020), "Festival Elements: A Source of Inspiration for Contemporary Fashionable Products," *Journal of Textile Science and Technology* 6 (4): 200–17, November, www.scirp.org. Zalmay, K. (2017), "Why Festivals Are Important," *The News*, February 25, www.thenews.com. Ejizu, C. I. (1990), "The Meaning and Significance of Festivals in Traditional African Life: Socio-Philosophical Perspective of African Traditional Religion," *New Age Publishers*, www.philpapers.org.
10 FlipFlop, V. (2019), "The Importance of Festivals for Society & Our Unique Cultures," January 14, www.vickyflipfloptravels.com. Adamu, Z. (2019), "6 Cultural Celebrations in Africa Everyone Should Experience," *Demand Africa*, January 19, www.demandafrica.com.
11 Hill, P. (1966), "Notes on Traditional Market Authority and Market Periodicity in West Africa," *The Journal of African History* 7 (2): 295–311, www.jstor.org. allAfrica (2020), "Africa Traditional Markets, Small-Format Shops Account for 90% of Urban Food Retailing in Africa," September 9, www.allafrica.com. Dream Africa (2019), "Africa's Top 10 Markets—Best Markets in Africa," August 21, www.dreamafrica .com. Diakote, P. (2019), "The Biggest Street Markets in Africa," September 23, www .travelnoire.com.

12 See Sen, K., M. Danquah, R. D. Osei, and S. Schotte (2021), "Ghana's Lockdown Hit Vulnerable Workers Hard: What Needs to Happen Next Time," March 22, www.theconversation.com. Egger, E. M., S. Jones, P. Justino, Ivan Manhique, and R. Santos (2020), "Working Paper, Africa's Lockdown Dilemma: High Poverty and Low Trust," *UNU-WIDER*, www.wider.unu.edu.

13 Ola, O. and E. Benjamin 2019, "Preserving Biodiversity and Ecosystem Services in West African Forest, Watersheds, and Wetlands: A Review of Incentives," May 31, www.mdpi-res.com. UNEP, "Supporting Sound Ecosystem Management: Why Do Ecosystems and Biodiversity Matter in Africa," *UNEP Newsletter*, www.unep.org; UNEP / S. Foote (2021), "In Africa Restoring Ecosystems Is Central to Green Recovery," *Nature and Action*, June 3, www.unep.org. World Bank Group 2019, "This Is What It's All About: Protecting Biodiversity in Africa," February 14, www.worldbank.org.

14 Nutakor, P. (2013), "Traditional Leadership and Development in Contemporary Ghana."

15 See www.thebusinessyear.com (2016) Economic Interview, Ghana.

16 See www.allafrica.com (2015), March 11.

17 See www.newswire.com (2021), February 1.

18 See Onukwe, A. (2022), "Sub-Sharan Africa Is the Only Region Where Out-of-School Children Keep Increasing," *Quartz Africa*, September 5, www.qz.com.

19 See www.bwindiugandagorillatrekking.com.

20 See Nutakor, P. (2013), "Traditional Leadership and Development in Contemporary Ghana."

21 Anani, K. V. (1999), "The Pursuit of Politics of Sustainable Livelihoods."

22 See Lamma, E. (2022), "Climate Solutions in Cameroon—Community Forestry and Rural Women," *Green Labs blog post*, August 8, www.babraham.ac.uk.

23 Obama, B. (2006), *The Audacity of Hope*, New York: Crown/Three Rivers Press, October 17.

24 AfCFTA (2013), "African Continental Free Trade Area."

25 See Katsaounis, N. and C. Muscarella (2022), "The Case for Investing in the Digitalization of Africa's Informal Retail Supply Chains," *How We Made It in Africa*, August 23, www.howwemadeitinafrica.com. See also Africa Center for Economic Transformation Final Report (2022), "Continental Regional Integration Support Program (CRISP) Initiative," prepared for the World Bank Africa Regional Integration Unit, September.

26 See Daily Sabah (2021), "A New Phase in Africa's Development: Free Trade Area," February 11. Daily Sabah (2021), "African Free Trade Block AfCFTA Opens for Business," January 1, www.dailysabah.com.

27 For example, see Ashe, M. O. and V. B. Ojong (2018), "Population Overhang and the Great Lakes Crisis: Rwanda and Her Neighbors," *Journal of African Union Studies* 7 (2): 127–47, August.

Chapter 10

1 See Campbell, J. and N. Quinn (2021), "What Is Happening to Democracy in Africa?."

2 UNICEF (2018), "Report on Reducing Stunting in Africa." Skoufias, E. (2018), "All Hands on Deck: Halting the Vicious Circle of Stunting in Sub-Saharan." CGTN

News (2020), "58.5 Million Children in Africa Suffering from Stunted Growth." Nshimyiryo, A., Bethany Hedt-Gauthier, and Ziad El-Khatib (2019), "Risk Factors for Stunting among Children under Five Years."

3   See Bayou, J. (2021), "No Bed Syndrome in Ghanaian Health Facilities: Time to Walk the Talk," May 30, www.africahealthpot.org. Akosa, A. B. (2018), "No Bed Syndrome, a Telling Phenomenon of Ghana's Health Care," June 16, www.graphic.com.gh. CitiNewsRoom (2018), "Ghana Health Service Reveals No Bed Syndrome Probe to be Ready July 6th," June 25, www. modernghana.com.

4   See examples from Ghana: Real Estate Times Africa (2022), "Bono East Leads with 330 Schools Under Trees," May 18, www.realestatestimesafrica.com. Eduwatch (2022), "There Are 5000 and 4500 Primary Schools Under Trees and without JHS Respectively," *Africa Education Watch*, www.eduandghana.net.

5   "While the global adolescent birth rate from 2015-2020 was about 44 births per 1000, girls aged 15 to 19, this figure peaked in regions in sub-Saharan Africa. West and Central Africa, for example, had the highest regional adolescent birth rate at 115 births per1000 girls aged 15 to 18," www.google.com.

6   Ashun-Sarpy, A. (2021), "Ghana's Youth: Resilience Despite the Odds."

7   See Turianskyi, Y. (2019), "African Peer Review: Progress Is Being Made, But There Are Problems," March 12, www.theconversationcom. Ramaphosa, C. (2021), "Opening Remarks by Chairperson of the African Peer Review Forum," March 25, www.thepresidency.gov.za.

8   For example, it will be recalled that in Ghana 'one of the major highlights of the budget (2022) statement is the scrapping or removal of road tolls. . . . Shortly after the Budget presentation, the Minister for Roads and Highways, Kwame Amoako-Attah, immediately issued a letter instructing the cessation of all road tolls effective Thursday, 18th November, 2021." For details, see Mariwah, S. (2021), "Scrapping Road Tolls in Ghana: What Are the Economic Costs," *Joy News*, November 19, www .myjoyonline.com. Adombila, M. A. (2021), "2022 Budget: Ghana Abolishes Road Tolls," *Graphic*, November 17, www.graphic.com.

9   See Abdelhadi, M. (2021), "Sudan on the Brink amid Scramble for Democracy," *BBC News*, October 20, www.bbc.com. Kirby, J. (2021), "The Coup in Sudan, Explained," *Vox*, October 29, www.vox.com.

10 Joy News (2021), "Be Honest about Campaign Promises That Can be Fulfilled and Those That Cannot—Franklin Cudjoe to Government," October 21, www .myjoyonline.com. Akwei, I. (2017), "New Ghana Government Says It Fulfilled over 100 Promises in First 100 Days," April 18, www.africanews.com.

11 Lee, M. (2021), "In Africa, Blinken Sees Limits of US Influence Abroad," *AP News*, November 22, www.apnews.com.

12 Ibid.

13 See DW News (2019), "South Africa's Youth Disillusioned with Politics, Shun Politics," May 6, www.amp.dw.com. Campbell, J. (2017), "South African Youth Fed Up with Formal Politics," June 28, www.cfr.org.

14 Ake, C. (1997), "The Unique Case of African Democracy," 42–5.

15 Ibid.

16 Classical contextual reference is the chronicles of Ogoniland in Nigeria. For details, see "The Ogoni Struggle," www.platformlondon.org. UNPO (2018), "Ogoni: Timeline of the Ogoni Struggle," March 30, www.unpo.org. UNPO (2018), "Ogoni: A Struggle against Oppression and Fossil Fuels," December 17, www.unpo.org. DW News (2020), "Nigeria: Ogoni 9 Activists Remembered 25 Years On," November

9, www.dw.com. Gomis, M. and E. Sodji (2021), "Revisited, Polluted by the Oil Industry: Life in Nigeria's Ogoniland," February 7, www.amp.france24.com. "Right Livelihood, Ken Saro-Wiwa/Movement for the Survival of the Ogoni People," www .rightliveliood.org.

17 Kefgan, K. (2021), "The Myth of Crisis Leadership."

18 See Felter, C. (2021), "Africa's Leaders for Life," June 20, www.cfr.org. Ohan, S., M. Kruhly, and H. Olivennes (2016), "Yoweri Museveni and Other African Presidents for Life," *The New York Times*, May 12, www.nytimes.com. Washington Post (2021), "Africans Don't Support 'Presidents for Life' Survey Shows," November 5, www .washingtonpost.com.

19 For details, see the e-levy saga in Ghana: Onukwue, A. (2021), "Ghana's Lawmakers Got into a Fight Over a Proposed Tax on Electronic Transactions," *Quartz Africa*, December 21, www.qz.com. Odour, M. (2021), "Brawl in Ghana's Parliament Over a Proposed e-levy," *Africa News*, December 21, www.africanews.com.

20 Politico Staff (2021), "The Man behind Bidenomics."

21 The Paris Agreement is a legally binding international treaty on climate change. It was adopted by 196 at COP21 in Paris on December 12, 2015, and entered into force on November 4, 2016. Its goal is to limit global warming to well below 2, preferably to 1.5 degree Celsius, compared to preindustrial levels. For details, see the United Nations Framework Convention on Climate Change (UNFCCC), www .unfcc.int.

22 World Bank (2013), "Unlocking Africa's Agricultural Potential—An Action Agenda for Transformation," *Sustainable Development Series*, Africa Region, World Bank, Washington DC, https://openknowledge.worldbank.org/bitstream/handle/10986 /16624/769900WP0SDS0A00Box374393B00PUBLIC0.pdf;sequence=1.

23 Morsy, H., A. Salami, and N. Mukassa (2021), "Opportunities amid COVID-19: Advancing Intra-African Food Integration," *World Development* 139, March, https:// www.sciencedirect.com/science/article/pii/S0305750X20304356#!.

24 African Union (2013), "Agenda 2063: The Africa We Want."

25 See www.visualcapitalist.com.

26 Menkiti, I. A. (1984), "Person and Community in African Traditional Thought." Ghosh, A. (2022), "European Colonialism Helped Create a Planet in Crisis."

27 Kakonge, J. O. (1992), "Traditional African Values and Their Use in Implementing Agenda 21," *Indigenous Knowledge Monitor* 3 (2), www.nuffics.nl/ciran/ikdm/articles/ kakonge.com.

28 Nef, J. (1994), "Human Security and Mutual Vulnerability in a New World Order," *Worldscape*, Fall, 4–5. Guelph, Canada: University of Guelph.

29 Logan, C. and J. Appiah-Nyamekye Sanny (2021), "China Has Invested in Africa. We Checked to See Whether That Is Undermining Democracy," *The Washington Post*, October 29, www.washingtonpost.com.

30 See Sachs, G. (2021), "Speech at the UN Food Systems Pre-Summit," July 27, www .jeffsachs.org.

31 See Manyika, J., J. Mischke, J. Bughin, J. Woetzel, M. Krishnan, and S. Cudre (2019), "A New Look at the Declining Labor Share of Income in the United States," *Discussion Paper, McKinsey Global Institute*, May 22, www.mckinsey.com. de Mooij, R. (2018), "How Much Can We Shift Taxes from Labor to Capital," *KPMG*, November 2, www .responsibletax.kpmg.com. Hergovich, P. and M. Merz (2018), "The Price of Capital, Factor Substitutability, and Corporate Profits," *IZA Institute of Labor Economics*, August, www.ftp.iza.org.

Epilogue

1 Washington Post (2020), "Who Won Ghana's 2020 Election?," December 16, www
.washingtonpost.com.

2 See BBC News (2022), "Kenya Election 2022: Were Result Sheets Altered as Odinga
Claims?," September 2, www.bbc.com.

3 See Smith, P. (2013), "Politics, Damned Lies and Statistics," *the Africa Report*, April
8, www.theafricareport.com. Afari, K. (2013), "Ghana: The Biggest Lies," *Ghanaian
Chronicle*, May 9, www.allafrica.com. Graphic (2022), "Malawi Bishops Accuse
President of Broken Promises," October 11, www.graphic.cpm.gh.

4 See Judson, S. D., J. Torimiro, and K. Njabo (2022), "COVID-19 Data Reporting
Systems in Africa Reveal Insights for Future Pandemics," National Institutes of Health,
June 16, www.ncbi.nim.nih.gov.

5 See Petetsi, J. Y. (2022), "Ghana: EC Planning to Compile New Voters' Register for
2024 Polls—Minority Alleges," *Ghanaian Times*, July 14, www.allafrica.com.

6 Stodolska, M. (2021), "#QuarantineChallenge2k20: Leisure in the Time of the
Pandemic," *Leisure Sciences* 43, www.tandfonline.com.

7 Brooks, S. K. (2022), "Challenges and Opportunities Experienced by Performing
Artists during COVID-19 Lockdown: Scoping Review," *Social Sciences & Humanities
Open* 6 (1), www.sciencedirect.com.

8 Ghanaweb (2020), "Reports We Shared Different Macroeconomic Data with IMF Are
False—Finance Ministry," May 10, www.ghanaweb.com.

9 See Ghanaweb (2022), "IMF Boss Was Being Diplomatic, Any Negative Comment
from Her Will Collapse Ghana's Economy," September 8, www.ghanaweb.com.
Ghanweb (2022), "Akufo-Addo Has Now Corrupted Even the IMF—Dr. Amoako
Reacts to IMF Statement on Ghana's Economy," September 8, www.ghanaweb.com.

BIBLIOGRAPHY

Abdelhadi, Magdi (2021), "Sudan on the brink amid scramble for democracy," *BBC News*, October 20, http://www.bbc.com.

Abebe, Michael A., Amanuel G. Tekleab, and Augustine A. Lado (2020), "Multilevel perspectives on leadership in the African context," *Journal of Management* 6 (3): 145–60.

Abor, J. and P. Quartey (2010), 'Issues in SME development in Ghana and South Africa," *International Research Journal of Finance and Economics* 39 (6): 215–28.

ACCA - the Association of Chartered Certified Accountants - (2020), "New report, accountability in Africa," December 10, http://www.accountabilitycounsel.org.

Achebe, C. (1958), *Things Fall Apart*, Oxford: Heinemann.

Achebe, C. (1974), *Arrow of God*, Oxford: Heinemann.

Acheng, R. (2014), "A moral consciousness: A leadership approach for a new Africa?," *Journal of African Union Studies* 3: 115–32.

Adam, S., D. Adom, and Asare Baffour Bediako (2016), "The major factors that influence basic school dropout in Rural Ghana," *Journal of Education and Practice* 7 (28): 1–8.

Adams, Samuel and Berhanu Mengistu (2008), 'The political economy of privatization in Sub-Saharan Africa," *Social Science Quarterly* 89 (1): 78–94.

Adamu, Zaina (2019), "6 cultural celebrations in Africa everyone should experience," *Demand Africa*, January 19, http://www.demandafrica.com.

Adeleye, Ifedapo (2011), "Theorizing human resource management in Africa: Beyond cultural relativism," *African Journal of Business Management* 5 (6): 2028–39.

Adeyemi, Sam (2017), "Africa doesn't need charity, it needs good leadership," *World Economic Forum*, May 04, http://www.weforum.org.

Adibe, Clement Eme (2020), "Accountability in Africa and the international community," *Social Research, From Impunity to Accountability in Africa's Development in the 21st Century* 77 (4): 1241–80, http://www.jstor.org.

Adombila, Maxwell Akalaare (2021), "2022 Budget: Ghana abolishes road tolls," *Graphic*, November 17, http://www.graphic.com.

Afari, Kwadwo (2013), "Ghana: The biggest lies," *Ghanaian Chronicle*, May 09, www .allafrica.com.

AfDB -African Development Bank (2021), *African Economic Outlook 2021, From Debt Resolution to Growth: The Road Ahead for Africa*, http://www.afdb.org.

Africa Business Insider (2021), "Ghana, Tanzania, Ethiopia and 30 others are on the World Bank's heavily indebted poor countries' list," November, http://www.africa .businessinsder.com.

Africa Center for Economic Transformation (2022), "Final report, Continental Regional Integration Support Program (CRISP) initiative," prepared for the World Bank, Africa Regional Integration Unit, September, www.acetforafrica.org.

African Studies Center (2016), *African Constitutions*, Leiden, October, http://www
    .ascleiden.nl.
African Union (2013), "African Continental Free Trade Area (AfCFTA)," http://www.au
    .int.
African Union (2013), "Agenda 2063: The Africa we want," http://www.au.int.
Afrobarometer (2018), "Africans increasingly support multiparty democracy, but trust in
    political parties remains low," June 14, http://www.afrobarometer.org.
Afrobarometer (2021), "Women's political participation," March 18, http://www.idea.int.
AFSA- Alliance for Food Sovereignty in Africa (2019), "Towards a food policy for Africa,"
    May 29, http://www.afsafrica.org.
Agbor, Julius, Olumide Taiwo, and Jessica Smith (2012), "Sub-Saharan Africa's Youth
    Bulge: A Demographic Dividend or Disaster?," in *Foresight Africa: Top Priorities for the
    Continent in 2012*. Brookings Institute, Africa Growth Initiative, http://www.brookings
    .edu.
Agyeman, Opoku (1988), "Setbacks to political institutionalization by Praetorianism in
    Africa," *The Journal of Modern African Studies* 26 (3): 403–35, http://www.jstor.org.
Ake, C. (1997), "The unique case of African democracy," *Africa World Review* 44: 42–5.
Akintan, Oluwatosin Adeoti (2013), "Traditional religious festivals and modernity: A case
    study of female-oriented cults annual festivals in Ijebuland of South Western Nigeria,"
    International Journal of Humanities and Social Science 3 (9): 267–76, http://www
    .ijhssnet.com.
Akinwumi, Femi Sunday (2010), "Proliferation of higher education in Nigeria;
    implications for quality education," June, http://www.researchgate.net.
Akosa, Agyeman Badu (2018), "No bed syndrome, a telling phenomenon of Ghana's
    health care," June 16, http://www.graphic.com.gh.
Akumatey, Samuel (2022), "Togbe Afede XIV to establish African Leadership Institute,"
    Ghana News Agency (GNA), September 09, www.gna.org.gh.
Akwei, Ismail (2017), "New Ghana government says it fulfilled over 100 promises in first
    100 days," April 18, http://www.africanews.com.
Al Jazeera Staff (2021), October 12, http://www.aljazeera.com.
Alemazung, Joy Asongazoh (2011), "Leadership flaws and fallibilities impacting
    democratization processes, governance and functional statehood in Africa," *African
    Journal of Political Science and International Relations* 5 (1): 30–41.
allAfrica (2020), "Africa: Traditional markets, small-format shops account for 90% of
    urban food retailing in Africa," September 09, http://www.alafrica.com.
Almazon, J. U., J. P. Cruz, M. S. Alamri, J. S. M. Alotaibi, A. S. B. Albougami, R. Gravoso,
    F. Aboceejo, K. Allen, and G. Bishwajit (2019), "Predicting patterns of disaster-related
    resiliency among older adult Typhoon Haiyan survivors," *Geriatric Nursing* 39 (6):
    629–34, Google Scholar.
Amalric, F. (1998), "Sustainable livelihoods: Entrepreneurship, political strategies and
    governance," *Development* 41 (3): 31–44, http://www.jstor.org.
Amin, S. (1972), "Underdevelopment and dependency in Black Africa: Origins and
    contemporary forms," *The Journal of Modem African Studies* 10 (4): 503–24, http://
    www.jstor.org.
Amnesty International (2015), *Impunity vs Immunity: Africa and the ICC*, June 24, http://
    www.amnesty.org.
Anani, Kofi (1992), "Transnational elite interests as manifested in the socio-economic
    recovery programs in Sub-Saharan Africa," unpublished MA thesis, Guelph, Canada:
    University of Guelph.

Anani, Kofi V. (1999), "The pursuit of politics of sustainable livelihoods: Focus on governance in Ghana," unpublished PhD dissertation, Guelph, Canada: University of Guelph.

Andrews, Matt (2010), "How far have public financial management reforms come in Africa," *HKS Faculty Research Working Paper Series*, John F. Kennedy School of Government, Harvard University.

Angai, Catharine Kyenret (2016), "West Africa's. Promise trackers hold politicians to their word," November 04, http://www.openfoundations.org.

Ani, Kelech Johnmary (2013), "Globalization and its impact on African political culture," *World Affairs: The Journal of International Issues* 17 (2): 44–61.http://www.jstor.org.

APET – African Union High Level Panel on Emerging Technologies - Secretariat (2020), "Is Africa addressing the food security dilemma through modern agriculture technologies," December 18, http://www.nepad.org.

Aremu, Adeyemi Oladapo and Nox Makunga (2022), "Africa is a treasure trove of medicinal plants: Here are seven that are popular," July 13, www.thisisafrica.me.

Arhin, Kwame (1985), *Traditional rule in Ghana: Past and present*, Accra: Sedco, http://www.worldcat.org.

Asante, M. (2017), *An Afrocentric Manifesto: Toward an African Renaissance*, Cambridge: Polity Press.

Ascroft, Rachel (2022), "Michel de Montaigne and Socrates on know thyself," *The Collector*, October 18, www.thecolector.com.

Ashe, Muesiri Oberorakpovioma and Vivian Besem Ojong (2018), "Population overhang and the Great Lakes crisis: Rwanda and her neighbors," *Journal of African Union Studies* 7 (2): 127–47.

Ashmos, D. and D. Duchos (2002), "Spirituality at work," *Journal of Management Inquiry* 9 (2): 134–45, Google Scholar.

Ashun-Sarpy, Abigail (2021), "Ghana's youth: Resilience despite the odds," *NewAfrican*, November 08, http://www.newafricanmagazine.com.

Associated Press and Charetta Bellamy (2022), "US museums return African bronzes stolen in 19th Century," *NBC News*, October 13, www.nbcnews.com.

Athal, Krishna (2021), "Why Servant Leadership is becoming the leadership style of the future," October 02, http://www.entrepreneur.com.

Atta Mills, Cadman (2018), "Politics, policy, and implementation: The Ghanaian Paradox," July 18, http://www.brookings.edu.

Atuoye, K. N. and F. S. Odame (2013), "Queen-mother concept in the upper west region of Ghana: Is this advancement or an emerging conflict with tradition in a patriarchal society?," *European Scientific Journal*, 9 (35), December, www.eujournal.org.

Aviles, William (2008), "US intervention in Columbia: The role of transnational relations," *Bulletin of Latin American Research* 27 (3): 410–29.

Ayesu, Solomon Marfo, Mercy Ampofowah Osei, Cynthia Akua Chichi, and Richard Acquaye (2020), "Festival elements: A source of inspiration for contemporary fashionable products," *Journal of Textile Science and Technology* 6 (4): 200–17, http://www.scirp.org.

Ayittey, G. (1990), "Guns, idiots, screams," *New Internationalist* 8, June, http://www.jstor.org.

Ayittey, G. (1991), *Indigenous African Institutions*, New York: Transnational Publishers.

Badu, Kwaku (2020), "Ghana: Why did an eminent JSC label NDC create, loot and share?," October 13, http://www.ghanaweb.com.

Baker, Bruce (2004), "Twilight of impunity for Africa's presidential criminals," *Third World Quarterly* 25 (8): 1487–99, http://www.jstor.org.

Baldoni, John (2017), "Fostering the sense of belonging promotes success," January 22, http://www.forbes.com.

Baloyi, Tshepang Brigid (2016), "The Role of Traditional Leadership in Local Government," A research report submitted to the Faculty of Commerce, Law and Management, University of Witwatersrand in partial fulfilment of the requirement for the Master of Management in the Field of Public Management and Development degree, January.

Basheka, Benon C. and Kedibone Phago (2014), "What constrains effective public financial management in African democracies?," *Africa Insight* 43 (4): 154–70

Bass, Bernard and Ronald E. Riggio (1998), "Transformational leadership: A comprehensive review of theory," http://www.goodreads.com.

Bawelle, Eugene B. G. (2022), "Ghana: Is the preferred investment destination becoming Africa's fading star?," January 18, http://www.thefricareport.com.

Bayou, Jonathan (2021), "No bed syndrome in Ghanaian health facilities: Time to walk the talk," May30, http://www.africahealthpot.org.

BBC News (2022), "Kenya election 2022: Were result sheets altered as Odinga claims?," September 02, www.bbc.com.

BBC News (2022), "Why Ghana government assign Toyota V8 vehicle which dey transport Prez Akuffo-Addo office chair everywhere," January 11, http://www.bbc .com.

Beckman, Bjorn and Gbemisola Adeoti, eds. (2000), *Pretensions and Resistance in African Politics. Africa in the New Millennium*, October 01, http://www.bloomsbury.com.

Benjamin, Nancy and Ahmadou Aly Mbaye (2020), "The Informal Sector in francophone Africa: The other side of weak structural transformation," July 07, www.brookings.edu.

Bennell, Paul (1997), "Privatization in Sub-Saharan Africa: Progress and prospects during the 1990s," *World Development* 25 (11): 1785–801.

Bobbio, N. (1989), "The Upturned Utopia," *New Left Review* 177: 37–9.

Bold Expert (2021), "Rethinking higher education in Africa – 21st century skills," February 04, http://www.bold.expert.com.

Bongila, Jean-Pierre K. (2012), "Grounding leadership ethics in African diaspora and election rights," *Journal of Third World Studies* 29 (1): 263–86.

Boone, Catharine (2009), "Electoral populism where property rights are weak: Land politics," *Contemporary Sub-Saharan Africa* 41 (2): 183–201, http://www.jstor.org.

Bratton, Michael and Carolyn Logan (2006), "Voters but not yet Citizens: The Weak Demand for Political Accountability in Africa's Unclaimed Democracies," *Afrobarometer Working Paper 63*, September, http://www.afrobarometer.org.

Britannica, The Editors of Encyclopedia (2018), "African religions," February 23, 2018, http://www.britannica.com (Accessed January 12, 2022).

Brooks, Samantha K. (2022), "Challenges and opportunities experienced by performing artists during COVID-19 lockdown: Scoping review," *Social Sciences & Humanities Open* 6 (1), www.sciencedirect.com.

Brown, Charlie (2014), "If you want your brand to succeed, make it aspirational, not inspirational," December 04, http://www.fastcompany.com.

Brown, Siobhan (2014), "Sustaining change by achieving critical mass," *TidalShift*, http://www.tidalshift.ca.

Business Financial Times (2021), "Cedi sinks further against dollar despite strong buffers," October 11, 2021, http://www.mobile.ghanaweb.com.

Campbell, John (2017), "South African youth fed up with formal politics," June 28, 2017, http://www.cfr.org.

Campbell, John (2018), "Rural Poverty in Sub-Saharan Africa," December 28, http://www.cfr.org.

Campbell, John (2021), "Coups are back in West Africa," September 08, http://www.cfr.org.

Campbell, John and Nolan Quinn (2021), "What is happening to democracy in Africa?," *Council on Foreign Relations*, May, http://www.cfr.org.

Carr, Evan W., Andrew Reece, Gabriella Rosen Kellerman, and Alexi Robichaux (2019), "The value of belonging at work," December 16, http://www.hbr.org.

Cascade (2012), "Leadership structure: The African experience," April 02, http://www.cascade.org.

CGTN News (2020), "58.5 million children in Africa suffering from stunted growth," February 10, http://www.newsaf.cgtn.com.

Chambers, R., ed. (1979), "Rural development: Whose knowledge counts?" *Special issue of IDS Bulletin, University of Sussex, Institute of Development Studies* 10 (2): 1–3

Chambers, R (1983), *Rural Development: Putting the Last First*, New York: Longman.

Chan, Stephen (2017), "Africa's elderly leaders get no prizes for hanging on," *SOAS*, London: University of London, March 03.

Chihuri, Silence (2014), "Sycophantic praises and bootlicking: The curse of African politics," March 06, http://www.newzimbabew.com.

Chikerema, Arthur Fidelis and Ogochukwu Nzewi (2020), "Succession politics and state administration in Africa: The case of Zimbabwe," http://www.eisa.org.

Chirwa, D. M. and L. Nijzink, eds. (2012), *Accountable Government in Africa: Perspectives from Public Law and Political Studies*, United Nations University, http://www.i.unu.edu.

Cho, Wonbin (2010), "Citizens' perceptions of government responsiveness in Africa: Do electoral systems and ethnic diversity matter?," *Comparative Political Studies*, June 28, http://www.journals.sagepub.com.

Chulu, Jimmy (2015), "Africa is largely influenced by foreign culture especially western culture. Has Africa now sacrificed her own culture on the altar of expediency?," October 13, www.papers.ssrn.com.

CitiNewsRoom (2018), "Ghana Health Service Reveals 'No bed syndrome' Probe to be ready July 6th," June 25, http://www.modernghana.com.

Clementi, Joe (2021), "Greatness is not primarily a matter of circumstances," January 09, http://www.joeclementi.com.

CNN (2021), "Why are coups making a comeback in Africa?," September 13, http://www.cnn.com.

Collin, Douglas, Martina Kirchberger, and David Lagakos (2017), "Measuring living standards in African cities and rural areas," October 02, http://www.voxdev.org.

Collins, Tom (2022), "Economic Outlook 2022: Africa faces rickety rebound," *African Business*, January 10, http://www.african.business.

Constitute Project (2021), "Ghana's constitution of 1992 with amendments through 1996," August 26, http://www.constituteproject.org.

Corrigen, Caitlin C. (2014), "Breaking the resource curse: Transparency in the natural resource sector and the extractive industries transparency initiative," *Resources Policy* 40: 17–30.

Crisis Group (2009), "The politics of ending impunity," *Aegis Trust*, February, http://www.crisisgroup.org.

Cropley, Ed. (2021), "Africa's digital payments race becomes a scramble," *Reuters*, May 05, http://www.reuters.com.

Cross, Hannah (2015), "Divisive democracy and popular struggle in Africa," *Review of African Political Economy* 42 (143): 1–6.

Curtis, Mark (2019), "LSE controls US$1 trillion worth of Africa's resources in Just 5 commodities," *HuffingtonPostUK*, http://www.ghanafinancialmarket.org.

Daily Champion – Lagos (2002), "Nigeria: Sycophancy is an art," May 28, http://www.allafrica.com.

Daily Sabah (2021), "A new phase in Africa's development: Free trade area," February 11, http://www.dailysabah.com.

Daily Sabah (2021), "African free trade block AfCFTA opens for business," January 01, http://www.dailysabah.com.

Darko, Kenneth Awotwe (2021), "Empower citizenry, not create – Loot- and -share schemes disguised as investments – Sam Jonah," April 25, http://www.myjoyonline.com.

David, Oladipo Olalekan and Wynand Grobler (2021), "Information and communication technology penetration level as an impetus for economic growth in Africa," *Economic Research* 33 (1): 394–1418, http://www.tandfonline.com.

Davidson, Basil (1961), *The African Slave Trade*, Suffolk: Boydell & Brewer Ltd., Google Books, https://books.google.com.

Davies, Joanne (2009), *Parliamentarians and Corruption in Africa: The Challenge of Leadership and the Practice of Politics*, Ottawa: The Parliamentary Centre.

de Mooij, Ruud (2018), "How much can we shift taxes from labor to capital?." http://www.kpmg.com.

de Vries, Deanne (2020), "A classical grounded theory study of how heads of state in Africa lead: A new theory of political leadership," Eastern University ProQuest Dissertations Publishing, Well-Grounded, Leadership Development, http://www.well-grounded.org.

Deloitte Insights (2021), "Africa economic outlook," December 02, http://www.deloitte.com.

Deutsche Welle (DW) News (2017), "In Kenya politics split on ethnic divide – Africa," October 26, http://www.amp.dw.com.

Deutsche Welle (DW) News (2019), "South Africa's youth disillusioned with politics, shun politics," May 06, http://www.amp.dw.com.

Deutsche Welle (DW) News (2020), "Nigeria: Ogoni 9 activists remembered 25 years on," November 09, http://www.dw.com.

Dia, M. (1991), "Development and cultural values in Sub-Saharan Africa," *Finance and Development*, Washington DC, December, 10–13.

Diakote, Parker (2019), "The biggest street markets in Africa," September 23, http://www.travelnoire.com.

Diane, Akua (2011), "Education in Africa is failing its people," August 09, http://www.newafricanmagazine.com.

Diop, Makhtar (2022), "Africa's pandemic recovery requires investments that build the foundation for the region's future," in *Foresight Africa: Top Priorities for Africa*. Foresight Africa, January, http://www.brookings.edu.

Diop, M. Bachir (2021), "The role of African elites in West African countries," July 07, http://www.afropolicy.com.

Dream Africa (2019), "Africa's top 10 markets – Best markets in Africa," August 21, http://www.dreamafrica.com.

Dungy, Tiara Nicole and Hermann Achidi Ndofor (2019), "A dialogue on the informal economy in Africa," *Africa Journal of Management* 5 (4): 401–7.

Dzobo, N. K. (1997), *African Proverbs: The Moral Value of Ewe Proverbs. Guide to Conduct Vol. II*, Accra: Bureau for Ghana Languages.

Ebert, Roger (2022), "The Woman King movie review and film summary," September 16, www.rogerebert.com.

Edinger, Scott (2021), "Good leaders know you can't fight reality," *Harvard Business Review*, October 08, http://www.hbr.org.

Eduwatch (2022), "There are 5000 and 4500 primary schools under trees and without JHS respectively," *Africa Education Watch*, www.eduandghana.net.

Egger, Eva Maria, Sam Jones, Patricia Justino, Ivan Manhique, and Ricardo Santos (2020), "Africa's lockdown dilemma: High poverty and low trust," *Working Paper*, UNU-WIDER, http://www.wider.unu.edu.

Ehui, Simeon, Holger Kray, and Elliot W. Mghenyi (2020), "Policy priorities for achieving food and nutrition security in Africa by 2030," *World Bank Blogs*, January 22.

Ejiogu, Amanze Chibuzo and Ambisisi Ambituuni (2019), "The dark side of transparency: Does the Nigeria extractive industries transparency initiative help or hinder accountability and corruption control?," *The British Accounting Review* 51 (5): 100811.

Ejizu, C. I. (1990), "The meaning and significance of festivals in traditional African life: Socio-philosophical perspective of African traditional religion," New Age Publishers, http://www.philpapers.org.

El Ouassif, Amal (2021), "The challenge of the youth bulge in Africa and the Middle East: Migration and the brain drain," January 29, http://www.africaportal.org.

Ezra Coaching (2021), "Where sycophancy thrives, innovation dies," June 08, http://www.helloezra.com.

Fabricius, Peter (2020), "Africa's youth bulge alone won't deliver economic growth," March 19, http://www.issafrica.org.

Fabricus, Peter (2022), "Time for Africa strategies on the big powers," *ISS Today*, September 09, www.issafrica.org.

Fanon, F. (1963), *The Wretched of the Earth*, New York: Grove Press Inc.

Faria, Julia (2021), "Internet penetration rate in Africa 2021, by region," *Statista*, March 12, http://www.statista.com.

Faucon, Benoit, Summer Said, and Joe Parkinson (2021), "Military coups in Africa at highest level since end of colonialism," *Wall Street Journal*, November 03.

Felter, Claire (2021), "Africa's leaders for life," July 30, http://www.cfr.org.

Ficht, A. and M. Ponton (2015), "Identifying primary characteristics of servant leadership: Delphi study," *International Journal of Leadership Studies* 9 (1): 44–61, Google Scholar.

Finch, Anne Marie (2021), "How belongingness can drive business success," August 18, http://www.unleash.ai.

Fitch Ratings (2021), "Ghana to opt for IMF financing if liquidity strains mounts," November 2, http://www.norvanreports.com.

Fitzgibbon, Will and Debbie Cenziper (2021), "American lawmakers denounce South Dakota, other US states as hubs for financial secrecy," *International Consortium of Investigative Journalists (ICIJI) Pandora Papers*, December 08, http://www.icij.org.

FlipFlop, Vicky (2022), "The importance of festivals for society & our unique cultures," January 14, http://www.vickyflipfloptravels.com.

Fox, Louise and Thomas S. Jayne (2020), "Unpacking the misconceptions about Africa's food imports," Brookings Institute, December 14, http://www.brookings.edu.

Fredua-Kwarteng, Eric (2020), "In Africa, university proliferation is not an unqualified good," April 27, http://www.timeshighereducation.com.

Gastineau, Benedicte and Valerie Golaz (2016), "Being young in Rural Africa," *Afrique Contmporaine* 259 (3): 9–22, http://www.cairn-int.info.

Gbadegesin, Job and Lochner Marais (2020), "The state of housing policy research in Africa," *International Journal of Housing Policy Research* 20 (4): 474–90, http://www.tandfonline.com.

George, S. (1988), *A Fate Worse than Debt: A Radical New Analysis of the Third World Debt Crisis*, London: Penguin.

Ghana News Agency (2019), "Okyenhene calls for inclusion of chiefs in local governance," December 4.

Ghana News Agency (2022), "Stick to commitment to reallocate SDR $ 100 billion to Africa – President to G20 leaders," February 07, http://www.mobile.ghanaweb.com.

Ghanaweb (2022), "All mining concessions should be granted with consent of Paramount Chiefs – Akufo-Addo orders," October 14, www.ghanweb.com.

Ghanaweb (2022), "Asantehemaa stops election of new Kumasi City Market leaders," October 14, www.ghanaweb.com.

Ghanaweb (2022), "Mahama, Godfried Dame face off in stiff fight," September 13, www.ghanaweb.com.

Ghanaweb (2022), "Odenho Kwafo Akoto III calls for reforms to reclaim respect for chieftaincy institution," October 21, www.ghanaweb.com.

Ghanaweb News (2020), "Where Ghana stands in the middle of the 4 coup countries," January 26, http://www.ghanaweb.com.

Ghanaweb News (2022), "Togbe Afede XIV to establish African Traditional Leadership Institute," 08 September, www.ghanaweb.com.

Ghins, Leopold and Jill Bouscarat (2021), "How should we understand sustainable food systems in West Africa?," May 13, http://www.blogs.lse.ac.uk.

Ghosh, Amitav (2022), "European colonialism helped create a planet in crisis," *The Guardian*, January 14, http://www.theguardian.com.

Global Witness Briefing Document (2009), "Natural resource exploitation and human rights in the DRC, 1993–2003," December 17, http://www.globalwitness.org.

Gomis, Moise and Emmanuelle Sodji (2021), "Revisited, polluted by the oil industry: Life in Nigeria's Ogoniland," February 07, www.amp.france24.com.

Graphic (2022), "Malawi bishops accuse president of broken promises," October 11, www.graphic.com.gh.

Graphic Online (2019), "What Nana SKB Asante told National House of Chiefs on December 17 referendum," January 19.

Graz, Jean-Christophe (2003), "How powerful are transnational elite clubs? The social myth of the World Economic Forum," *New Political Economy* 8 (3): 321–40.

Greenleaf, Robert K. (1998), *The Power of Servant Leadership*, New York: Berrett-Koehler Publishers Incorporated.

Greenleaf, Robert K. (2002), *Servant Leadership: A Journey into the Nature of Legitimate Power and Greatness (25th anniversary Ed.)*, New Jersey: Paulist Press.

Gumede, Vusi (2016), "Leadership for Africa's Development: Revisiting Indigenous African Leadership and Setting the Agenda for Political Leadership," *Journal of Black Studies*, November 21, http://www.journals.sagepub.com.

Gyimah-Boadi, E. (2021), "Good Governance: Building trust between people and their leaders," January 21, http://www.brookings.edu.

Hanley, Ryan P. (2019), "What is national greatness," *National Affairs*, http://www
.nationalaffairs.com.

Haque, Syed Wasimul (2017), "Greatness of a nation," May 26, http://www
.fredericknewspost.com.

Harcourt, W. (1998), "Editorial- sustainable livelihoods and governance: Our role as
intermediaries," *Development* 41 (3): 3–5, http://www.jstor.org.

Hayes, Adam (2020), "Comparative advantage," October 26, http://www.investopedia.com.

Hayter, T. (1981), *The Creation of World Poverty*, London: Pluto.

Hayzlett, Jeffrey (2019), "4 principles of servant leadership," October 16, http://www
.entrepreneur.com.

Hendrickson, Joy and Hoda Zaki (2013), "Modern African ideologies," in Michael Freeden
and Marc Stears (eds.), *The Oxford Handbook of Political Ideologies Online*, December
2013, http://www.oxfordhandbooks.com.

Herman, Edward S. and Noam Chomsky (1988), *Manufacturing Consent: The Political
Economy of the Mass Media*, New York: Pantheon Books.

Hesse, Herman (2003), *The Journey to the East*. Translations H. Rosen, Picador. (original
work published 1932)

Hill, Polly (1966), "Notes on traditional market authority and market periodicity in West
Africa," *The Journal of African History* 7 (2): 295–311, http://www.jstor.org.

Houeland, Camila and Sean Jacobs (2018), "The 'Big Man' Syndrome in Africa," March 11,
http://www.africascountry.com.

Hurndall, Suzanne (2021), "Transformational leadership and its benefits to your business,"
November, http://www.breathehr.com.

Ibrahim, Mo and Special to CNN (2013), "Africa's elderly leaders 'risk more revolutions,"
September 17, http;//www.cnn.com.

IDEA Policy Brief (2016), "Democratic accountability in service delivery-lessons from
Africa," *International IDEA*, http://www.idea.int.

Ighobor, Kingsley (2013), "Politics of succession: Coping when leaders die," *Africa
Renewal*, January, http://www.un.org.

Inoue, K. (2015), "Why do Sub-Saharan African youth drop out of school?," April 2015,
http://www.elibrary.worldbank.org.

Institute of Local Government Studies (ILGS) and Friedrich Ebert Stiftung (2016), "A
guide to district assemblies in Ghana."

International Monetary Fund (IMF) (2022), "Tackling the Global Food Crisis: Impact,
Policy Response and the Role of IMF," Washington, DC, September 29, 1–98.

International Peace Institute (IPI) (2011), "Elections in Africa: Challenges and
opportunities," September 2011, http://www.ipinst.org.

Isaksson, Ann-Sofie (2014), "Political participation in Africa: The role of Individual
resources," *Electoral Studies* 34: 244–60, http://www.sciencedirect.com.

Izugbara, Chimaraoke O., Mary O. Obiyan, Tizta T. Degfie, and Anam Bhati (2020),
"Correlates of Intimate partner violence among urban women in sub-Saharan Africa,"
PloS one 1 (3): 1–21.

Jackson, Terence (2016), "Why the voice of Africa's informal economy should be heard,"
January 21, http://www.theconversation.com.

James, Peter Bai, Jon Wardie, and Jon Adams (2018), "Traditional, complementary and
alternative medicine use in Sub-Saharan Africa: A systematic review," BMJ Publishing
Group, August 27, http://www.ncbi.nlm.nih.gov.

Joy News (2021), "Be honest about campaign promises that can be fulfilled and those that
cannot – Franklin Cudjoe to government," October 21, http://www.myjoyonline.com.

Judson, Seth D., Judith Torimiro, and Kevin Njabo (2022), "COVID-19 data reporting systems in Africa reveal insights for future pandemics", National Institutes of Health, June 16, www.ncbi.nim.nih.gov.

Kakonge, J. O. (1992), "Traditional African values and their use in implementing Agenda 21," *Indigenous Knowledge Monitor* 3 (2), http://www.nuffics.nl/ciran/ikdm/articles/kakonge.com.

Katsaounis, Nikos and Chris Muscarella (2022), "The case for investing in the digitalization of Africa's informal retail supply chains," *How we made it in Africa*, August 23, www.howwemadeitinafrica.com.

Kauppi, Niilo and Mikael Rask Madsen (2013), "Transnational power elite: The new professionals of governance, law and security," *Transnational Power Elites*, 12–26, http://www.taylorfrancis.com.

Kefgan, Keith (2021), "The myth of crisis leadership," May 01, http://www.forbes.org.

Keita, Mohamed and Alex Gladstein (2021), "Macron isn't so post-colonial after all," August 03, 2021, http://www.foreignpolicy.com.

Kessy, Ambrose T. (2020), "The demand and supply sides of accountability in local government authorities in Tanzania," *Public Integrity* 22 (1): 1–20, http://www.researchgate.net.

Khan, S. E., K. E. Khan, and A. J. Chaudhry (2015), "Impact of servant leadership on workplace spirituality: Moderating role of involvement culture," *Pakistan Journal of Science* 67 (1): 109–13, Google Scholar.

Khwaja, Maria (2014), "Jack in the box: The failure of education in Sub-Saharan Africa," September 25, http://www.fairobserver.com.

Kirby, Jen (2021), "The Coup in Sudan, explained," *Vox*, October 29, http://www.vox.com.

Kodero, Cliff Ubba (2020), "Review – authoritarian Africa: Repression, resistance and the power of Ideas," August 30, http://www.e-ir.info.

Koh, Aaron and Jane Kenway (2012), "Cultivating national leaders in an elite school: Deploying the transnational in the national interest," *International Studies in Sociology of Education* 22 (4): 333–51.

Kolko, J. (1988), *Restructuring the World Economy*, New York: Pantheon Books.

Krawczyk, Kelly Ann and Jennie Sweet-Cushman (2016), "Understanding political participation in West Africa: The relationship between good governance and local citizen engagement," *International Review of Administrative Sciences*, April 07, http://www.journals.sagepub.com.

Kroeker-Falconi, Caroline, Rachel Canclini Kettle, ACT-es, Gyorgy Sumeghy, ed. (2021), *Compendium of Best Practices for Housing in Africa*, February 2021, http://www.habitat.org.

Lamma, Ewi (2022), "Climate solutions in Cameroon – Community forestry and rural women," *Green Labs blog post*, August 08, www.babraham.ac.uk.

Lancaster, Andy (2012), "The divisive nature of ethnicity in Ugandan politics, before and after independence," May 25, http://www.e-ir.info.

Landell-Mills, P. (1992), "Governance, cultural change and empowerment," *The Journal of Modem African Studies* 31 (4): 543–67.

Landell-Mills, P. and I. Serageldin (1991), "Governance and the external factor," *World Bank's Annual Conference on Development Economics*. Washington DC, April 25–26.

Lauer, Helen (2007), "Depreciating African political culture," *Journal of Black Studies* 38 (2): 288–307, http://www.jstor.org.

Leatt, James, Theo Kneifel, and Klaus Numberger (1987), "Contending ideologies in South Africa," *International Journal on World Peace* 4 (2): 181–4.

Lee, Matthew (2021), "In Africa, Blinken sees limits of US influence abroad," *AP News*, November 22, http://www.apnews.com.

LeHane, Miles (2020), "4 characteristics of transformational leadership," December 09, http://www.mileslehane.com.

Levy, Brian, Alan Hirsch, Vinothan Naidoo, and Musa Nxele (2021), "When strong institutions and massive inequalities collide," March 18.http://www.carnegieendowment.org.

Lewis, W. A. (1965), *Politics in West Africa*, London: Oxford University Press.

Lickonia, Thomas (2000), "A comprehensive approach to character building in Catholic schools," *Catholic Education: A Journal of Inquiry and Practice* 4 (2): 259–71.

Lindberg, Staffan I. (2006), "The surprising significance of African elections," *GSDRC Applied Knowledge Series*, http://www.gsdrc.org.

Loanes, Ellen (2022), "How to understand the recent coups in Africa," February 05, http://www.vox.com.

Lodge, Tom (1998), "Political corruption in South Africa," *African Affairs* 97 (387): 157–87, in M. Utas (ed.), *African conflicts and informal power: Big Men and networks*, DiVA portal, http://www.uu.diva-portal.org.

Lodge, Tom (2013), "Alternation and leadership succession in African democracies," *Irish Studies in International Affairs* 24 (1): 21–40.

Logan, Carolyn and Josephine Appiah-Nyamekye Sanny (2021), "China has invested in Africa, we checked to see whether that is undermining democracy," *The Washington Post*, October 29, http://www.washingtonpost.com.

Luna, Joseph (2015), "Constituency service in Ghana – Scholars at Harvard," August 20, http:// www.scholar.harvard.edu.

Maglione, Joyce L. and Kathleen Neville (2021), "Servant leadership and spirituality among undergraduate and graduate nursing students," *Journal of Religion and Health* 60: 4435–45.

Majambere, Silas (2021), "Ending malaria in Africa needs to focus on poverty: Quick fixes won't cut it," October 14, http://www.theconversation.com.

Makinda, Samuel M. (1996), "Democracy and multi-party politics in Africa," *The Journal of Modern African Studies* 34 (4): 55–73, http://www.jstor.org.

Malatji, Khashane Stephen (2016), "Moving away from Rote learning in the University Classroom: The use of cooperative learning to maximize students' critical thinking in a rural university of South Africa," *Journal of Communication* 7 (1): 34–42.

Malpass, David (2021), "World Bank chief calls for comprehensive debt relief for poor countries," October, 11, http://www.moneycontrol.com.

Mampilly, Zachariah (2021), "The promise of Africa's Youth Bulge," July 07, http://www.foreignaffairs.com.

Managa, Azwifaneli (2012), "Unfulfilled promises and their consequences: A reflection on local government performance and the critical issue of poor service delivery in South Africa," May 01, http://www.africaportal.org.

Manyika, James, Jan Mischke, Jacques Bughin, Jonathan Woetzel, Mekala Krishnan, and Samuel Cudre (2019), "A new look at the declining labor share of income in the United States," *Discussion Paper, McKinsey Global Institute*, May 22, http://www.mckinsey.com.

Mariwah, Simon (2021), "Scrapping road tolls in Ghana; what are the economic costs," *Joy News*, November19, http://www.myjoyonline.com.

Marley, Robert (1980), "Redemption Song," *Uprising Album*, June 10.

Marley, Robert and the Wailers (1983), "Lyrics of Stiff-necked fools," *Confrontation Album*.

Mbaku, John Mukum (1996), "Bureaucratic corruption in Africa: The futility of cleanups,"
    The Cato Journal 16 (1), http://www.dlib.indiana.edu.
Mbaku, John Mukum (2021), "Entrenching democracy in African countries: Policy
    imperatives for leaders in 2021," March 18, http://www.brookings.edu.
Mbaye, Ahmadou Aly, Stephen Golub, and Fatou Gueye (2020), "Formal and informal
    enterprises in Francophone Africa: Moving toward a vibrant private sector," July 10,
    http://www.brookings.edu.
Mbeki, Moeletsi (2021), "How South Africa's elites are stunting the economy and
    democracy," July 29, http://www.theafricareport.com.
McCain, James A. (1975), "Ideology in Africa: Some perceptual types," *African Studies
    Review* 18 (1): 61–87.
McClean, Ruth (2020), "With elections ahead, some African presidents try engineering
    results," October 11, http://www.nytimes.com.
McNeil, Mary (2010), "Demanding good governance: Lessons from social accountability
    initiatives in Africa," *Open Knowledge Depository*, http://www.worldbank.org.
Melber, Henning (2019), "Has the relationship between Namibia and Germany sunk to a
    new low?," *The Conversation*, August 04, http://www.theconversation.org.
Mellon, David, Yves Van Durme, and Maren Hauptmann (2020), "Belonging: From
    comfort to connection to contribution," May 15, http://www.deloitte.com.
Menkiti, I. A. (1984), "Person and community in African traditional thought," in R. A.
    Wright (ed.), *African Philosophy: An Introduction*, 171–81, Lanham: University Press of
    America.
Mennasemay, M. (1982), "Political theory, political science and African development,"
    Canadian Journal of African Studies 16 (2): 223–44.
Michalopoulos, Stelios and Elias Papaioannou (2019), "Historical legacies and African
    Development," March, http://www.voxdev.org.
Mikdad, Mohammed (2013), "A modest proposal: Create! Loot! Share," December 05,
    http://www.modernghana.com.
Mikell, G. (1991), "Equity issues in Ghana's rural development," in D. Rothchild (ed.),
    Ghana: The Political Economy of Recovery, 85–100, Boulder: Lynne Rienner.
Mire, Sada (2022), 'Africa's heritage is humanity's – And it's been overlooked for so long',
    The Guardian, January 03, http://www.theguardian.com.
Mishera, Abhishek (2021), "Coups are making a comeback in Africa, but what's driving
    them?," November 01, http://www.orfonline.org.
Mitra, Aniban (2017), "The infamous Macauley speech that never was," February 19,
    http://www.thewire.in.
Moosa, Fareed (2016), "Understanding the 'Spirit, Purport and Objects' of South Africa's
    bill of rights," *Journal of Forensic Legal & Investigative Sciences Herald*, December 26,
    http://www.heraldopenacess.us.
Morsy, H., A. Salami, and N. Mukassa (2021), "Opportunities amid COVID-19:
    Advancing intra-African food integration," *World Development* 139, March, https://
    www.sciencedirect.com/science/article/pii/S0305750X20304356#.
Muller-Crepon, Carl (2021), *State Reach and Development in Africa since the 1960s: New
    Data and Analysis*, Cambridge: Cambridge University Press, November 10.
Munshi, Neil and Andres Schipani (2021), "Failure of democracy?: Why are coups on the
    rise in Africa," *Financial Times*, November 14, http://www.ft.com.
MyNewsGh (2021), "Create, Loot & Share: How weeks old company won GHc518
    million govt. laptop contract on Sole-sourcing," November 21, http://www.mynewsgh
    .com.

Naseer, S., F. Syed, S. Nauman, T. Fatima, I. Jameel, and N. Riaz (2020), "Understanding how leaders' humility promotes followers' emotions and ethical behaviors," *Journal of Positive Psychology* 15 (3): 407–19, Google Scholar.

Ndaba, Vuyani (2021), "Sub-Saharan Africa to see mixed economic recovery into 2022," *Reuters* October 27.

Ndue, P. (1998), "Best practices in institutional reform," *Development Policy Studies* 4 (3): 16–22.

Ndulo, Muna (2019), "Constitutions and constitutional reforms in African politics," July 29, http://www.oxfordre.com.

Nef, J. (1989), "Development processes: Contradictions between theory and practice," *Worldscape* 3 (1), University of Guelph.

Nellis, John (2005), "Privatization in Africa: What has happened? What is to be done?," January, http://www.researchgate.net.

Nelms, L. W., E. Hutchins, D. Hutchis, and R. J. Pursley (2007), "Spirituality and the health of college students," *Journal of Religion and Health* 46 (2): 249–65, Google Scholar.

Neophytou, Nadia (2021), "okayafrica," October 04, http://www.okayafrica.com.

Ng, John (2021), "What Is Greatness? (What you must comprehend)," January 20, http://www.worldscientific.com.

Ninsin, Kwame (1991), *The Informal Sector in Ghana's Political Economy*, Accra: Freedom Publication.

Nisihara, H. N. (2001), "The significance of constitutional values," http://www.ajol.info.

Nsereko, Norman David (2018), "Proliferation of university institutions in Africa: Student academic life and mental health challenges," October 03, http://www.researchgate.net.

Nshimyiryo, Alphonse, Bethany Hedt-Gauthie, and Ziad El-Khatib (2019), "Risk factors for stunting among children under five years: A cross-sectional population-based study in Rwanda using the 2015 Demographic and Health Survey," *BMC Public Health* 19 (175), February 11, http://www.bmcpublichealth.biomedcentral.com.

Nutakor, Praise (2013), "Traditional leadership and development in contemporary Ghana," Feature Article, *Modern Ghana*, March 21, http://www.modernghana.com.

Nwagwu, N. A. (1976), "African students' attitudes towards school teaching as a career," *Educational Review* 29 (1): 47–57.

Obama, Barack (2006), *The Audacity of Hope*, New York: Crown /Three Rivers Press, October 17.

Odour, Michael (2021), "Brawl in Ghana's parliament over a proposed e-levy," *Africa News*, December 21, http://www.africanews.com.

OECD (2005), "Managing conflict of interest in the public sector," http://www.oecd.org.

Ogbenika, Gregory E. (2020), "Festivals in Africa and social mobilization," *International Journal of Research and Innovation in Social Science* 4 (3): 291–5, http://www.rsisinternational.org.

Ogunkola, Isaac Olushola, Yusuff Adebayo Adebisi, and Don Eliseo Lucero-Prisno (2021), "Rural communities in Africa should not be forgotten in responses to COVID – 19," *The International Journal of Health and Management*, July 10, http://www.ncbi.nim.nih.gov.

Ohan, Sewell, Madeleine Kruhly, and Hannah Olivennes (2016), "Yoweri Museveni and other African Presidents for life," *The New York Times*, May 12, http://www.nytimes.com.

Ojiakor, Ifeoma C. (2012), "Sycophancy and objective journalism," *Advances in Applied Sociology* 2 (3), September.

Ola, Oreoluwa and Emmanuel Benjamin (2019), "Preserving biodiversity and ecosystem services in West African forest, watersheds, and wetlands: A review of incentives," May 31, http://www.mdpi-res.com.

Olewe, Dickens (2019), "Is Africa going backwards on democracy?," *BBC News*, February 22, http://www.bbc.com.

Olowu, D. and J. Erero (1996), "Governance of Nigeria's villages and cities through indigenous institutions," *African Rural and Urban studies* 3 (1): 99–121.

Onukwue, Alexander (2021), "Ghana's lawmakers got into a fight over a proposed tax on electronic transactions," *Quartz Africa*, December 21, http://www.qz.com.

Onukwue, Alexander (2021), "Microsoft is leading Big Tech's push to relocate African developers to North America," *Quartz Africa*, August 19, http://www.qz.com.

Onyinkwa, Benard (2017), "The nature of political parties in Africa: What is the role of political parties in a democratic process?," December 14, http://www.papers.ssrn.com.

Opalo, Ken (2021), "It's time to democratize public finance management systems in African States," *IMF Finance and Development Special Series*, http://www.imf.org.

Owusu, M. (1992), "Democracy and Africa: A view from the village," *The Journal of Modem African Studies* 30 (3): 369–96.

Ozawa, C., T. Suzuki, Y. Mizuno, R. Tarumi, K. Yoshida, K. Fudjii, J. Hirano, H. Tani, E. B. Rubinstein, M. Mimura, and H. Uchida (2017), "Resilience and spirituality in patients with depression and their family members: A cross-sectional study," *Comprehensive Psychiatry* 77: 53–9, Google Scholar.

Pandey, Kiran (2021), "Sub-Saharan Africa's debt burden increased to record $702 billion in 2020 – Highest in a decade," October 14, http://www.downtoearth.org.in.

Parekh, Nidhi and Aimee Hare (2020), "The rise of mobile money in sub-Saharan Africa: Has this digital technology lived up to its promises?," *J-PAL*, October 22, http://www.povertyactionlab.org.

Park, Alex and Siera Vercillo (2021), "African agriculture without African Farmers," October 09, http://www.Aljazeera.com.

Patterson, Rebecca (2021), "9 reasons to invest in transformational leadership," March 25, http://www.lifeintelligence.io.

Paunesku, Dave (2011), "5 strategies for changing mindsets," May 30, http://www.medium.com.

PEFA (2016), "Framework. Public Expenditure and Financial Accountability," http://www.pefa.org.

Peterson, Stephen (2011), "Reforming public financial management in Africa," January 11, http://www.hks.harvard.edu.

Petetsi, Julius Yao (2022), "Ghana: EC planning to compile new voters' register for 2024 polls – Minority alleges," *Ghanaian Times*, July 14, www.allafrica.com.

Pew Research Center (2021), "Beliefs and Practices," December 21, http://www.pewresearchcenter.org.

Politico Staff (2021), "The man behind Bidenomics," December 17, http://www.politico.com.

Prah, K. K. "Multi-party democracy and it's relevance in Africa," *Center for Advanced Studies of African Societies*, http://www.elections.org.za.

Pratt, Kwesi (2022), "Bagbin is not a 'king' in Parliament," January 27, http://www.mobile.ghanaweb.com.

Public Service Commission (2008), "Report on the Management of Gifts in the Public Service – South Africa," March 2008, http://www.gov.za.

Pulse (2017), "Have Ghana's foremost hospitals become death traps?," *Business Insider Africa*, February 15, http://www.pulse.com.gh.

Pulse (2019), "Referendum: Otumfuo slams neglect of chiefs in local government reforms," November 23.

Rahmati, A., M. Sajjadi, and A. Negarestani (2022), "A spiritual approach to job satisfaction and motivation among special education teachers," *Health, Spirituality and Medical Ethics Journal* 5 (3): 29–35, Google Scholar.

Ramaphosa, Cyril (2021), "Opening remarks by chairperson of the African peer review forum," March 25, http://www.thepresidency.gov.za.

Ranger, Terence O. (1986), "Religious movements and politics in Sub-Saharan Africa," *African Studies Review* 29 (2): 1–69, http://www.jstor.org.

Rau, B. (1991), *From Feast to Famine*, London: Zed Books Ltd.

Razzetti, Gustavo (2019), "How to upgrade your mindset to succeed in life," November 12, http://www.psychologytoday.com.

Real Estate Times Africa (2022), "Bono East leads with 330 schools under trees," May 18, www.realestatestimesafrica.com.

Reddy, A. V. (2019), "Servant leadership and spirituality at workplace: A critical review," *International Journal on Leadership* 7 (1): 8–12, Google Scholar.

Resnick, Danielle and Daniela Casale (2011), "The political participation of Africa's youth: Turnout, partisanship protest," http://www.gsdrc.org.

Reuters Africa (2021), "Text of de Klerk's video message to South Africa," November 11, http://www.reuters.com.

Right Livelihood (1995), "Ken Saro-Wiwa / movement for the survival of the Ogoni people," http://www.rightliveliood.org.

Riley, M. (1993), "Indigenous resources in a Ghanaian town: Potential for health education," *The Howard Journal of Communications* 4 (3): 249–64.

Rodney, W. (1972), *How Europe Underdeveloped Africa*, Dar es Salaam: Tanzania Publishing House.

Roming, S. and K. Howard (2019), "Coping with stress in college: An examination of spirituality, social support, and quality of life," *Mental Health, Religion, and Culture* 22 (8): 832–43, Google Scholar.

Rostow, W. W. (1960), *The Stages of Economic Growth: A Non-Communist Manifesto*. Cambridge: Cambridge University Press.

RT News (2022), "West destroying its own privileges – Lavrov," September 21, www.rt.com.

Rukuni, Mandivanba (2002), "Africa: Addressing growing threats to food security," *The Journal of Nutrition* 132 (11): 34435–85.

Sachs, Geoffrey (2021), "Speech at the UN Food Systems Pre-Summit," July 27, http://www.jeffsachs.org.

Sackey, Frank Gyimah (2021), "Impact of African leaders' characteristics and regime transitions on economic growth in Africa: A dynamic model approach," *Social Sciences and Humanities Open* 4 (1): 1–10.

Saldinger, Adva (2020), "How can the US help address Africa's youth bulge?," February 17, http://www.devex.com.

Samba, Sylla Ndongo (2017), "The CFA Franc: French monetary imperialism in Africa," July 12. http://www.blogs.lse.ac.uk.

Sanders, D. M., C. Todd, and M. Chopra (2005), "Confronting Africa's health crisis: More of the same will not be enough," http://www.ncbi.nim.nih.gov.

Scott, Richard G. "The transforming power of faith and character," www.churchofjesuschrist.org.

Sen, Kumal, Michael Danquah, Robert Darko Osei, and Simone Schotte (2021), "Ghana's lockdown hit vulnerable workers hard: what needs to happen next time," March 22, http://www.theconversation..com.

Sibani, Clifford Meesua (2016), "Impact of Western culture on traditional African society: Problems and prospects," *Journal of Religion and Human Relations* 10 (1), www.ajol .info.

Siegle, Joseph and Candace Cook (2020), "Assessing Africa's 2020 elections," November 03, http://www.africacenter.org.

Signe, Landry (2018), "Accountability and demand for democracy drive leadership changes in Africa," June14, http://www.brookings.edu.

Signe, Landry (2018), "Accountable Leadership: The key to Africa's successful transformation," January 05, http://www.brookings.edu.

Signe, Landry (2019), 'How the France-backed African CFA franc works as an enabler and barrier to development?," December 07, http://www.brookings.edu.

Signe, Landry and Ameenah Gurib-Fakim (2019), "Africa is an opportunity for the world: Overlooked progress in governance and human development," January 25, http://www .brookings.edu.

Silvey, Jonathan (1969), "Unwillingly from school: The Occupational Attitudes of Secondary School Leavers in Uganda," *Unemployment Research in Africa* 2 (1): 2–16, http://www.jstor.org/stable/43390826.

Sindiga, I. (1994), "Indigenous (Medical) Knowledge of the Masai," *Indigenous Knowledge Monitor* 2 (1), http://www.jstor.com.

Skoufias, Emmanuel (2018), "All Hands on deck: Halting the vicious circle of stunting in Sub-Saharan Africa," November 28, http://www.blogs.worldbank.org.

Smarp Blogs (2020), "Transformational leadership: The secret to organizational success," November 17, http://www.blog.smarp.com.

Smit, Sarah (2021), "GDP Stats: Economy grows, but not enough to secure jobs and long-term recovery," September 07, http://www.mg.co.za.

Smith, Patrick (2013), "Politics, damned lies and statistics," *the Africa Report*, April 08, www.theafricareport.com.

Sommers, Marc (2011), "Governance, security and culture: Assessing Africa's youth bulge," *International Journal of Conflict and Violence (IJCV)* 5 (2): 292–303.

Songwe, Vera (2013), "The Mandela Rule- A legacy to African leaders," December 06, http://www.brookings.edu.

Songwe, Vera (2022), "Strategies for financing Africa's health sector," *Foresight Africa*, February 03, http://www.brookings.edu.

Staatz, John and Frank Hollinger (2016), "West African food systems and changing consumer demands, FAO and OECD," http://www.wathi.org.

Stallings, B. (1978), *Class Conflict and Economic Development in Chile. 1958–1973*, Stanford: Stanford University Press.

Stodolska, Monika (2021), "#QuarantineChallenge2k20: Leisure in the Time of the Pandemic," *Leisure Sciences* 43, www.tandfonline.com.

Suleiman, Muhammad Dan and Stephen Maiangwa (2021), "History of divisive ethnic identities shows it's time Nigeria admits its role in enforcing them," February 24, http:// www.theconversation.com.

The Africa Leadership Forum, http://www.africaleadership.org.

The Cities Alliance (2018), "Assessing the Institutional Environment of Local Governments in Africa, United Cities and Local Governments of Africa," November, www.citiesalliance.org.

The Democratic Alliance DA (2018), "#Healthcarecollapse: Public Hospitals have become a death-trap for the poor. Time for action," June, http://www.da.org.za.

The Economist (2017), "Africa's ageing leaders don't know when to quit," December 07, http://www.economist.com.

The Economist (2021), "Pricey politics: Why does it cost so much to be an African MP?," February 27, http://www.economist.com.

The Ghana National House of Chiefs, http://www.nhoc.org.

The Global Knowledge Partnership (GKP), https://m.facebook.com.

The Globe and Mail, Toronto, Canada, http://www.theglobeandmail.com.

The Infrastructure Consortium for Africa (ICA), "ICT financing needs and trends," http://www.icafrica.org.

The International Monetary Fund (IMF), Washington, DC, http://www.imf.org.

The Ogoni Struggle, http://www.platformlondon.org.

The Paris Climate Agreement, www.unfccc.org.

The Punch (2021), "Nothing to celebrate at 61, poverty, insecurity, poor leadership still thrive – Nigerians living abroad," October 2.

The World Bank (2015), "Half of youth in Sub-Saharan Africa are out of school," July 15, Washington DC, http://www.worldbank.org.

The World Bank (2021), "Ensuring a strong recovery for developing countries," October 15, Washington DC, http://www.worldbank.org.

The World Bank Group (2013), "Unlocking Africa's agricultural potential – An action agenda for transformation," *Sustainable Development Series*, Washington DC: Africa Region, https://openknowledge.worldbank.org/bitstream/handle/10986/16624/769 900WP0SDS0A00Box374393B00PUBLIC0.pdf;sequence=1.

The World Bank Group, Washington DC, http://www.worldbank.org.

The World Bank Group (2019), "This is what it's all about: Protecting biodiversity in Africa," February 14, Washington DC, http://www.worldbank.org.

The World Bank Group (2021), "Climate Change Action Plan 2021–2025, - Supporting Green Resilient and Inclusive Development," Washington DC, http://www.worldbank.org.

The Young African Leadership Initiative, http://www.yali.state.gov.

Thurlow, James and Valerie Mueller (2020), "Does rural Africa have a youth problem?," February. http://www.theafricareportt.com.

Thomas, Abdul Rashid (2018), "When Leaders tolerate sycophants – The nation perishes," November 18, http://www.thesierraleonetelegraph.com.

Thompson, Lena (2014), "Examining government and public officials' accountability and responsiveness," Afrobarometer Briefing Papers 131, http://www.afrobarometer.org.

Tih, Felix and James Tasamba (2019), "8 African nations to withdraw cash reserves from France," November 15, http://www.aa.com.fr.

Traub, Lulama Ndibongo, Edward Mabaya, and Wandile Sihlobo (2021), "What it will take for Africa's agri-food systems to thrive," January 11, http://www.theconversation.com.

Turi, Guyo Chepe (2020), "Kenyan Voters need leaders focused on equity and inclusivity," October 06, http://www.issafrica.org.

Turianskyi, Yarik (2019), "African peer review: Progress is being made, but there are problems," March 12, http://www.theconversationcom.

UNEP (2022), "Supporting sound ecosystem management: Why do ecosystems and biodiversity matter in Africa," *UNEP Newsletter*, http://www.unep.org.

UNEP and Stephanie Foote (2021), "In Africa restoring ecosystems is central to green recovery," *Nature and Action*, June 03, http://www.unep.org.

UNICEF (2018), "Report on reducing stunting in Africa," November28, http://www.unicef
    .org.
United Nations (2001), *Public Service Ethics in Africa Vol. 1*, New York, http://www
    .administration.un.org.
United Nations (2017), "Health care systems: Time for a rethink," *Africa Renewal* 30 (10),
    December, http://www.un.org.
United Nations (2021), "Policy brief: Africa and food security," October, http://www.un
    .org.
UNPO (2018), "Ogoni. A struggle against oppression and fossil fuels," December 17,
    http://www.unpo.org.
UNPO (2018), "Ogoni. Timeline of the Ogoni struggle," March 30, http://www.unpo.org.
Vaill, Peter B. (1998), "Foreword," in Larry C. Spears (ed.), *Robert Greenleaf, The Power of
    Servant Leadership*, 1–13, New York: Berrett-Koehler Publishers, Inc.
Van Alstine, James (2017), "Critical reflections on 15 years of the Extractive Industries
    Transparency Initiative – EITI," *The Extractive Industries and Society* 4 (4): 766–70.
van Wyk, Jo-Ansie (2007), "Political leaders in Africa: Presidents, patrons or profiteers?,"
    Accord 2 (1): 1–38.
Vaughan, O. (1995), "Assessing grassroots politics and community development in
    Nigeria," *African Affairs* 94 (77): 501–18, http://www.jstor.org.
Visual Capitalist, http://www.visualcapitalist.com.
Wa Thiong'o, Ngugi (1993), *Moving the Center: The Struggle for Cultural Freedoms*,
    London: James Curry.
Wallerstein, I. (1974), *The Modem World System Vol. 1*, New York: Academic Press.
Washington Post (2020), "Who won Ghana's 2020 election?," December 16, www
    .washingtonpost.com.
Washington Post (2021), "Africans don't support "presidents for life" survey shows,"
    November 05, http://www.washingtonpost.com.
Watkins, Kevin (2013), "Too little access, not enough learning: Africa's twin deficit in
    education," January 16, http://www.brookings.edu.
Weber, Max (1864–1920), "Protestant ethic thesis - Protestantism was the seedbed of
    character traits and values that under-girded modern capitalism," http://www.eh.net.
WhatsApp posts: Origin and dates unknown.
White, Mike and Mary Robson (2014), "The 'Critical Mass' initiative – helping promote an
    international new understanding in arts in health," *Journal of Applied Arts and Health* 5
    (3), December.
White House Archives (2009), "Remarks by the President to the Ghanaian Parliament,"
    July 11, http://www.obamawhitehouse.archives.gov.
Wignaraja, P. (1984), "Towards a theory and practice of rural development," *Development*
    2: 3–11, http://www.jstor.org.
Wignaraja, P. (1998), "Revisiting the Grassroots Initiatives and Strategies Program (GRIS)
    of the Society for International Development," *Development* 41 (3): 6–11, http://www
    .jstor.org.
Wikipedia, http://www.en.m.wikipedia.org.
Wiles, Jackie (2020), "Build a sense of Belonging in the Workplace," August 04, http://www
    .gartner.com.
Woode, S. N. (1997), *Values, Standards and Practices in Ghanaian Organizational Life*,
    Accra: Asempah Publishers.
World Vision (2021), "Seven million people at risk of starvation across six countries in
    East Africa," Nairobi, April 01, http://www.worldvision.org.

Wu, X, M. Hayter, A. J. Lee, Y. Yuan, S. Li, Y. Bi, L. Zhang, CI. Cao, W. Gong, and Y. Zhang (2020), "Positive spiritual climate supports transformational leadership as a means to reduce nursing burnout and intent to leave," *Journal of Nursing Management* 28 (4): 804–13, Google Scholar.

Yamson, Ismael (2022), "Our problem is bad leadership corruption," *Ghanaweb*, September 23, www.ghanaweb.com.

Yukl, G. (1999), "An evaluation of conceptual weaknesses in transformational and charismatic leadership, Langston University Transformational leadership theories," *Leadership Quarterly* 10: 285–305, http://www.langston.edu.

Zalmay, Kahar (2017), "Why festivals are important," *The News*, February 25, http://www.thenews.com.

Zed, Rajan (2017), "Faith Forum: What should be the role of religion in society?," February 24. http://www.amp.rgj.com.

Zeinab, N. B., H. M. Khorasan, and F. A. Eskandani (2019), "Investigating the effect of transformational leadership on employees' communicational performance," *Revista Orbis* 14 (42): 40–52.

Zulu, Andile (2020), "Prosperity gospel: Excusing poverty and its true causes in Africa," January13, http://www.premiumtimesng.com.

Zwane, Thuletho (2021), "Jobless growth stymies SA," *City Press*, December 05, http://www.news24.com.

INDEX

Note: Page numbers followed by 'n' refer to notes

accountability
  and belongingness 145–9
  budgets 146
  civil society organizations
    (CSOs) 148
  horizontal accountability
    measures 149
  at local and national levels 97, 99
  nongovernmental organizations
    (NGOs) 148
  parliamentary brakes and
    controls 148
  for policy outcomes 52–3
    democratic wave of 1990s 53
    electoral votes solicitation 53
    forms of community
      empowerment 52
    proliferation of social media 53
    social inclusion initiatives 52
  public press briefings 146–7
  revenue generation and
    taxation 146–7
  specialized commissions and task
    forces 148
  State of the Nation, constitutional
    mandate 146
Achebe, Chinua 7, 34
Africa Continental Free Trade Area/
    Agreement (AfCFTA) 7, 20,
    42, 125, 134–5, 152–3, 155, 157,
    180 n.39
Africa Leadership Forum (ALF) 79, 81,
    187 n.1
African Green Revolution 44
African personhood, virtues 111–12
  personhood, definition 111
  practice of religiosity and
    spirituality 111

Tran-Serve leadership 1–2, 13–5,
    19–20, 25–6, 33, 64, 68–9, 71–2,
    75–6, 91–105, 107, 109–12, 125–
    31, 134, 145–6, 148–61, 172 (*see*
    transformational and servant
    (Tran-Serve) leadership)
African Studies Association of the US
    academic community 127
African Traditional Leadership Institute
    (ATLI) 20, 84, 127–8
African Traditional Leadership Union
    (ATLU) 20, 125, 127, 175 n.34
Africa Continental Free Trade Area/
    Agreement (AfCFTA) 134–5
African Traditional Leadership
    Institute (ATLI) 127
African Union, efforts of 125–6
African Union Commission
    (AUC) 127
altruistic behavior and
    development 131–3
BRP (*see also* blended representation
    principle (BRP))
  benefits for rollout of 128–30
  -driven reforms 127–8
  opportunity for enhancing ideals
    of 127
  propellers for boosting 130–5
  rationale and synergy with 125–
    30
center of excellence on Tran-Serve
    leadership 127–8
common property resource (CPR)
    management 133
communities of learning and practice
    (CLP) 127
collective welfare of African
    societies 130–1

colonial commercial order of free
  trade   134
enthusiasm at continental level   133
as faith in collective possibilities   133
participation in decision-making   133
partnerships and associations or
  affiliations   128
roles of chiefs   126
African Union (AU)   20, 48, 125–8, 168
African Union Commission (AUC)   127
"Africa We Want"   20, 48–9, 125–6, 134,
  168
Agbogbomefia   84
Agenda 2063   48
altruism   49
Amazon   14
Annan, Kofi   32
2021 Annual Conference   54
Apartheid   7
"asafo" groups   92
Asantehene   84
Asian Tigers' narratives   7
Asokorehene   84
authoritarianism   2, 139–40, 160
avian flu   7

Beyond Certifications Programs
  (BCP)   155
big man syndrome   39, 179 n.30
Black colleges and universities
  (HBCU)   127
blended institutions
  mission   108–9
    blended rulership
      institutions   108–9
    communities of learning and
      practice (CLP)   109
    formulation, articulation, and
      adoption   108
    National Task Force on
      Operationalization (NATFO),
      set up of   109
  vision   110–11
    engendered adaptation
      capabilities   111
    service delivery outcomes   110
blended representation principle (BRP)
  Africa Leadership Forum,
    engagements with   81

arrangement of democracy practice
  3
borrowed forms of government   5
communal and multiparty-based
  representatives' selection
  principles   4
construct   21 (*see also* BRP construct,
  analytical framework)
country cases   80
features   2–3
Ghana (*see* Ghana)
Global Knowledge Partnerships
  for Development (GKD)
  initiative   80–1
implications of adopting BRP   88–90
  customized institutional
    reforms   89–90
  district assemblies, composition
    and functioning   88
  institution of chieftaincy, reforms
    and adaptation   88–9
indigenous leadership
  arrangements   6
institutional dividends with
  operationalization of   11–12
interrelated issues   80
leaders of local assemblies, selection
  of   3–4
local government institutions   12
logic of the BRP framework   3
Mobilizing African Diaspora for
  Development program   81
modern forms of leadership and
  governance   4–5
multiparty-based elections   81
national-local partnership value
  chain   12
operationalizing (*see* operationalizing
  BRP)
political participation by ordinary
  people   12
regional ruling councils (RRC) of
  target societies   4
semi-urban settings   4
Structural Adjustment Programs
  (SAPs)   80
three-phased set of activities   79
transformational process, features
  90

World Bank Group programs   80
Young African Leadership Initiative
       (YALI)   80
Bretton Woods Twins   7, 43
BRP construct, analytical framework
   centrality of participation in
       governance   26–7
   collective actions, restrained capacity
       for   24–5
   creativity and entrepreneurship   24
   crisis in global political economy   32
   design and operations bias,
       administrative state   32–3
   Euro-American version of
       participation in governance   29
   fair access to resources for inclusive
       growth   25
   fit-for-purpose seedling
       conceptualizations   24
   inadequacy of borrowed forms of
       government   31–2
   indigenous forms of representation
       and participation   30–1
   institutional resilience and
       empowerment, mechanisms   26
   literary nuances   23
   modernization "stages of growth"
       development paradigm   24
   modern leadership arrangements   33
   primacy of quality well-being   25
   public administration and affairs,
       conduct of   33
   resources for sustaining and
       transforming lives   28
   rural-urban migrations   32
   thoughts of social and political
       relationships   27
   traditional and multiparty forms of
       organizing society   28
BRP-induced participation, transparency,
       and accountability   26
BRP-inspired interventions   95, 123
BRP-inspired practice of democracy
   accountability (*see* accountability)
   Africa Continental Free Trade Area
       (AfCFTA)   157
   authoritarianism   139
   challenges and hopefulness   137–9
   derision-laden approach   140

dogmatic ways of doing things   159–
       61
   ecological institutional integrity and
       resilience   160–1
   economic institutional
       resilience   159–60
   endogenizing governance   159
   food and nutrition   152–5
   high school fees and dropouts   138
   high-value education   155–8
   institutional resilience   159
   outsourcing   160–1
   participation in democracy
       (*see* democracy, effective
       participation in)
   positive trends of democratization   140
   service provision and delivery   138
   status quo, saving grace in   139–40
   StP (*see* Seed-to-Plate (StP) agriculture,
       key elements)
   transparency (*see* transparency)
   youth bulge (*see* youth bulge, creativity
       and innovations)
BRP-inspired rulership   19, 91
Bulange-the Buganda Parliament   132
Busumakura II, Osahene Katekyi   132

cash crops   38, 44, 70
Chirac, Jacques Rene   6
civil society organizations (CSOs)   7, 148
collective welfare of African societies
   annual and periodic festivals   130
   community markets   130
   conformity with local norms and
       practices   131
   Covid-19 measures   131
   end-of-life celebrations (funerals) in
       communities   131
   traditional leaders as custodians of
       land   131
common property resources (CPR)   133
communal bonding   63–5
communal bonding and institutional
       synchronization   63–5
   socioeconomic fulfillment and
       improvisation   64–5
   transformational regenerative
       process   63–4
   value of communal bonding   64

communities of learning and practice
(CLP)   19, 69, 107, 109, 112,
114, 127
confusing and difficult leadership and
governance challenges   16–17
Constitution 1992   8, 84, 86, 88
constitutional coups   11, 138
country cases
Botswana   81
Namibia   81
Sierra Leone, Cote d'Ivoire, Liberia,
and Benin among others   81
South Africa   80
Zimbabwe   80
Country Partnership Strategy (CPS)   51
County Assistance Strategy (CAS)   50–1
COVID-19 pandemic   7, 55–6, 95, 105,
131, 169, 170–1
cultural heritage, assault on   36–8

democracy, effective participation
in   140–2, *see also*
BRP-inspired practice of
democracy
communal and multiparty-based
representatives selection   140
Constitutional Amendments and
Enactments Reports   141
independence of ruling
institutions   141
quality of participation   142
universal adult suffrage   140
derision-laden approach   140
district assemblies, composition and
functioning   83–4, 88, 98, 115,
173 n.4, 188 n.17

Ebola outbreak   7
educating educators   69, 109
education, high-value   155–8
Africa Continental Free Trade Area
(AfCFTA)   157
ecological management regimes
158
positive environmental adaptation and
transformation   157
preservation of plant species for
medicinal properties   157–8

responsibility for public goods and
welfare   155
talent access programs (TAP)   156
technological advancements   157
electoral politics, participation in   53–4
lack of enthusiasm toward voting   54
nationwide civic education
programs   54
periodic voting processes   54
women's participation   54
empowerment   26
collective   34
community   7, 52
institutional resilience and   15, 26–7
proactive   159
types of empowerment modality   28
Extractive Industries Transparency
Initiative (EITI)   7, 51, 183 n.27

Fact Check Ghana   147, 171
faith, practice of   62–3
character formation   62
collective visioning of greatness   63
ethics of work   62
institutional channels   63
trends in   62–3
fintech   7
food and nutrition   152–5
food market integration, Africa
Continental Free Trade Area
(AfCFTA)   153
intra-African food trade   153
non-food agricultural commodities
and services   153
social enterprise business service
facilities   152
StP agriculture products and
services   152 (*see also* Seed-
to-Plate (StP) agriculture, key
elements)
fragile, conflict, and violence (FCV)   75

get-rich-quick attitude   156
Ghana, *see also* representation and
participation in governance of
Ghana
BRP in practice, elements of   86–8
critical features   87–8

earlier post-independence
period   87
representation of majority of the
people   88
resilience of institutions of
chieftaincy   87
suitability for case study   86–7
traditional African and "Western"
principles   87
local governance (LG) in   82–6
competitive partisan politics   86
conscientious patriotic
interventions   85–6
indigenous leadership for
transformative or regressive
politics   85
institution of chieftaincy,
involvement of   84
local governance arrangements,
undermining features   83
local governance subpar
performance problematic   83–
4
mandated leadership
arrangement   83
parallel leadership syndrome   84–
5
systemic leadership design
anomaly   84
transformative development and
indigenous leadership   86
unofficial and informal leadership
arrangements   86
vote-grabbing efforts and voter
turnouts   85
Ghana 1992 Constitution   8, 84, 86, 88
Ghana Refugee Board (GRB)   80
Glasnost   7
Global Knowledge Partnerships for
Development (GKD)   79, 81,
187 n.2
global political economy   5, 25, 32
goal, case of Ghana   117–22
Great Lakes region   75–6
Greenleaf, Robert   99, 110
G5 Sahel countries   75
guardrail channels and avenues   12, 21,
145
"gun boat" policy   43, 77

Highly Indebted Poor Countries
(HIPC)   7
hometown associations (HTA)   93
Horn of Africa   75

independence and self-rule   57
institution of chieftaincy (IoC)   9–10,
21, 48, 82–8, 90, 92, 96, 107,
113–15, 116, 123, 163, 167–8
frontline involvement of   84
orienting and adapting   114–15
reforms and adaptation   88–9
International Monetary Fund (IMF)   54–
6, 80, 95, 102, 113, 170–1
intra-African food trade   153
"inward retreat" strategies   105

just energy transition (JET)   150

Kabaka's Palace-Twekobe   132
Kenya elections 2022   164
Kufour, John Agyekum   139

Lake Chad Basin   75
landscape, background development   6–
7
biographical reflections and
observations   6
military dictatorships   7
leadership and governance, fundamentals
of
accountability   52–3
democratic wave of the 1990s   53
electoral politics (*see* electoral politics,
participation in)
electoral votes solicitation   53
forms of community
empowerment   52
ideals of the "promised land"   48
leadership, grounded system   47–9
leadership expressions of
gratitude   48
ruled and the rulers,
dysfunctionality   47
rulership (*see* rulership)
social inclusion initiatives   52
social media   53
tenets of communal mode of
coexistence   48

transparency in PFM (*see* public
  financial management (PFM),
  transparency in)
leadership interests, imbalanced   65–6
  legitimacy of the nation-state   65
  local-level   65
  logic of BRP framework   66
  national   65
  sense of collective purpose   65
Lee Kuan Yew   2, 11, 49, 61, 101
living standards, appreciable sector   12–
  14
  adherence to nutritional guidance   13
  digitalization   13
  education system   13
  global stigmatization   14
  health policy   13
  labor market for youth   13–14
  peaceful coexistence   12
  StP (*see* Seed-to-Plate (StP) agriculture,
    key elements)
  Tran-Serve system (*see*
    transformational and servant
    (Tran-Serve) leadership)
local government systems (LGS) in
  Ghana   166
local leadership councils (LLCs)   166
low-income developing country
  group   55

Malpass, David   43
Mandela, Nelson   61
Microsoft   14
1Million Teachers (1MT)   132
'Mobilizing the African Diaspora for
  Development' program   81
modernization "stages of growth"
  development paradigm   24
Mohamed, Mahathir   2, 49, 61, 101
multinational companies (MNCs)   7
multiparty-based elections   1, 82

Nantawetwa Monument   132
National Identification Authority
  (NIA)   168
National Patriotic Party (NPP)   139
National Task Force on Operationalization
  (NATFO)   19, 107, 109,
  113–15

coordination efforts in Ghana   115
  role of   113–14
nation life choices and alternatives
  food policy strategy from seed to
    plate   70–1
  health policy   72
  medicinal properties   71–2
  orthodox and herbal medicine   72
  out-patient department (OPD)
    visitations   72
  spiritual   76–8 (*see also* spiritual
    materialism)
  technology (*see* technology)
Nkrumah, Kwame   2, 49, 61, 101
No Bed Syndrome   138, 194 n.3
Non-Aligned Movement (NAM)   7
nongovernmental organizations
  (NGOs)   7, 148
no-street communal communities in
  Kpandu   7
Nyerere, Julius   61

Obama, Barack   8, 80–1
Okyehene   84
Open Government Partnership   80
operationalizing BRP
  blended institutions (*see* blended
    institutions)
  communities of learning and practice
    (CLP)   107, 109
  efficacy of IoC   116
  female traditional chiefs and gender
    balance   123
  goal, case of Ghana   117–22
  legitimacy and credibility of
    institution of chieftaincy
    (IoC)   116
  NATFO   107–9
  partnerships and resource mobilization
    targets   115–16
  readiness actions (*see* readiness
    actions, operationalizing BRP)
  risks and mitigation measures   116–23
  virtues, African personhood   111–12

Paris Agreement   150, 195 n.21
participation in governance
  centrality of   26–7
  in decision-making   133

in democracy (*see* democracy, effective
        participation in)
in electoral politics   53–4
Euro-American version of   29
formalized structures of
        communication and   38
governance of Ghana (*see*
        representation and participation
        in governance of Ghana)
in politics, by ordinary people   12
Perestroika   7
"pin-stripe suits" policy   44
politics of sustainable livelihoods   15, 23,
        174 n.30, 175 n.1
politics of words and not swords   33, 148
positive trends of democratization   140
Poverty Reduction Strategy Papers
        (PRSPs)   7
Price Waterhouse Coopers (PwC)   132
principle of collective responsible
        reciprocity   63
principles of representation, transparency,
        accountability, and participation
        (RTAP)   1
Project Development Fund Facility
        (PDFF)   76
"prosperity gospels" in churches   96
Public Expenditure and Financial
        Accountability (PEFA)   7, 183
        n.23
public financial management (PFM),
        transparency in   50–2
    Country Partnership Strategy
        (CPS)   51
    County Assistance Strategy
        (CAS)   50–1
    Extractive Industries Transparency
        Initiative (EITI)   51
    guidance on international best
        practices   51
    lack of transparency   51–2
    transparency in decision-making   51–
        2
public financial management (PFM)
        systems   50–2
public work space, professionalism
        in   68–70
    abysmal sense of purpose   68
    educating the educators   69

media houses and personnel   69
    self-introspection of officials   69
    sense of belonging   69–70

readiness actions, operationalizing BRP
    BRP-themed events   114
    Communities of Learning and Practice
        (CLP)   112
    constitutional amendments and
        enactments   113–14
    guidelines for media engagement   114
    institution of chieftaincy, orienting and
        adapting   114–15
    national command papers   112–13
    National Task Force on
        Operationalization (NATFO)
        coordination efforts in Ghana   115
        role of   113–14
    news-making virtual conferences   114
    operational manuals and handouts for
        education   114
    payments of debt   113
    periodic press releases   114
    public education, activities for   114
realities and success
    caring for people   60
    communal bonding (*see* communal
        bonding and institutional
        synchronization)
    consistency of purpose   61
    desired results and outcomes   66
    drivers of success   60
    existential trajectory of individuals and
        nations   60
    leadership interests, imbalanced   65–6
    nation life choices and alternatives
        (*see* nation life choices and
        alternatives)
    notion of ever-presence of God   61–2
    participation and involvement   66–7
    practice of faith (*see* faith, practice of)
    public work space (*see* public work
        space, professionalism in)
    restrictions for high-level
        participation   67
    sense of belonging   61
    underperformance of leadership
        (*see* representative leadership,
        underperformance of)

visions and values 61–2
realities of African within global
        community
    access to higher social order 40
    "big man" syndrome 39
    continental initiatives, African
        Common Free Trade Agreement
        (AfCFTA) 42
    electioneering 41
    formal development strategies 39
    globally aligned interests 42
    "gun boat" policy "pin-stripe suits"
        policy 43
    jobless growth situations 41
    operations of trust companies and
        locations 43
    post-independence pyramidal school
        system 39
    post-independence two-world
        syndrome (*see* two-world
        syndrome)
    private apprenticeship system 39
    schooling 39–40
    transformation, laboring for 40–1
    urban bias of development focus 41
regional ruling councils (RRC) 4
representation and participation in
        governance of Ghana 8–11
    competitive partisan politics 10
    1992 Constitution 8
    district chief executives (DCEs) 8
    divisive and acrimonious
        tendencies 10
    facts 9–10
    forms of democracy 11
    governance at the local level, features
        of 8–9
    inability of national leadership 9
    incessant individualism 10
    institution of chieftaincy 10
    presidential term limits 11
    systemic leadership design
        anomaly 9
    TAP (transparency, accountability,
        and participation)
        principles 11
    transformational process 10
    unofficial and informal
        leadership 10–11

representative leadership,
        underperformance of 67–8
    "heritage nothingness" 67
    innovations in leadership selection
        process 68
    participation in local governance by
        target communities 68
    poverty and societal ills 67
Rhodes Scholarship 177 n.6
risks and mitigation measures 116–23
    efficacy, legitimacy and credibility
        of institution of chieftaincy
        (IoC) 116
    gender balance and female traditional
        chiefs 123
Royal Mile 132
rulership
    synchronous 49–50
        asynchronous rulership 50
        collateral casualty 50
        concept of public servants 49
        trust, respect, and loyalty 50
        values of the rulers 49
    unequal distribution 54–7
        agriculture system 56
        household amenities 57
        journalistic activities and
            media 56
        low-income developing country
            group 55
        public education system 55–6
        quick fixes 55
        sentiments 57
        sub-Saharan Africa's debt
            burden 56
        technology applications 56–7
rural-urban migrations 5, 32
Russian-Ukraine War 56, 105, 171

Sahel region 75
Sanusi II, Muhammad 132
SAPs, *see* Structural Adjustment Programs
        (SAPs)
SARS 7
schooling 39–40, *see also* realities
        of African within global
        community
    "big man" syndrome 39
    formal development strategies 39

post-independence pyramidal school
    system 39
private apprenticeship system 39
Seed-to-Plate (StP) agriculture, key
    elements
    food production 153–4
    fruit trees plantation and agri-
        forestation 154
    harvest assistance 154
    livestock and fish/mushroom
        farming 154
    makeshift irrigation measure 154
    marketing facilities and channels 154
    seeds 154
    targeted artisan labor force
        program 154–5
    training and skills acquisition
        initiatives 154
seed-to-plate food strategy 71
servant leadership 1, 38–9, 48–9, 68,
    99–100, 102, 110
Sino-Soviet conflict 7
Sino-Western development financing
    trapping 160
skepticism 91, 93
social inclusion 7, 52
social media 7, 42, 53, 56, 73–4, 78, 92,
    138–9, 147, 168
spiritual materialism 76–8
    all-day fasting and all-night prayer
        sessions 77–8
    miracle churches 77
    religious leaders 77
    through prophecies and instant
        gratification 78
statehood in Africa, practical lessons of
    inconvenient truths
    acts of impunity under BRP-inspired
        regime 170–1
    decision-making, issues 170
    #AdoptBRP 168
    Covid-19 pandemic 169
    decision-making, issues 170
    empty political promise and
        society 168–9
    independence 172
    International Monetary Fund
        (IMF) 171
    lockdown compliance 169

    management of public
        resources 166–7
    multiparty politics 167–8
    responsive designs of statehood is
        traditional leadership 165–7
    local government systems (LGS) in
        Ghana, 166
    local leadership councils
        (LLCs) 166
    management of public
        resources 166–7
    revolution of the mind 171–2
    state structures of governance 164–5
    volunteerism
        Covid-19 pandemic 169
        lockdown compliance 169
status quo, saving grace in 139–40
Strategic African Securities (SAS) 132,
    175
Structural Adjustment Programs
    (SAPs) 7, 80
Sunon-Asogli Power Ltd 132

Takoradi Institute of Science and
    Technology (TIST) 132
talent access programs (TAP) 156
TAP (transparency, accountability, and
    participation) principles 11,
    57, 99
technology
    cellphone and social media
        technology 73–4
    in construction business 74
    fragile, conflict, and violence
        (FCV) 75
    idleness and vulnerability 73
    minimal deployment of 76
    power generation and
        transmission 73
    priority fragile, conflict, and violence
        (FCV) zones 75
    Project Development Fund Facility
        (PDFF) 76
    smart mobile technologies 74
    social media technology 73–4
    technology-aided approaches 73
    utilization in household amenities 76
    venture capital fund 76
'Tied-Aid' industries 7

Togbe Afede XIV 84, 132
transformational and servant (Tran-Serve)
    leadership
    accountability at local and national
        levels 97, 99
    administrative efficiency, increase
        in 98
    alternatives and options 15
    assessments of civic duties
        responses 98
    BRP-inspired interventions 95
    characteristics of servant
        leadership 100
    common goal of fulfilling needs of
        society 101
    distinctive components of a
        transformational leader 99
    distinguishing features of 1–2
    as driver of BRP 102–4
        earn respect and trust
            voluntarily 104
        focus on solutions, communities
            and empowering spaces 102–3
        high-level buy-in and sense of
            belongingness 104
        improved outcomes, satisfaction,
            and performance 103
        individual's needs 103–4
        motivation to serve others 103
        public service 104
        sets aside self-interests 103
    economic recovery 95
    execution skills 100
    freedom of the press 95
    game-changing services
        provisions 14–15
    increased buy-in and sense of
        belonging 98
    parallel leadership syndrome,
        elimination of 97–8
    policing and enforcement of rules 95
    political participation by ordinary
        people 97
    "prosperity gospels" in churches 96
    public office occupants 2
    quality education 95–6
    rulership institutions 102
    servant leadership 99

solutions-focused leadership 100
solutions to problems of
        governance 14
    and spirituality 100–1
    for steering affairs 99–102
    structures of authoritarianism
            camouflaged in democracy
            garbs 2
TAP principles of governance 99
target groups, sentiments
    African diaspora 93
    international community 93–4
    ordinary Africans 93
    public sector officials 93
    reactions 94
    ruling elites/political class 92
    traditional leaders 92
    women 92
    youth 92
transparency 97
unofficial and informal leadership
        arrangements 96
transformational leader 17, 59, 99
Transnational Elites Interests as
        Manifested in the Socio-
        Economic Programs in Sub-
        Saharan Africa 79
transparency
    coalitions and partnerships 143
    effective public service provisions and
        delivery 143
    extractive policies 143
    leadership performance 144
    neighborhood developmental
        interests 143
    in PFM (*see* public financial
        management (PFM),
        transparency in)
    privatizing the management 143–4
    TAP (transparency, accountability, and
        participation) 11, 57, 99, 115
    and trustworthiness 142–4
two-world syndrome 16, 35, *see also*
        realities of African within global
        community
    African Green Revolution 44
    assault on cultural heritage 36–7
    cash crops production 44

divide-and-rule tactics 36–7
formalized structures of communication
        and participation 38
freeing oneself from mental
        enslavement 36
inferior African practices 36
intersections of 43–4
navigating life in both 37–8
notion of servant leadership 38
protections from volatility and
        instability 44
straddling between 36–7
structural delineations 37
value-added processed goods and
        products 43–4

United Nations Children Fund
        (UNICEF) 138, 174 n.21
United Nations Mission in Kosovo
        (UNMIK) 8
unofficial and informal leadership
        arrangements 10, 20, 86, 96, 135

voluntarism 17, 21, 47, 97, 132, 142,
        163

"Western" models of democracy
        practice 2
World Bank 13, 43, 51, 55–6, 80–1, 102,
        113
World Bank Group 8, 18, 79–80

Yamson, Dr. Ishmael 7
"Young African Leadership Initiative"
        (YALI) 81, 188 n.6
youth bulge, creativity and
        innovations 149–52
    digital skills, green and technology-
        enabled investments 149
    employment and job creation
        151
    formal and informal education
        strategies 150–1
    just energy transition (JET) 150
    peer-to-peer training 150